Black Range Tales

Black Range Tales

By James A. McKenna

High-Lonesome Books
Silver City, New Mexico

Library of Congress Card Catalog Number 37-15022

ISBN-13: 978-0-944383-60-5
ISBN-10: 0-944383-60-2

First Published by Wilson-Erickson, NY, 1936

Illustrated with Numerous Woodcuts by
Howard Simon

This printing, 2014
by
High-Lonesome Books
P.O. Box 878
Silver City, New Mexico 88062

INTRODUCTION

Much remains to be learned about James A. "Uncle Jimmie" McKenna. The first edition of *Black Range Tales* (Wilson-Erickson, New York, 1936), offered nothing about the man, or the writing of his book, beyond what the author himself had to say concerning his years in the Gila Region of southwest New Mexico. A subsequent edition (Rio Grande Press, Glorieta, 1969) included a *Welcome to the Black Range* by Ms. Lydia G. Key of the Black Range Museum, Hillsboro, New Mexico. Within this *Welcome*, Ms. Key told of interviewing W.J. "Oxy Bill" Hamlet of Silver City, described as a blacksmith, 82, and an old friend of Uncle Jimmie. Mr. Hamlet told Ms. Key that he and Uncle Jimmie – "they two" -- wrote the "Tales" out on scraps of paper in the blacksmith shop in Silver City. Later, when McKenna was retired to the Holy Cross Sanatorium in Deming, the handwritten notes were typed for publication by a Sister Foley, one of the caregivers at the sanatorium. In the late 1930s the sanatorium burned down, whereupon McKenna went to live with a niece in St. Petersburg, Florida. From Ms. Key's *Welcome:* "Oxy Bill says the change broke (Uncle Jimmie's) heart, and a few years later he went over the hill to the great roundup." Ms. Key reports his death as November 1941.

All this sounds plausible and generally fits with other sources, with the possible exception of Mr. Hamlet's claimed contributions to the writing of *Black Range Tales*. The tales concern the life and times of James McKenna and Oxy Bill is not mentioned in the text.

High-Lonesome Books went looking for more information and just prior to publication of this edition of *Black Range Tales* some newspaper items surfaced, compliments of Susan Berry, Director of the Silver City Museum (Retired). Together they provide some additional background and biography of James McKenna and suggest avenues for further inquiry. We will quote the news stories in their entirety.

From: Silver City *Independent*, February 11, 1930

> "Uncle Jimmie" McKenna of Deming, famous pioneer prospector of Grant County, mining man and Indian fighter, visited friends in

Silver City Wednesday on a business trip here in connection with numerous mining leases which he holds in this vicinity.

"I came first to Silver City on Christmas day 1877," said Mr. McKenna to the *Independent*. "I spent about a year at that time at Pinos Altos where I did placer mining. In 1879 I went to Hillsboro and worked for George Wells on the Flapjack and Poor Man's Gulch claims, which he owned.

"In 1880 we had the Kingston mining excitement, created first by the operations of Bob Forbes and Harry Elliot, who came over from Tombstone. Their three best claims then at Kingston were the Brush Heap, Andy Johnson and the Black Eyed Susan. These were great lead and silver properties and were later sold to an English syndicate for $700,000. They produced heavily for a time, but were later sold for taxes to the Empire Zinc Company.

"I located at Kingston on Kentuck Mountain. With me in the same cabin on Percha Creek were Johnny Roach, Ed Doheny and Tom Grady. Doheny was teaching school and receiving a salary of $40.00 a month. It was at that time that he was married to his first wife. It seems funny now, but out of the 27 claims at Kentuck Mountain all were producers except the two owned by Doheny, the Mountain Chief and the Miner's Dream.

"There were between 500 and 600 miners at work then in Kingston. My operations were successful. Roach and I would locate and sell, which method proved to be very profitable. Roach became a great gambler. There were ten or fifteen faro games running in Kingston at one time. It was at that period that the stone hotel, still standing, was built by two Swedes. Kingston was beautiful, and was watered by a large stream, which ran down from Kelly Spring.

"In 1883 and 1884 I located a ranch at the Gila Hot Springs, and spent most of those two years there. About this time I became interested in the Snively Diggings. A man named Snively appeared at Pinos Altos in 1876 with $20,000 in native gold. He explained that the gold was discovered 100 miles north of Pinos Altos. Snively, a little later started for California, and nothing more was ever heard of him.

"We decided to try and locate the diggings. Three of us set out on an expedition northward. I was accompanied by J.J. Baxter and Wood Poland. Baxter had come to this country in 1886. He had served in the Confederate army under Quantrell. Poland was a placer miner from Alabama.

"We thought that we had located the Snively diggings, but there had been some sort of cloudburst, flood or earthquake, which had torn things up in such a fashion that we were obliged to give up the search. We were in north of the Datils. Baxter had been in that same section 12 years before that, and discovered gold there, but the Indians ran him off.

"We started back home heading for Gila Hot Springs. We trailed along through Turkey Feather Pass, Iron Creek, Snow Creek and down on the west fork of the Gila. We noticed moccasin tracks, but believed we were being watched by persons, who thought we were successful in our search for gold.

"Everyone wore moccasins in those days, and we did not realize these tracks were made by Indians. We were attacked on the Gila at a point where Jenks cabin is now located. I saw both Geronimo and Nana during the battle. Nana was tied to his horse. Baxter was killed; I managed to escape death or capture and Poland also made a getaway to spread the word down at Gila Hot Springs of the presence of Indians and of the attack on our party. Baxter was buried there at Jenks cabin by soldiers who answered the alarm created through the Gila country by Poland."

Mr. McKenna is hale, hearty and rosy cheeked today. He is 77 years of age, and is probably one of the greatest living authorities on southwestern New Mexico's early history. He has been blessed with a remarkable memory, and he reconstructs early events and scenes with almost photographic accuracy. His column in the Deming *Graphic* has been widely read, and is a valued contribution to the history of this section.

From: The Connellsville *Daily Courier*, Pennsylvania, August 25, 1931

The 32nd anniversary of the capture of Manila in the Philippine Insurrection was fittingly observed Thursday, August 13, by Colonel Crawford Camp, United Spanish War Veterans, at a dinner at Marietta Tea Garden.

Among the distinguished guests present was none other than the dean of the regiment who was introduced as the "most popular member of the Old Fighting Tenth Pennsylvania and the grizzled veteran of three wars, James McKenna of Deming, New Mexico."

Mr. McKenna served in the Indian Wars under General Lawton and later served in the Spanish War and finally wended his way across the Atlantic Ocean to do his bit in the World War. His services saw action in many countries and far-off foreign lands. Mr. McKenna was the first speaker and he related very interesting experiences.

Incidentally "Jim" was the first private to have been elected commander of the Old Tenth. He has been in New Mexico for the past eight years where he has been following his old pursuit of mining, real estate and farming. He is planning to attend the annual reunion of the Fighting Tenth that will be held at Waynesburg on August 22. He is an uncle of Dr. H.J. Coll (Call?) of this city and _______ Lynch of Greensburg.

Ms. Key gives James McKenna's place of birth as Greensburg, PA and the year as 1851, making him 90 years old at the time of his death. The birthplace is correct but, for the record, we now know that "Uncle Jimmie" was born November 6, 1853, not 1851, and died November 4, 1940, making him 87 (and missing his 88th birthday by two days!) at the last roundup (see the last page of this book).. His obituary in the Silver City *Independent* names his niece in St. Petersburg as Miss Sarah Call and says that McKenna was buried at the Bay Pines Cemetery, Florida, with full military honors, and corroborates his service as an "Indian fighter" and as a soldier in the Spanish American War.

Another interesting biographical reference to James McKenna has come to light. Visitors to the Gila Wilderness are familiar with McKenna Park and McKenna Creek, so named on the various maps of the area. These landmarks were named after Uncle Jimmie, but apparently by mistake. Old Timer Jack Stockbridge, in *Wilderness of the Gila* by Elizabeth McFarland, tells the story.

"The soldiers and I left Jenks Cabin next morning and went through McKinney Park. It was named for Joe McKinney who built a cabin here. He was an old Civil War veteran who was a scout in this country when the 8th Cavalry was following the Apaches. McKinney had some close calls – one was in 1885 near Lee Meader's place on Big Dry. The Apaches ambushed the soldiers and killed several of them.

"There was another old feller named James McKenna who lived up in the same part of the wilderness during the Indian raids. He homesteaded on the West Fork and also located up on McKenna Creek – he told me later he had figured on selling that big area of timber in there. He convinced folks that it was named McKenna Park for him instead of McKinney Park. McKenna was quite a story teller, and some of his stories of them days was published as *Black Range Tales*."

Rounder, miner, Indian fighter, Spanish-American War Vet, raconteur *par excellence*, Uncle Jimmie was still the yeoman volunteer in 1918, doing service in World War I in France as a volunteer "missionary" and fountain of entertainment whether through the written word or when he told the story aloud round the fire where the soldiers warmed their hands. From the Deming *Headlight*, December 10, 1918:

"No more entertaining story tellers ever worked among the soldiers than Mac, and he held all of his experiences down to the truth as he had known and lived it in the Southwest, and his example was one that appealed to every clean thinking, clean living boy in the camp."

After the war Uncle Jimmie spent much of the 20's knocking about his real estate properties and ventures, most of which were mining claims, but in the early 1930's, when he was approaching 80 years old, he got the political bug. The 1932 Democratic ticket in New Mexico included such notables as McKenna for State Representative District 21; Joseph Hodges for District Attorney, 6th Judicial District; Dennis Chavez, U.S. Congress; and Arthur Seligman, Governor. All won. The *Headlight* commented on McKenna's platform: "McKenna believes that if people want prohibition it should be enforced by love and good example rather than by force; therefore he believes the 18th amendment should be repealed." The paper also noted that of McKenna, "It was said that in his early days he ate turkey every meal and had two chickens in the pot, but most of the time he was like most prospectors, taking a side leap at a rind of bacon. He at times had many good stakes but he says that the Hoover administration has nearly made his pile strike bedrock."

McKenna served one term (2 years, sessions 1933 & 1934), got a commendation from the Governor, but declined to run again due to a heart attack and other health concerns. He would eventually spend his final years with relatives in Florida, but not before a grand personal achievement—which was nonetheless celebrated by many in Deming, Luna County, New Mexico, and beyond—the publication in 1936 of *Black Range Tales.* The *Headlight* opined that Uncle Jimmie, "has told the story of his out-of-the-way and frequently diverting experiences in a narrative whose directness and simplicity, as well as never failing humor, will give it a place among the books, few and select, which are sure to stand the test of years….."

M.H. Salmon, Publisher
High-Lonesome Books

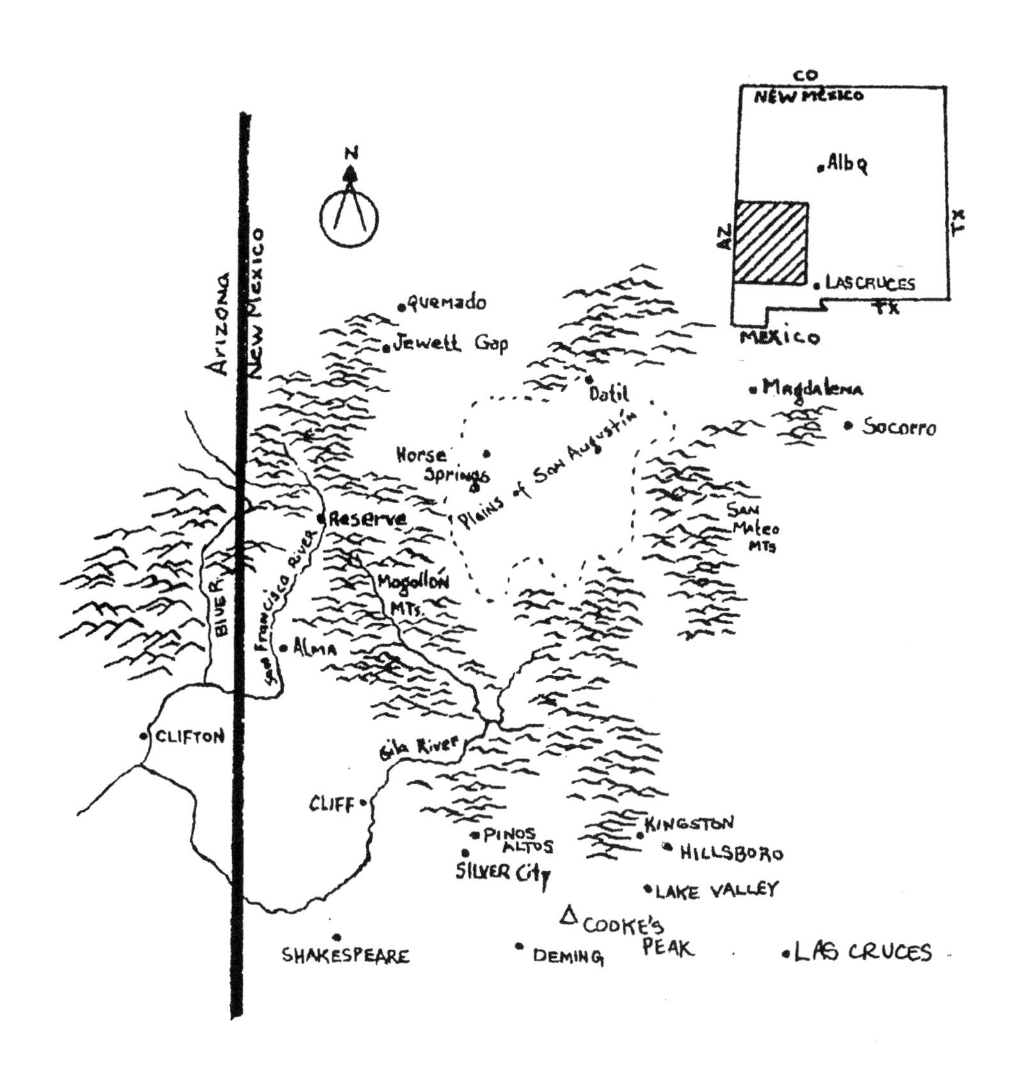

James A. McKenna's Southwest.

JAMES A. MCKENNA

TO

THE SISTERS OF THE HOLY CROSS
HOLY CROSS SANATORIUM
NEW MEXICO

The Old-time Prospector

"As you come to know him better, you must love him for the kindliness, the simple honesty, the modesty, and the charity that he seems to draw from his mountain environment. There are hundreds of him buried in the great canyons of the West."

—Stewart E. White.

CONTENTS

ILLUSTRATIONS

Black Range Tales

Black Range Tales

Pioneering from 1877 to 1887

1. *I Go West*

IN the fore part of 1877 I went to work on a steamboat which ran from Pittsburg, Pennsylvania, to St. Louis, Missouri. In St. Louis I got a chance to go on the *Far West*, a steamer carrying supplies to the different forts on the Missouri River. I shipped as a weigh clerk as far as Kansas City. There I took note of the crowds getting ready to head for the West, and I made up my mind to go along and try my luck in the mining camps of Colorado or New Mexico. A wagon outfit was about ready to pull out for Trinidad, Colorado, so I bought a pony and agreed to ride herd for my bed and board, the wagon boss furnishing me with a rifle, saddle, and bridle, and other things needed for the trip.

There were over thirty covered wagons in the outfit, and we made about twenty miles a day. At dusk the wagons drew up in a circle and we went into camp. Then I would crawl out of the wagon where I had been sleeping and make ready to ride herd all night. Feed and water were plentiful until we reached Dodge City. Part of the wagon train left us here, but I kept with the balance until we reached Trinidad. There were many contractors in that section looking for men to help build the railroads, and most of the men in the outfit were picked up by them. Myself and three other men who were foot-loose and without families pitched together and hired a bull team. Loading up what we needed in the way of blankets and food, we pulled out for Elizabeth Town, a gold diggings in the main Rockies, a hundred miles west from Trinidad.

It took us about fifteen days to get there, the bullwhacker being in no hurry, for the bulls were poor and the grass was good. I was in no rush to get work, as I had about fifty dollars in greenbacks to go on, though I soon found out the hotels and restaurants discounted paper money, many of them paying only four dollars in silver or gold for a five-dollar bill. Mexicans would not take it at all.

When we got to Elizabeth Town I took up with a man named Allen, who had a piece of ground on Ute Creek not far distant, that panned out fairly well. As he wanted a partner who would do the mucking, or shovelling, I agreed to take an interest in his diggings, promising to pay him twenty-five dollars from the dust we took out. Placer mining was new to me, and I spent several days looking around before I went to work.

A placer is a gravelly sandbank, generally located in an ancient river bed, where loose gold is found. A diggings, as the word shows, is one of those spots where gravel has been dug and sifted in the search for yellow treasure. The terms, placer and diggings, mean one and the same thing. Placer gold, or free gold, was supposedly washed into the creeks and gullies during the alluvial age, but a placer is sometimes formed by erosion also. These beds of sand-bearing gold occur in scattered areas in the United States from the Rockies to the Pacific. The gold generally lies thickest on bed-rock and is known as paystreak. The gravel or wash is found in depths ranging from a few inches to three or four hundred feet. A deposit that is not too deep can be worked by pick and shovel, but thick or heavy diggings from ten feet to hundreds of feet deep have been worked by hydraulic pressure since the earliest days of mining history in the West. Outfits and companies often build immense reservoirs high up in the mountains, piping the water to the diggings for hydraulic purposes. In hydraulic mining a strong current of water is forced into the placer, dislodging the sand and gravel, which is caught in a sluice-box.

I took note of hundreds of sluice-boxes in the vicinity of Elizabeth Town, ranging all the way from three or four hundred feet to less than fifty feet in length. When Allen took me out to his claim I saw he had a fair outfit—long tom, sluice-box, and flume. The long tom made me think of a coffin. It was set up on a trestle four feet high and was tipped just a little towards the sluice-box. One end was closed, but the one that put into the sluice-box was covered by a wire screen to let in the sand and water and to keep out the rocks and gravel.

The sluice-box was built of plain rough lumber like a trough with both ends left open. Slats, or riffles, which were blocks of wood, rails, poles, iron bars, and often sacking, matting, or hides with the hair up, were laid crosswise on the bottom of the sluice-box, being farther apart at the end of the box than at the beginning. The riffles caught the free gold. Mercury was sometimes put into the grooves to help catch the gold, especially if it was light in weight, as gold has an affinity for quicksilver. Allen's sluice box was fitted with wooden riffles, and he had no need of quicksilver to catch the free gold.

Through the sieve in the end of the long tom the sand was forced into the sluice-box by a stream of water. As it passed by a slight incline through the sluice-box, gold being slow of movement dragged back and lodged against the riffles. When quicksilver was used an amalgam was formed. Clean-ups were made every so often, generally once a week. Allen made his clean-up every Sunday. Once I went with him to town to see how the quicksilver and other foreign metals were separated from the gold. This was called cupelling. The gold was emptied into a porous cup made of bone ash, put into the furnace, and exposed to a blast of air. The oxidized metal dropped into the pores of the cup, and the quicksilver passed into vapor, which was caught in the chimney, to be used again. Only the pure gold was left in the cupel. In the rich, coarse golds of California placers, and even in the diggings around Elizabeth Town and Pinos Altos in New Mexico, the gold caught easily on the riffles without the aid of mercury.

When a miner found a paystreak on bed-rock under debris such as sand and gravel, if there was enough water in a near-by creek, he generally built a dam upstream to get pressure to carry away this debris instead of shovelling it off. Sometimes he would build a trough called a flume to lead the water to the diggings.

In California, near Nevada City, I have seen natural sluice-boxes on the clean bed-rock where hydraulic pressure was used, the stream being forced through immense cracks, or fissures, in the river bed. When the "Little Giant" was turned on the pressure sometimes tore down big mountains. This debris, when carried by river freshets into the Yuba, American, and Sacramento Rivers, filled and raised their bottoms, causing them to overflow and carry ruin to rich farming valleys. This ended in an

Act of Congress, forbidding hydraulic mining, but it was taken up again when elevators were brought in to pick up the debris and build new hills in place of letting it fill up the river channel.

Many placers in the vicinity of Elizabeth Town were worked without the long tom and sluice-box—the miner's pan, his horn, and his pick and shovel being all the tools he needed. The prospector's pan was made of shiny black Russian iron and averaged about eighteen inches across the top with a steep incline to the bottom, which was close to fifteen inches in diameter. The pan was about three and one half inches deep. Miners became expert at picking out the colors in the pan, knowing just how to shift the gravel to show them up. Some prospectors could find even one color in the pan. They learned to judge both weight and value by the number of colors in the pan and never wasted time over sands that did not show up black with the first turn of the pan.

When a prospector went on a short trip he generally carried a horn to test the sands and gravels. This was the shallower half of a cow's horn cut lengthwise and scoured to a smooth white finish. With the horn, which the prospector valued for its light weight, he tested in the same manner as with the pan—scooping up the sand, gravel, and water, shaking the mixture, and casting off till only the precious bit of color was left in the bottom of the vessel. This he emptied into the little vial he carried for the purpose. Many a time I have panned in an old saucer or a broken teacup. In the Philippines I saw the natives catching the gold of their rivers in a polished wooden dish called a bateau, which looked like a toy boat.

At times the prospector did not have at hand either pan or horn, or he ran across an interesting section where water for testing could not be reached. If bed-rock was close and the sand looked good he probably tried it by taking up a handful which he rolled about in the palm of his hand, at the same time blowing off the light material with his breath. This left only the heavy sand in the palm of his hand. By moving this about with his fingers, he could pick out promising colors. In the dry washes gold was sometimes taken from the sand and gravel by blowing through a pipestem or a small tube into the loose sand that covered bed-rock, in this way uncovering nuggets and particles of gold. The bits of gold were then picked up with the fingers or with a small stick moistened at one end with the tongue.

In a day or so after going out to Allen's claim I caught on to my job—shoveling off the overhead debris which lay on top of the paystreak in the creek bed. As soon as I came to black sand Allen would take the shovel from me and put the paystreak into the long tom. Then he would turn in the water from the flume, washing the black sand from the long tom into the sluice-box, where the free gold caught on the riffles. He always gathered the grains of gold in a snuff bottle. We averaged about a half ounce of gold a day.

I soon got so I could tell a rich paystreak from a poor one. Before long I could pan the black sand and even count the colors to the pan. I liked the West from the first, and I took to mining like a duck takes to water. I soon owned half the claim. I had been used to mountain scenery in Pennsylvania, but I was struck with the immensity of these western mountains, mighty piles of rock splashed with colors that would shame a rainbow. Allen showed me which colors a prospector should take note of and told me what they meant.

Elizabeth Town had been the center of a big excitement in '67, and I came across some old timers who could talk by the hour of the years in this section when even a tenderfoot stood a fair chance of picking up a hundred dollars a day in coarse gold. I knocked up against some pretty tough customers while I was in the Cimarron country, but I was told Elizabeth Town was tame then, compared to the days of the big rush—that in those days shootings were as common as meetings in the streets and saloons. I did not stay long around Elizabeth Town, but I still have a warm spot in my heart for that section. It was there that I panned my first gold, came to know what was meant by a diggings, and stored away bits of mining lore that I picked up here and there among veteran prospectors. It was there that I sat for the first time before a golden camp-fire and listened to blood-curdling tales of raiding Indians, of heartless cutthroats, of daring outlaws, of dashing cowboys, of painted women, of dead shots, and of regular old sourdoughs and desert rats, some good and some bad.

As I was working day after day in water I soon felt the pangs of rheumatism and decided to pull out for a mining camp farther south. One day while I was working in the flume a regular old sourdough drifted to our camp looking for work. He was a Californian named Martin, a big fellow with shoulders like a wall and an immense brushy beard. We hired him on shares, giving him a piece of ground to work, and he agreed to give us a royalty of one third of all he produced. He helped to increase our profits. It was now September and the nights were turning cool. Some pilgrims drifted into camp and made us a fair offer for our diggings. As both Martin and Allen dreaded the winters of this high altitude they decided to go south with me.

My horse was out on pasture, so we bought a second horse and a pack mule, also two riding saddles and a packsaddle. Before we had everything we needed for the trip I had to let go of one of my ten-dollar greenbacks. We bought only one second-hand shotgun.

"I've been in this country for twenty years," said Martin, "and I've gone from the Pacific to the Rockies and from the Arctic to Mexico without ever needin' a gun. It's a damn sight better to keep our money for feed and grub."

Whatever money Martin and Allen had failed to show up on the trip, and it was up to me to fork over one greenback after the other. As there was an excitement down in the southwest corner of the State we headed for there. The only groceries we carried were a bag of coffee, a slab of salt bacon, and a twenty-five-pound sack of flour. As there was no butter in the country at that time, we bought a keg of syrup for our flapjacks. We figured we could get supplies along the road if we ran short.

We struck out for the Rio Grande, intending to follow it south nearly to Las Cruces, as we knew some prospectors at a placer camp called Hillsboro, a distance of over three hundred miles. One of us at all times walked ahead to punch the mule, and what a mule! He must have been with Noah in the Ark, for he was as gray as a badger. But he was a good pack animal and kept his paunch filled with grass or brush. The pinto horse was a fine-looking animal but soon got leg-weary. My pony was at home, and like the mule, could eat almost anything and held up well. In a short time we reached Taos and from there on followed the river to Socorro, missing Santa Fe. We went through many Indian pueblos.

Several incidents of that trip I will never forget. We had camped over night a short distance above an Indian village called, I believe, San Domingo, not far from Santa Fe. Getting an early start the next morning, we came into the village about eight o'clock. The pack mule had taken the lead, seeming to be on the lookout for some of his former owners. When he reached the plaza we saw an Indian run him back. Everything was quiet as we neared the plaza. What a surprise we got! It must have been their patron saint's day, or fiesta. In front of the church there were at least a hundred bucks down on their knees, all wearing their best togs. But it was a sight that nearly caused us to burst out laughing, for each and every buck had on a pair of step-ins, or pants, made out of a muslin flour sack, and facing us from the backside of every Indian was a picture of the Pride of Denver! It surely was a sight. At that time there was a brand of flour by that name milled in Denver, with the head of a beautiful woman painted on one side of the sack. One of the sub-chiefs led us away, but we surely had a good laugh.

As virtually no United States paper money was in use in the Southwest at that time we could not pass our greenbacks in the Mexican *tiendas,* so at last we could get nothing to eat except squash and rabbits. The corn patches along the way were filled with squash and pumpkins, and rabbits and quail could be seen at all hours of the day. We soon had more than enough of this diet. We must have crossed the river more than fifty times before we reached the end of our trip. What a time we had! There were no bridges, and we missed the big towns on account of trying to keep where there was grass for our animals. I had it in mind that old man Martin could speak Spanish after living so long in these parts, but I soon found out he did not even know the meaning of the word *sabe.*

When we came to the river there was usually a house close by, and the whole Mexican outfit would come rushing out to see us wade across, the old grandfather and grandmother in the lead. Martin, whose voice was very loud and coarse would call, "Is this river very deep?" The answer would nearly always be, "*No sabe. Que es, quien sabe.*" Then you would hear some tall swearing while Martin pulled off his overalls and waded into the river. When he reached the middle it would generally be only four or five inches deep. At the next crossing he would start over with all his clothes on, and would be forced to swim half the distance. I took note of a peculiar thing about most burros and mules. No matter how deep or swift the stream, they nearly always stopped to void right in the middle of it, and all hell could not move them until they got ready to push on. By that time the bedding would be wet through, and often the flour would be ruined.

As we neared Bernalillo we came to some wheat fields, and just beyond them to a small *tienda* with a lot of chickens picking in the dust around the wheat stacks. As the diet of squash and rabbits had become very monotonous, we thought we might be able to buy a few eggs. Martin and Allen went ahead of me into the *tienda* where a big, fat *dona* was in charge. They tried hard to make her understand, but she shook her head, *no sabe.* Not more than a hundred feet away from the store stood a small school. While Martin and Allen were putting themselves through all kinds of motions the school was dismissed, and the young ones came flocking around them, giggling and staring. I know now the woman was laughing up her sleeve at them the whole time, for before we left she gave herself away.

When I took note of the trouble Martin and Allen were having I picked up a sack and headed for the straw stack. When I came back I pulled out some straw and made a nest. Then I got down on my hunkers and cackled like a hen that has just laid an egg. Oh, what fun it was for those young ones! I surely raised a noise. Some of the boys ran into the chicken coop shouting with glee and brought out four or five eggs. In all they rounded up about two dozen eggs for us. Our next trouble was trying to pay for them. We could not get the *dona* to take paper money, but finally by scraping out our pockets we raised two bits, enough to satisfy her.

We wanted to buy coffee, but it was almost as hard to get it from her as the eggs had been. Finally we went off with a package of dandelion, a substitute for coffee, which must have been put up during the Civil War. The paper around it was so covered with fly dirt that we could not make out the original color.

The next day we got to Bernalillo, where I learned my first Spanish. A tall Missourian kept a store there right on the road we were travelling. He had a large corral and sold feed. Our pinto horse was virtually played out, so we made up our minds to rest up for a few days and try to trade him off. This Missourian was a regular, galvanized greaser, and there was no other American in the town. He was very glad to see us. He traded me silver for my paper money, and he even gave a *baille* for us with a choice of nearly fifty *senoritas* to dance with. He wanted me to stay and offered me a job in his store. He argued that the Indians were out and that it was not safe for us to push on. But we had the mining bug and could not see things his way.

When he saw he was not making any headway with us he pitched in and virtually taught me more Spanish in a few days than I have ever learned since. When we pulled out I knew how to ask the way to good water and feed. He also made a fair trade with our pinto horse, saying it had been alkalied and needed to be put on good grass and pure water. Although we stayed with him nearly a week he would not take a cent for our bed and board. We bought quite a bill of goods from him when we were leaving.

After pushing on past Albuquerque we saw many Indian signs, but the Indians themselves seemed always to keep ahead of us. When at last we pulled into Socorro we found the town full of excitement, the Indians having massacred some Mexicans not a great distance down the river from this town. Though the stage ran from here to Silver City, we kept on down the river to Ft. Craig, where some troops were stationed. At the Fort they told us there had been several killings of late between there and Hillsboro.

In Socorro we had heard considerable about the Black Range from some of the old timers there, and many of them still spoke of the range as the Sierra Diablo, or Devil Mountains, telling us the whites had never had any settlements there until the year 1872. From the time we left Socorro we could see the range from the river like a fringe of black curves. Here and there a white streak would break the blackness and shoot upward, showing a change in the formation, no trees or vegetation being on these barren granite peaks. Other sections would show a heavy black appearance at the head of some stream or at the edge of some park in the forests of fir, spruce, and pine that covered the mountains. At times we could make out a light-leaved aspen on a snow-capped peak.

The wily and murderous Apaches, led by Mangas Coloradas, Cochise, Nana, Victorio, and later by Geronimo, were never willing to let the Mexicans or Americans settle in these mountains. The beauty of the Black Range cannot be described by man, for at times, especially after a rainy reason, with its forests, flowers, and wild animals, it is a perfect paradise. It is no wonder the savage did not want to be moved away from his strongholds in these sylvan beauties. The Mimbres and the Animas are the only good-sized streams that head in the Black Range, and as far as I know there are no good-sized fish in them. Most of the streams that head in the Black Range put into the Rio Grande, though many of them sink long before they reach it. The range is about one hundred and twenty-five miles long, and not more than twelve miles across at its widest parts. It runs almost north from Cook's

Peak, a granite knob not far from Deming, New Mexico, that can be seen for miles. The north end is not a great distance from the San Augustine Plains in Socorro County. Sawyer's Peak, about ten thousand feet above the sea, is the highest point in the range.

A short distance from Ft. Craig we left the Rio Grande River, going up on a mesa and following the wagon road to Palomas Spring. We knew by the signs there had been a killing there not more than two days before. We were beginning to find out what it meant to go into the Black Range. From Palomas Spring we headed for the Animas River, and followed it till we struck the Hillsboro trail. We got into the town about sundown, where we soon fell in with some friends of Martin's and Allen's, among them Old Kentuck. He invited us up to his camp for supper, and I never will forget my feelings when I saw him dishing up rabbit and squash. Martin stayed in the Black Range mining district for several years, but Allen drifted on to Arizona and thence to California. I got into placer mining near Hillsboro, but I did not stay there long, going on to Silver City, Pinos Altos, and Tombstone, back to Lake Valley, down to Hachita, and up again into the Black Range, becoming, like all other prospectors, a rover.

The Black Range mining district, following the east slope of the Continental Divide, may be said to begin at Cook's Peak, famous for its lead mines. Running north from Cook's Peak the great fault again shows up at Tierra Blanca, and a little farther north on the Percha Creeks, where it carries gold, silver, and copper with a manganese base. Famous mines of the Kingston group are the Grey Eagle mine on the South Percha, the Virginia and the Comstock on the North Percha, and the Bullion, the Superior, the Comstock, the Brush Heap, and the Lady Franklin on Old Kentuck Mountain. Eastward on an off-shoot lies the town of Hillsboro, with the placers of Animas Peak near-by, and nine miles southeast of the main range on a volcanic butte is Lake Valley with the empty but once celebrated Bridal Chamber of silver ore. The Black Range mining district ends near Fairview and Chloride. All these mines have brought millions to their owners, and large sections of the Black Range may still be developed. In virtually all these camps of the Black Range I have had my day. The booms in these districts came between the years 1882 and 1896. Many a time I was carried along in a round of excitement that went with a strike.

The mountains of the Southwest were filled in those days with a set of men who had to face all kinds of danger from Indians, wild beasts, horse thieves, and outlaws. They had to suffer more than the 49'ers who crossed the plains in their covered wagons. The pioneer prospector in the Southwest not only had to put up with a bleak and desolate country, a land of deserts, but he often had to get along without water, and many times without wood or brush to cook a bite; he had to be on the watch for the savage Apache, who carried the latest firearms; and he was never safe from thieves or renegades who would not think twice about killing the prospector for his ammunition. The loss of a horse or an outfit often meant death on these deserts.

Who were these pioneers, where did they come from, and what has become of them? Some came from Virginia City, Nevada, and a few from Colorado, but most of them were men who helped to build the Continental railroads in the early eighties. Not a few Texans drove their herds of cattle into the mountains, took up ranches around water holes and later on became prospectors. And why not? There is the story of the cowboy who picked up a nugget of pure gold to throw at a mean cow, and he was only one of many who struck it rich by a turn of good luck.

Many were the hardships of these early prospectors in the Southwest! The minerals were not easy to get at like the placer ores of California and Elizabeth Town, nor did they resemble the free-milling quartz ores of Colorado, Montana, and Nevada. They were all smelting, or refractory ores, and the character of the mineral was different. They had to be assayed by fire, and often it was weeks after making a strike before the prospector found out its value.

The old-timer knew nothing of horn silver, chlorides, bromides, or bornites, and what he did know often did him little good. On account of the long hauls to Denver or Omaha, the cost of building the roads, and the high treatment charges, the ore had to be rich. Ores were often thrown over the dumps that are good pay to-day. Many of these dumps have since been shipped and fortunes made from them. The pioneer became an expert judge of ore. Mistakes cost too much. Though he could not talk about his specimen in terms of science he seldom made a shipment that did not pay.

And what producers these Black Range mines became! The district around Kingston had twenty-seven mines, and the lessors at Georgetown kept the mill running for years with everyone getting better than day's pay. Most of these ores ran more than a hundred ounces in silver to the ton.

Pioneers had plenty of coin in those days, and a more honest group of men never lived. The merchant knew their word was as good as gold, and until the depreciation in the price of silver, the business men of frontier days never lost a cent. The demonetization of silver was the death-blow to many a settlement and brought ruin to many a well-to-do miner. Most of the mines closed down, and men with means left the country. Those who had to stay for want of money, or because it was tied up in the mines, barely managed to get enough for bed and board. A few who had water on their claims took up either cattle or goats on shares, but many of the older men who were Civil War veterans, went into a soldier's home or became a charge on the county or State.

Some of those who left the country became rich in other ventures, either in the gold fields of Alaska or far off in South Africa, but I have never heard of any of them who gave of their wealth to the broken pioneers they knew in the past except Ed Doheny, the oil magnate of Los Angeles.

For the most part the Government also has forgotten them in its pensions, though any fair-minded man or woman will agree that the early prospectors did almost as much warring and scouting as the militia. Sometimes they furnished the troops with food and horses; very few times did those in authority take note of it, nor did the settlers expect it. Several reasons are given for this treatment of the pioneer Indian fighter of New Mexico. Few could prove they had been out for thirty days at a time, which is the law. When marauding Indians appeared neighbors banded together, and in a few days had generally driven them out of the vicinity, but not always before robbery and murder had been done.

Records of old militia companies were destroyed by fire in Santa Fe, and virtually no proof is left of the services of some of these volunteers. Many were not properly sworn in, though they never failed to answer a call for help. I myself went out several times under Captain Cantwell on the Gila, again under Captain Russel of Socorro, whose superior officer was Colonel Blake, and again under Captain Highland of Kingston. I am only one of many whose services have never been noted.

The Indian feared the prospector, yet he persecuted him. It was the prospector's cabin that was burned; it was his stock that was stolen; and his life was always in danger. The men of this group who are left are now between the ages of seventy and eighty-five. Who will deny that they deserve the care of their Government? Soon they will be forgotten, though every dale, every ridge, and every gulch of the Southwest bears their mark. Cowboys and hunters often come upon abandoned cabins, shafts, and drifts in lonely spots that were deserted by hunted owners more than fifty years ago. Will their places ever be filled?

Something bigger than gold was behind the search of the old-time prospector and led him up and down the world looking for the hidden treasures of the earth. Leading the solitary life of a hermit for months at a time, frugal, hard-working, observant, kind, thoughtful, and brave—did he not take to himself virtue from the mighty works of God among which he wandered? Was he the vagabond he is sometimes made out, or was he, perhaps, a soul reaching out for the Creator, like all humans, as St. Augustine says, "Restless till we rest in Him"?

2. *The Gila Country*

While working at the Iron King Mine at Kingston in 1883 I got a touch of lead poisoning and decided to go with a party of miners and muckers for a few baths in the Gila Hot Springs. In the fore part of May we loaded pack animals with blankets, groceries, and other supplies; and having bought us some good riding horses and mules, we struck out for the Gila country, about seventy-five miles north and west of Kingston.

The best springs lay on the Middle Fork of the Gila River near the north line of Grant County. At that time they were owned by the Hill brothers, who had a home there on twenty-five acres of tilled land. A small herd of their cattle grazed near by. The Hill brothers had bought the springs from John Perry and catered to visiting miners. They kept a good supply of groceries in their strong adobe house, built a sixteen-mile road from Sapello Creek across the flat to the Hot Springs, and set up adobe bath houses, each with a deep pool dug out of solid rock and supplied with a constant flow of hot water. The water that bubbles from the largest of these springs is about one hundred degrees Fahrenheit and contains sulphur, iron, calcium, and soda in small amounts.

Its waters are good for rheumatism and other troubles of the human body. These springs are now on the National Forest Reserve but are owned by a woman in Silver City, fifty miles to the south.

It is said these hot springs were known to the early Spaniards, but the waters were never tested by them, for the Gila country was one of the favorite strongholds of the Apaches during two and a half centuries of warfare with the white man. The Indians took note of the health-restoring properties of these waters and brought their sick to the springs to be cured of pneumonia and other fevers, bathing and sweating them until they either got well or passed in their chips. After the discovery of Pinos Altos and other mining districts in the Mogollon and Black Ranges, miners used to go to the springs to boil out during the lulls in Indian fighting.

Between baths my companions did considerable hunting and fishing. Even down to the present day the Gila Forest is a paradise for sportsmen. The snow-cooled waters of the Gila River and its tributary creeks that head high up in the Mogollons are filled with rainbow, steelhead, and speckled trout. The hunter may spend days in the evergreen forest that covers the mountain sides, straggles through deep canyons, crosses over the mesas, and edges the parks. The Gila National Forest takes in a part of the Datil Range and all of the Mogollon and Black Ranges, with a jumble of ridges and foothills that lie between them. A thousand square miles of this immense wilderness is broken only by the trails of wild animals and forest rangers.

Below an altitude of six thousand feet are found scrub oak, pinon, juniper, mahogany trees, and cottonwoods. In the belt between six and nine thousand feet are thousands of yellow pine and groups of alders, wild cherries, and mountain maples. Near the Canadian Zone the tall spires of the balsam fir and Engleman spruce seem to pierce the blue sky. In the same altitudes as these evergreens grows the quaking aspen, which turns so yellow on the mountain tops in late October that it fairly blazes.

At a distance yellow pine puts me in mind of the live oak on account of its stocky look and round top. Some say this tree is named for its bark, while others claim it is named for the yellow tinge on the underside of its needles. It grows best on sunny slopes with good drainage and likes plenty of room. The yellow pine has a friendly way about it, and people love to wander among the bronze trunks. The best place in the world to get a good sleep is on a bed of brown pine needles. This strong-limbed tree has three powerful enemies,—wind, water, and fire—and of these fire is the most deadly. A cigarette stub, a camp fire not put out, or a blast of lightning can bring ruin to hundreds of pine-covered acres. Still, the yellow pine is A-1 among evergreens at fighting fire, as proven by the telltale cat-faces, or fire scars that one sees on the lower part of the trunk. The yellow pine often lives through many a round of hard luck to a great age. Like a stocky giant, he stands for hundreds of years with his feet gripping the soil and holds his own against the mountain torrents that try to tear away his foothold.

This evergreen forest is the stamping-ground of an immense number of wild animals that water in the mountain streams and feed on the mast. Here the hunter may stalk the bear, the fox, the cougar, and the wildcat, or he may start a covey of Gambel quail or Merriam turkey. Other game birds found here are the band-tailed pigeons, the white-winged dove, the mourning dove, and the Mearns quail. Those who like nature will note many birds and animals they do not see in other sections. Hundreds of beavers dam up the water and by doing so, help to control forest fires, to add to the duck supply, and to stop erosion. Thousands of squirrels chatter among the pine boughs, among them the tassel-eared Abert species which lives on pine twigs, bark, and nuts. He seems to know how handsome he is, for he makes a great fuss to get one's attention. The gray and red squirrels live in sycamore, walnut, spruce, and fir trees.

After three weeks of bathing, hunting, and fishing in the bracing air of the pine forest, the miners were ready to go back to Kingston. Realizing the value of these hot springs in an area noted for fish, game, and beauty, I came to the conclusion to settle in the Gila country. I found out from the Hill brothers that there was a tract of Government land still open to settlement with several springs on it and at least forty acres of good farm land.

I went back to Kingston with the party of miners, settled up my affairs there, and got Bradford, a surveyor, to return with me to the Gila country. He marked off one hundred and sixty acres of land, which I took up as a homestead, putting down my location logs. Shortly after that I rode to Las Cruces to file my claim.

Oh, the hardships of that trip! After loading my pack mule

with a pair of blankets, a loaf of Dutch oven bread, and a few other supplies I mounted my faithful Buck and struck out on the three-hundred-mile trip. It rained nearly all the way. More than once on the slippery trail across the Black Range I thought my last hour had come. But western horses are sure-footed and I got over the range in good shape. In a way the rain was a help, for it kept the wild animals under cover and there was less danger of meeting marauding bands of Apaches.

I got into real trouble in crossing the Rio Grande. There was no bridge nearer than El Paso, and I found the river at flood stage when I got to Rincon. The Rio Grande has many beds of treacherous quicksand. I could get no one to guide me over. I met only Mexicans who told me in bad English and with many motions that I might be able to cross a few miles below at San Juan. I thanked them in bad Spanish and splashed away through the rain. At San Juan I had no better luck in getting a guide. It was late in the day when I finally headed my horse into the river.

The horse led, I hung to his tail, and the mule followed me, all drenched with rain and splattered with mud. A crowd of excited Mexicans had gathered under a dripping tree waiting for the worst to happen. It did. First the mule got into quicksand and then myself, but I hung on to Buck's tail like a flea. The Mexicans set up a yell from the bank that was meant to help me out. It only put my nose out of joint along with everything else.

After a mighty pull my horse's feet struck hard-pan and we were out. The mule was still pulling and straining, but at last he worked into deep water and swam down the river. I followed until he, too, struck hard-pan and could be coaxed up the slippery bank. It had been hell both for myself and the animals. To this day when I think about it I can feel the quicksand sucking me in, and I get all choked up. I stayed several days in Las Cruces after filing my claim, resting up, and getting my animals into condition to make the trip back. The waters had lowered a little by that time, and two men offered to ford the river with me above Rincon.

It was virtually three weeks before I got back to the Gila country. There I met a man named Grudgins who was taking the baths. He was in need of money, so I hired him to help me cut logs for a cabin. Timber was close and plentiful. Soon we had chopped down enough logs to put up a twelve by fourteen room, eight feet high to rafters, and had cut lumber for a hip roof—

beams, braces, and shived shingles. We dragged all of these timbers out of the near-by woods and peeled off the bark before hauling them to the cabin site. Wood Poland, the three Grudgins brothers, and the two Hill brothers pitched in and helped to set up the logs and chop out openings for two windows, a door, and a fireplace. Several of the boys rigged up a sled, so I could haul stone for the chimney.

While laying the chimney rocks I still cooked in the open. One morning after a heavy rain I was standing over the fire frying bacon when I heard "Peep! Peep!" Looking up, I saw a dozen or more full-grown turkeys coming towards me Indian-file. Grabbing up my rifle I fired at least ten shots without getting a single bird. Each one of those wise old codgers lifted his head ever so little just at the right instant. None of them was able to fly, but it looked as if they were going to make a safe getaway in spite of their rain-sodden wings. At last I banged wildly into the flock and brought down a fine bird with the stock of my gun.

That day Grudgins and myself worked harder than ever, looking ahead to the turkey stew we would have for supper. I was busy at the rock chimney and Grudgins was splitting the shingles with a frow. These shingles, about three feet long and a half inch through at the thickest end, were split from pine blocks held in a handmade horse, much in the way a cooper reduces his staves with a drawing knife. Each shingle had to be smoothed down so it would lie flat on the roof. I have known roofs made with this kind of shingle to last fifty years without leakage in rain or snow. Many roofs like this, moss-grown with age, can still be seen in the mountainous sections of Pennsylvania.

After we had hoisted the rafters and fitted them into the notches cut for them, we nailed on the braces, running them the opposite way to make a firm hold for the shingles. I built up the chimney at the back end of the cabin, with the fireplace going well into the room to save the heat. For the upper part of the chimney I used "cats and dogs", laying rough sticks of wood in rows, the long, narrow pieces being the dogs, and the smaller ones the cats. There was plenty of sticky adobe mud lying everywhere that I could use for mortar, or daubing material.

When the cabin was finished we stamped down the earthen floor. I hoped before long to cover it with one of puncheon. These puncheon floors, of logs hewn with a broad ax and smoothed with an adz, never wore out and were often finely grained. As soon as

I could get away I had it in mind to haul by burro from Silver City a door and two windows. In the meantime I moved into the cabin without them. I cut me some young pine branches for a mattress filler and covered them with my wagon sheet. It made me a good bed and I slept like a log. Every night I built up a big fire, boiling beans and baking potatoes in the hot coals of the fireplace.

The Hill brothers sold me some young pigs and a potato patch already planted. The pigs lived on the mast in the woods, growing fat and sleek on acorns and pinon nuts. They became so wild they would not stop at attacking a man if he happened to be in their way. About once a week they came to the cabin for a little corn or the few scraps I had saved up for them. I cultivated the potatoes, raising a fair crop, which I sold to visiting miners. Off and on I killed a shoat and cured the hams and bacon. I took note of the cold nights, so I cut and piled a stack of wood for the coming winter. I also picked out a range for my stock which it would be easy to fence.

One evening while I sat nodding before the fire I was aroused by a catlike patter. Through the open door came Mrs. Skunk and her family. You may be sure I did not bother her. She picked up some scraps of meat and bread that cluttered the floor and out she went. For many nights after that she made me a visit without in any way disturbing my comfort. She became very friendly, purring and rubbing my legs like a cat, while her kittens soon made themselves at home on my shoulder or in my lap. I called the mother "Scraps", and she learned to feed from my hand.

One evening when Scraps and her family came in Poland and Grudgins were there, having brought me a fresh supply of wild meat. It put Grudgins in mind that a man had of late been at his cabin offering him five dollars for a fat skunk. He wanted to render its fat, as he believed the skunk oil would cure his rheumatism. I said he could not have my pets, and we went ahead with our plans to get winter supplies.

I was virtually out of food, but I did not want to go to Pinos Altos till I could take in a load of turkeys and venison to meet Thanksgiving demands. Poland was to furnish the load, and I I was to share profits for packing it to the settlements. In order to get along till then, I came to the conclusion to go by burro to

Cantwell's ranch on the East Fork of the Gila. He was a newcomer in these parts and was reported to have a large outfit. He was located about fifteen miles northeast of my place on the site of old Camp Vincent. When Grudgins came along with the burro he said he knew of a trail to the ranch. About three in the afternoon we struck out. In order to be on the safe side we took along a pair of blankets, a few slices of bread and bacon, a frying pan, and a coffee pot.

Reaching the Zigzag Trail where it leaves the West Fork we headed across the mesa that lies between the West Fork and the Middle Fork of the Gila. Before long I could see that Grudgins had lost his bearings. About sundown we came into some low, rough hills. Among them on a small flat was a ramshackle cabin. It was a double log cabin; that is, it had two rooms with a driveway between them. Pulling off the packsaddle from Old Hog, the burro, we led him into the west room.

Having set up the rickety door in the east room, we bolstered it up with the packsaddle, taking note as we did so, of a deep hole in the doorsill where the wood had rotted away. I told Grudgins we ought to stuff up the hole after we had a bite to eat. While we sat before the fire waiting for the coffee to boil we took note of some queer-looking marks in the dust of the floor and came to the conclusion that an animal had rolled there to stir up the fleas on his body.

All of a sudden we got a whiff of air that made us hold our noses, and it set us talking about skunks. There are four kinds of skunks in New Mexico often found living together peaceably in the same canyon, valley, or gulch. They differ in size and in the coloring of their hair, but they all smell alike. My pet Scraps was a big, hog-nosed, or rooting skunk and was easy to pick out by her shabby white back and her size. The more common skunk, which is smaller, has two spreading white stripes on his back. A third kind, known as the hooded skunk, wears a white crest on his head and white stripes along his sides.

The little spotted, or hydrophobia skunk, as he is called by cowboys and prospectors, is the scarcest but the most troublesome of the skunks. He wears a patchwork coat of spots and stripes. He rids the country of many insects and rodents, but he makes himself a nuisance by robbing the nests of game birds. Old timers claim that the bite of the little spotted skunk will cause hydrophobia, but I have never known anyone to be bitten by him. All skunks have fine, long hair, and their black and white pelts are much in demand among furriers.

Still talking about skunks, which are often more dreaded by campers than really fierce animals of the woods and mountains, we made down our bed on the loose sands of the floor. We clean forgot to plug up the hole in the doorsill. We soon dropped off to sleep. About midnight we were both startled by a queer sound. Hands on our guns, we looked out from under our blankets. Standing over the frying pan smacking her chops was the largest skunk I ever saw. I hunted in the saddle pocket until I found a piece of candle. Some one had told me that a skunk would follow a lighted candle if it were held before its eyes. I told Grudgins to get in front of it and lead it to the door while I got ready to shoot it in the eye as soon as he had it into the right position.

We were slow and quiet in every move we made, and we spoke in whispers in order not to excite the skunk. All our plans worked fine except the one that mattered most—my bullet only creased the skunk. In other words the bullet passed through the upper crease of the neck above the cervical vertebrae, cutting a big nerve and dropping the skunk as though it had been shot in the brain. As a matter of fact, it was only stunned for the time being. Before either of us could grab a stick of wood to club it, it was afoot. Up went its tail. Oh, what perfume! My clothes and the bedding were soaked with it. Grudgins also got his share of the essence. There was no more sleep in the stench that filled the cabin, so we built up a fire and sat before it.

A couple of hours later we both jumped a foot when the weird cry of a night prowler went up before our rickety door. Looking through a crack I made out a fine specimen of the cougar, or mountain lion, with head up and tail lashing from side to side. In his own way he was telling us to get the dickens out of his rolling den. I knew the door would give way at the first touch of his paw, so I did not risk taking a shot at him. The burro in the next room, mad with fear, was striking sharp blows at the wall and screaming with all his might. He seemed to know that cougars would rather have burro meat than any other kind. It may be that our visitor got a good whiff of skunk odor, for, as a rule the cougar will hang around a cabin all night if he gets the scent of a burro, but this fellow, after a few more screams that fairly raised the hair on our head, ran off down the river. The rest of the night dragged peacefully to an end.

At daybreak we made an early start, getting to Cantwell's place in a few hours. Since our clothes could not stink any worse than they did already we packed the carcass of the skunk for our rheumatic friend. Cantwell smelt us coming and was more than willing to bring us a change of clothing before we went into his cabin. He knew of the hut where we had spent the night but could give no reason for its being there. I never could account for it in the barren gulch where there was neither water, wood, nor any signs of minerals.

When we went back to the Hot Springs we were as busy as nailers for a few days, storing away the supplies we got from Cantwell, washing our clothes and bedding, and rendering the skunk fat. Our rheumatic friend paid us five dollars for the skunk oil and came around after a while to say he was feeling better.

3. *Bears*

Soon after we got back from Cantwell's ranch I had another strange visitor. As I had not yet had a chance to get a door and windows, I was in the habit of hanging sacks in the doorway every night. My little Mexican mules sometimes stole away from the bell mare to call on me, knowing their visit meant salt, a chunk of bread, or a lump of sugar. I always caught them with this ruse and kept them tied up until I got time to run them back to the range. Otherwise I was sure to have a bill for damages in near-by cornfields. Sometimes they came in the middle of the night and and would then wake me up by bumping the sacks together in the doorway.

One morning about daybreak I was down on my knees with a turkey feather fanning the backlog to a blaze when I took note that the doorway had gone dark. Then I heard the sacks move. Supposing it was the mules, I did not look around. On getting up from my hunkers I found myself face to face with an immense silvertip. Oh, what a yell I gave! It was more powerful than a bullet, for the bear took action in flight. When he had gained the shelter of a near-by clump of brush he faced about to figure things out. Grabbing my rifle, I rushed from the cabin and climbed the ladder to the roof. Lying down I took a pot-shot, not aiming to hit him, for I knew he saw me, and if stirred up by a bullet, he might tear down the end of the cabin to reach me. Bears are mighty strong and have bigger things than that to their credit. A bear will fight with many minor wounds, and he is so well protected by his thick hide and rolls of fat that even a dead shot often fails to kill him. When my bullets began to patter the brush around him like hail he lumbered off through the woods shaking his head.

All bears are clumsy, probably because their fore legs are shorter than their hind legs. They walk on the whole sole of the foot and are generally slow of movement, but when angry or alarmed they can keep up with a horse for a distance of fifty to a hundred yards. The bear's teeth are made for vegetable rather than for fleshy foods. The five toes on each foot are fitted with sharp claws, better suited for digging in the earth or climbing trees than for seizing prey. His smooth, fleshy tongue was considered good eating among the Indians. The ears of the bear are small, round, and erect. His nose always put me in mind of a shepherd dog's. His thick, close-set shaggy hair makes the pelt very handsome and useful.

Bears are very curious, and I have known them to risk their lives to nose around a camp fire or the inside of a cabin. I often took note of them sporting like a crowd of boys in a good swimming hole in the Gila River. They are smart beasts but do not rank as high in that respect as a dog or a horse. At times they were very peaceful and would come close to camp without bothering anyone, but at certain seasons of the year, in particular during the breeding period, they seemed to carry a chip on their shoulders and the wise traveler gave them a wide berth on a mountain trail. I have never come upon a bear in his winter sleep, but I have talked with old timers who did. He seldom digs up the earth to make a den, seeming to like a hollow log or a shallow cave covered with brush. Some old timers claim that when the bear goes into winter headquarters he puts his paw into his mouth and draws through it the fat he has stored up in his body, but this is, probably, only a camp-fire tale. When a bear first leaves his den he looks fat in spite of his long fast, but he soon loses this flabby flesh, and within a week after leaving his winter hole is as lean as a wolf.

I took note of four kinds of bear in the Black and Mogollon Ranges. The silvertip, or mountain grizzly, so called because his long brownish-yellow hair is tipped with silvery white, is the largest and fiercest of the bears. In my time he was nearly always aggressive and would attack anyone who crossed his path. The average length of the silvertip is six and a half feet and his weight about six hundred pounds, but at times he gets to be eight feet long and to weigh over a thousand pounds. In the early days he would often go down to the plains to get him a buffalo which he would drag up to his den in the foothills. One still hears of grizzlies that become troublesome on cattle ranges, but for the most part they feed on rodents, insects, fish, fruit, berries, and grasses. As everyone knows, the bear has a sweet tooth and will stuff himself with honey whenever he can get it. I have taken note of a bear so smeared with honey he put me in mind of a two-year-old just out of its mother's jam pot. Once the ants get wind of the honey that has matted the bear's fur they give him no peace, and I have known a bear to roll an ant hill flat in his torment.

On bright moonlight nights I often watched a silvertip back himself slowly into a quiet pool in the Gila River, peering into the water for trout. When a few fish drifted by he would scoop into them with his fore paws and toss them to the bank. As soon as he had caught himself a good mess of trout he would clamber out and sit under a tree to feed himself. He often acted almost human.

I remember a man named John Lester who owned a small field of corn. He complained of thieves, so he and I stayed up one night to see if we could catch them. After a while we caught sight of an immense silvertip at the edge of the woods. He took down a section of the fence and was soon helping himself to the roasting ears. When he had built up a stack big enough to suit him he sat down on his hunkers and fed himself with his paws in the manner of a human. As he did not take note of us we were only too glad to let him fade out of the landscape. Besides, it seemed too bad to take away the life of such a fine big fellow.

One time I had an exciting race with grizzlies. At the head of the Mancos River in Colorado, where our luck at prospecting had dropped to the zero mark, Jim Wetherall and myself took a contract to furnish hay to Fort Lewis, a post on the La Platte River. The immense mesa where we cut this hay lay between Bear Mountain and Chicken Creek. For several weeks we were busy cutting and stacking the hay, but at last the job was done. We loaded the mules with mowers and hayrakes and sent them down to the settlement. Wetherall and myself stayed a day or two longer to measure the hay and hide a few tools we forgot to pack on the mules.

McGrew's dairy farm, the nearest ranch, was about fifteen miles across the mesa, on Chicken Creek. McGrew sold most of his dairy products in Silverton and Rico at a fine profit, sometimes getting over a dollar a pound for butter. To protect his milk cows from grizzlies, he had built extra strong corrals of rock. He also kept some fine shepherd dogs which were not afraid to drive off prowling bears. One of the dogs would run forward and nip the bear's feet, and when he snapped back a second dog would nip his nose, and so between them the dogs worried the bears until they trotted off in disgust. In time the silvertips gave up hunting beef in the vicinity of McGrew's corrals.

When our work was done we headed for the ranch, where we expected to rest up for a few days. It was about four in the afternoon when we struck the trail. We had not gone far when the sun dropped behind Bear Mountain. In the thick dusk we plodded on, wishing that we had our guns along, for the bears had been bad that summer, and several men had been killed in that section. Our object was to get out of the meadows as soon as we could, for we felt there was less danger in the willow brakes along the river, but we were still in the open when the full moon rose in the east, whitening the meadow like snow.

We had not gone more than five miles when we both got the hunch we were being followed. At the next rise we looked back. No wonder we felt uneasy! About three hundred yards to our rear an immense grizzly was lumbering along the trail. We were in for it and we knew it. Away we went without stopping till we reached the next rise. We now sighted a second grizzly loping along about a hundred yards behind the first, which had gained quite a little in this strange race. Knowing that a sudden run would quickly wear us out and bring on the bears with a rush, we kept the same pace. Before heading into the willow brakes at Chicken Creek we halted once more to take stock of our enemy. Four grizzlies were now in plain sight standing out in the moonlight on rises in the meadow.

The first one was within a hundred and fifty yards of us, just half as far from us as when we first sighted him. And we had virtually three more miles to cover before getting to McGrew's ranch! We began to shout, hoping that our cries for help would carry to the ears of the shepherd dogs. This roused the bears to a faster gait. At every turn or rise we took note that they had gained a few more yards.

About a mile from the ranch we heard the dogs barking, and they soon dashed by looking for the bears. The silvertips slowed up for a spell and then came on faster than ever, as if they had come to the conclusion not to give up. I still have it in mind that those silvertips knew we had no guns. But the dogs were giving them a song and a dance, to judge by the uproar, and we made a final spurt to reach the corrals.

By this time we had stumbled out of the brakes on to the mesa where the ranch lay. The bears roared, the dogs yelped, and we yelled, and McGrew told us afterwards, it sounded as if all hell had broken loose in the valley. The dogs could only head off one bear at a time, and the second bear soon passed the first. McGrew stood in the corral gate with his gun raised. With the nearest bear not more than twenty-five feet away we rushed through the gate, and McGrew slammed it shut just in the nick of time. Once inside the gate Jim and myself fell in a heap, too fagged out to move. McGrew fired towards the bears, being careful not to hit any of them, as he was afraid they would tear down his corrals if they got stirred up by wounds. The dogs kept after the silvertips till they finally shambled off, the losers in the most exciting race I ever took part in.

A few silvertips still live in the Gila Forest, but they have learned to fear the gun of the white man, and they find themselves dens far out of his reach. The silvertip has been almost wiped out, and where he does live in small numbers, as in the Gila Forest, his power is broken.

The black bear and the cinnamon bear are alike in every way except in color. In the early days the black bear was found in all the wooded sections of North America and in greater numbers than any other kind. Unlike the grizzly he was timid and would rather run away than fight, though he could be savage enough in self-defense or when called on to protect the cubs. The black bear is seldom more than five feet long. The flesh of a young, full-grown bear is not bad eating. I once saw a black bear hanging to the trunk of a tree feeding on juniper berries. A Mexican a short distance ahead of me grabbed a heavy stick and shinnied up the tree before the bear got sight or scent of him. He clubbed the animal till it dropped thirty feet to the ground. Then he slid down the tree trunk and put an end to the bear with a final clout on the head. By the time I came up to the tree the Mexican was on his way down the trail with the bear slung over his shoulder. The best of bear meat has a strong wild flavor and no American will eat it while he can get any other food.

The fourth kind of bear that I took note of was a little larger than the cinnamon, but was colored like him except that his reddish hair had silver tips. He may have been a young grizzly of that color or a cross between a grizzly and a cinnamon, though half-breeds among animals are not so common as among humans. Again, he might have been an extra large old cinnamon.

But I have gotten away from my story with all this talk about bears. I stayed on the roof of my cabin until I was sure the silvertip would not come back. That afternoon when Poland came around, we made up our minds to track the grizzly and get his pelt. Upon going over his tracks we found that he had a toe missing on his right fore foot. He had been near the range where I kept my horses, for we saw spoor and his telltale tracks close to the fence rail. Here and there we took note of trees that had been lately scratched by a bear, and from the height of the marks on the trunk and the telltale tracks it was plain our bear was boss in this section of the country.

The next morning we filled up with some extra tins of coffee to give us pep for the hunt, and having loaded up Poland's pack mule we struck off on the trail of the grizzly. Bears like a clearing, or meadow, where they can sleep in the shade. If the park has a marshy pool, such as one finds at times in these mountain meadows, the bear has a wallowing hole and he wants nothing better.

The park that our bear's tracks led to was edged with heavy junipers. Poland and I separated at the park; he headed for the ridge and I kept among the junipers. As I went along I took note of a slight movement among the trees and I watched my step, being careful to keep my scent from the bear. I almost fell over a pile of fresh spoor the size of a small keg, so I knew I was in the neighborhood of a silvertip. The next instant I caught sight of him standing on his hind legs under a juniper tree feeding on the berries. He stood facing me at a distance of about a hundred and fifty yards. I sighted for the right hand side of his breast. My shells were forty caliber and contained one hundred and five grains of powder with an explosive cap; they would tear a four-inch hole. I pulled the trigger, hitting the bear in the breast true to aim. He did not fall. I kept on firing until my cartridges were nearly out. He soon saw me and headed for me like a cyclone. I turned to run but tripped and fell. I was down but I kept on pumping bullets into him. He was as mad as the devil and roaring like a bull. I was caught in the brush and could not get up while I kept on firing. Poland at last heard the uproar and saw from the ridge what a fix I was in. With a shot from his long-range rifle he broke the grizzly's back, dropping him within twenty feet of me riddled with bullets. Every shell of mine had gone home but wounded bears and other wild animals never give up if they can sight the enemy. Probably only one of my shots would have killed this bear if he had not seen me, for he would have lain down and bled to death. In hunting it is well to keep out of sight as well as out of wind. This was the silvertip we were after, for his foot showed the absence of a big toe. The pelt, being full of holes, was no good; besides, the bear had been shedding during the warm weather, and his hair had not begun to set.

Poland had seen fresh deer signs and struck out on that trail. When he brought down a fine buck he called to me, and I went to him, leading the pack mule. After loading up the best portions of the deer we headed back to camp. At my cabin we found two miners from Pinos Altos, who had come for a few baths. Our bear story excited them, and they finally got us to go back for the pelt of the silvertip, promising to pay us well for our trouble, though we told them the pelt was worthless. The head was what they wanted most. We took along their big white burro to pack the pelt for us.

I packed a blinker, for I took note that the burro was a lively fellow, and I knew he would fight like mad against carrying the pelt of the grizzly. Burros have a great fear of bears and get their scent a long way off. We found the bear as we had left him and soon had him skinned, leaving the head untouched. Though very lean, this silvertip must have weighed close on to eight hundred pounds, the pelt alone being nearly a hundred and fifty pounds. After blinding the burro we had to punch and drag him to the pelt, and it was a fight to the finish before we got it loaded on him. Oh, what a time we had getting the pelt roped on! The burro bucked and snorted, but at last the pelt was made fast, and I pulled off the blinker. We took turns leading the burro with a strong rope. All went well till the saddle began to slip, on our way downhill. Then the fun was on. Poland tried to hogtie the burro, but he had no luck.

The burro was mad with fear. At last he forced the saddle over his head, but he could not get rid of it, for the cinch still held. The bear's head had worked around and its eyes now glared into those of the burro. The burro began to back away from the terrible head, but it kept the same distance from him, nodding and tossing savagely with each move he made. Then Poland began to laugh. In a minute the two of us were holding our sides, with the tears rolling down our cheeks. We had all we could do to keep out of the burro's way, let alone to give him any help.

At last he saw he could not get away no matter what he did, and he got as mad as the dickens, biting into the face of the bear. Soon the whole head looked as if it had been under the jaws of wolves. Poland and I finally got hold of ourselves and put an end to the fun. The bear pelt from the tip of the nose to the hind quarters looked as if it had gone through a threshing machine. We finally got the burro to my cabin. The miners paid us for our trouble and went off to Pinos Altos with the ragged pelt.

I had yet another experience with bears. One day later in the season, while I was sitting in the door of my cabin, I took note of what appeared to be two dogs rolling on the slope some distance below me. I thought to myself, "I wonder who's drifted into these parts now." Picking up my gun I struck off down the hill. The dogs proved to be silvertip cubs. They ran towards me, frisking and tumbling around my legs, but I tried to drive them off, for I expected at any minute than an angry mother would come at me to defend her cubs.

I looked in every direction without finding any trace of her, so I came to the conclusion she must have fed too close to the edge of a near-by cliff and toppled off in a rock slide. The cubs trailed me back to my cabin where I chained them to a pine tree. They must have been about six months old. I have never seen any very young cubs, but I have been told they are no bigger than kittens. As my cubs were old enough to eat solid food I was kept busy catching fish for them, hunting deer, and gathering berries, and tender twigs and grasses. They grew fast and were tame and smart. Both learned to dance and to wrestle with me.

The pigs did not like them and tried to drive them off. One day I came along just in time to save a shoat that was virtually squeezed to death by the stronger of the two cubs. Grabbing a piece of pipe, I struck at the bear, and without meaning to do it, I killed the cub in trying to free the pig. Teddy missed his pal, but it did not cure him of his mischief. The hens often tried to steal his corn, and he got even by having a couple of good chicken dinners. He got away with it, because I still felt bad about the end of his brother.

Several Irishmen who were taking baths drifted to my cabin one day for a visit. They took note of Teddy and one of them began to wrestle with the cub, though I warned him it might be dangerous. Teddy liked to show off, and when the stranger got rough with him, he came to the conclusion to prove his strength. Before I could stop him the Irishman got a regular bear hug, his face being purple by the time I pulled Teddy away.

At last I sold the cub for ten dollars to an agent looking for circus animals, but I missed him more than any pet I ever had.

Lost Canyon Diggings

1. *Baxter*

IN the summer of 1884 there drifted to the Hot Springs a man I hope to meet again when I cross my last divide. He was Jason Baxter, a great story-teller of early happenings in the West. Having whacked bulls across the plains from Missouri when only a boy, he had been at one time or another a Pony Express rider, scout, trapper, Indian fighter, and finally a prospector and mine-owner. Baxter was the swarthy type, about six feet tall, with very dark hair and eyes, and an extra long mustache, the kind that was all the go in the eighties.

During the Civil War he was one of Quantrell's men. He came back to the West when the war ended, but I never heard him talk of his Confederate leanings. I did, however, often hear him speak of having been with Sheridan on the Platte in his campaign against the Cheyennes. He was among the first in the rush into the Black Hills and also into Leadville, Colorado. At Antelope Hill he was with Weaver, and he was known among the pioneers at Tombstone, Arizona. It is claimed he made a rich stake near Taos, New Mexico, in the Red River district, and he was known to have made several fortunes which he spent like a stage robber. Baxter had never married, but like many another white man of frontier days, he took the woman he wanted and lived with her off and on. Among half-breeds in settlements like Taos, Santa Fe, Pinos Altos, or Tucson, there was no law but the gun, and they mated like the birds in the springtime. Baxter paid his respects to a good-looking *senorita* of mixed Irish and Mexican blood, named Barbarita. She was tall and slim with rosy cheeks and light hair. She was as neat as a pin and kept everything in apple-pie order. Besides, she was a fine cook, and the *chili con carne* joint run by her did fairly well. Baxter was very good to her except once in a while when he was hitting the jug. He never took up with any other woman. He often promised to settle down and stay with her, but in the end the roving fever always got him. Barbarita helped him spend his money while it lasted, saw to it that she had a place for him to eat and sleep, and took care of his horse and outfit during a carousal.

The old prospector who came in after a long trip often took too much red eye, or bad whiskey, for his own good, and it seems to me this fact has harmed him more than he deserves with a lot of people, who do not remember his life of hardship and danger. The old timer lived mostly on meat; he dressed in overalls and brogans, or in buckskin and moccasins; he slept with his gun beside him; and for months at a time, far away from any post or settlement, he neither drank nor dissipated in any way. Since human nature is what it is, it is not surprising that he cut loose when he got back to the frontier town. He could not carry his liquor so well as those who had it every day and he sometimes made a fool of himself.

These frontiersmen lived very close to nature, becoming sharp observers. Baxter was typical of this group of men. He could read Indian signs and knew several Indian dialects. As a prospector and miner he ranked in the A class. Honest as the sun, free, liberal, outspoken, quick to resent an injury—such was Baxter. He had plenty of grit and was known as a dead shot. All the different mining processes from arastra to cyanide were known to him, and pay ore he knew to the queen's taste as soon as he struck it.

Whatever Baxter put his hand to was well done, but his greatest gifts were his memory and imagination. Mountains, rivers, trails, and canyons—once he had seen them he could describe clearly even years afterwards. This was the man I met among the Gila Hot Springs, where he had come "to boil out", as he called it. I never tired of hearing him talk and would sit, Indian fashion, half the night before a blazing camp-fire listening to his tales.

Another old-timer around the evening camp-fire was Poland, gangling Alabaman, with a real southern drawl. He was a great hunter and trapper, famous as a dead shot. He traded and sold off the game meat which he killed in near-by mountains to the many campers who came to these springs every summer. Poland also set a lot of store by Baxter.

Judging from his talk, Baxter must have had a fair education, for he could keep the ball rolling on a wide range of subjects. He always packed a few books even on the roughest trails, and he always got himself a few new ones after making a stake.

During one of these evenings I recall he turned to me with the question, "Have you ever heard of the Adams diggings?"

I told him that I had.

"But I'll bet my bottom dollar you didn't know I'd met Adams himself in Arizona? He was O.K. then, but later when I saw him at Pinos Altos, he seemed a kind of loco. Indian experience had somehow affected his mind. He gave it out that he had found a rich diggin's and he even showed nuggets to prove it, gettin' some Arizona people to form a company with him, but the Indians drove them out of the country before they could find anything. From time to time since then one party or another has looked for the diggin's, but as you know, no trace of them has ever been found. For myself, I've never put much stock in Adams' tale. I've seen too many prospectors in my day lookin' for the pot of gold at the end of the rainbow. Many of them, like me, have grown so they hardly believe their own lies any more. Adams himself has set out several times from Silver City, but each time he gets lost on Cactus Flat and comes back to the settlement. Now I feel mighty sure if these diggin's are anywhere outside of Adams' head, they are the same as the Snively diggin's."

Baxter fell silent at the end of these remarks, staring into the red ashes of the camp-fire. Some of us got up to throw more wood on the fire and to call back a straying burro. When we were settled, Baxter again turned to me. "I reckon you've heard all about the Snively diggin's, too? They date much farther back, Snively havin' been one of the founders of Pinos Altos. I hev faith in those diggin's, for I knew Snively, also Houston and Thomas, both reliable men up here in Pinos Altos, as you'll agree. Thomas, Houston, and myself saw Snively and talked with him when he pulled his freight into Pinos Altos in the sixties with ten thousand dollars in gold nuggets. Cochise was raidin' the country at that time with his red devils and it was too dangerous to go back to look for the rich find. Thomas felt sure that Snively hed a sluice-box and he was certain that he hed a cabin. Snively told Thomas and Judge Houston that he believed Mexican sheep-herders also knew of this place, as when he first went into the gulch he found signs of a camp."

"Are the Snively diggin's by any chance the same as what they call the Nigger Diggings?" I asked Baxter.

"In my opinion the Nigger Diggin's, the Schaeffer Diggin's, the Snively Diggin's,—the Adams Diggin's, if they exist at all,—and my own diggin's, which I'll tell you about some time, are one and the same. There's not much known about the Nigger Diggin's, but I reckon from what I've been able to gather of the tale that the nigger while on detail as a trooper must hev happened into the same gulch that Snively tells about. Findin' coarse nuggets of gold, he located the place in his mind, by its distance from Island Mountain, and its direction from the mountain with the painted face of a woman on its eastern side. When he was discharged from the army he claims he went back there, but was chased out by Apaches the day after makin' a rich find. Well boys, it's time to roll in for the night—but if you care to hear it, I'll tell you to-morrow night the tale of the Schaeffer Diggin's."

2. *Baxter Tells McGurk's Story of the Schaeffer Diggings*

It was a fine evening for "swappin' lies". There was just enough tang in the air to make the fire feel good. A flock of turkeys in a near-by grove of pinons kept up their evening chant of "peep, peep". Some distance down the creek a mountain lion roared, and still farther away the sharp yap of the coyote broke the quiet of the evening. Quite a crowd had gathered around the fire to hear Baxter's tale of the Schaeffer diggings.

"Ay bain dreamin' last night," Swedish Nelson told us, "that ay bain to the lost diggin's an' chust as Ay bain about to leave with my sack of gould nuggets, them red Apaches come poppin' up out'n the ground like corn from a skillet, and every one o' them bain wearin' a bunch o' scalps at his belt and a long string o' human ears and fingers around his neck instead of beads. My goodness, but Ay was glad to wake up an' leave them nuggets where they be."

"And you weren't up against it in your dream," began Baxter, "any worse than the German whose story I heard from a friend of mine named McGurk. In the year 1876 I pulled in my freight and went into camp at an old government post, called Fort Thomas, on the Gila, near the spot where Duncan now stands. I soon began to knock around with some of the troopers there. One of them was an Irishman named McGurk. To-night I'm goin' to tell you the tale of the Schaeffer Diggin's as I got it from McGurk.

" 'I was a sergeant,' began McGurk to me, 'detailed to go in charge of some soldiers to he'p guard a band of wood choppers, sent from Fort Cummings in the fall of 1872. I was second sergeant in C Company of the Fourth Regiment under Captain Tucker. As there was no large timber nearer than the head waters of the Mimbres River, I was given ten men, and a farrier named Young, who hed done some scoutin' in this section. All hed good ridin' animals and there were enough pack animals to carry what supplies we needed. The captain give me leave to pick my own men, with orders to be ready to start the next evenin' at sundown. "Your duties," said the captain to me, "will be to see that camp is made, and to keep a close guard on your horses and stock, for maraudin' Apaches under Cochise and Victorio have a stronghold near these headwaters and may give you a deal of trouble."

" 'Young had a shepherd dog which was used by the troops at Ft. Cummings for herding. He asked to take the dog along, and the captain said O. K.

" 'Among those I picked for the trip was a German, named Jake Schaeffer, intendin' him for a cook, as it is well known among frontiersmen that Germans, as a rule, can cook, but are no good in the woods. They seem to get lost as soon as they are out of sight of camp. Takin' him along is the basis of this tale. Five of the ten men picked were all new in the country, and this was a fine chance to practice shootin', game bein' plentiful.

" 'I generally detail a rooky with a vet, my experience being that too many vets do not do so well as where there are a few rookies. The latter are more anxious and willin' to do what they are told, the old vets preferrin' to play cards and sleep while out on these details, especially when there are no Indian signs of danger. The rookies recitin' their guard duties and night experiences around the evenin' camp fire gave the vets many a laugh.

" 'We had been in camp some three months and seen no signs of Indians. Everything was peaceful and quiet. The game was easy to get, comin' often close to our camp. Jake Schaeffer, our German cook, got around me to let him go out and kill a deer or maybe a bear, he sayin' that he had never even shot at one, and would like to have a chance now as they were plentiful. He asked me to let him go with Young the next time he went out for game. I spoke to Young about Schaeffer's wish, Young sayin', "By cracky, let him have a chance. I'll take care of him."

" 'I told Jake he could go and he talked of nothin' else. At last the day came, they leavin' early in the morning, Jake takin' his carbine and a belt filled with cartridges. I was up to see them off and made the German fill his haversack with hard-tack, warnin' him to be sure to keep his canteen full of water. That was the last I saw of Jake for three months.

" 'Young came back in the afternoon as glum as hell, sayin' he could not find him. We saddled up the two best horses and Young and myself struck out to look for him, taking along the dog and a three-day supply of food. Ridin' direct to the point where Young claimed he heard the rifle report, we found no sign of Jake. Both of us fired our rifles but we got no answer. The dog seemin' to know what we wanted, started to circle, finally givin' out some loud yelps and barks. On goin' up to him we found the German's tracks. Soon we sighted blood on the trail, and seein' the deer tracks we followed slow, at times firin' our rifles, but got no answer.

" 'The dog finally trailed the deer to where it lay dead, but no Jake was to be found. The moon had gone down by this time, so we lit a fire and roasted some of the venison. We then pulled the saddles off our horses, hobbled 'em, and turned 'em loose, havin' made up our minds to wait till daylight. The dog seemed uneasy, whinin' at times. As soon as we laid down he kept pokin' his cold nose into our faces; at times he would bristle up and growl as if afraid.

" 'Young said nothin' but he seemed worried. About an hour before daybreak he sent the dog for the horses, though he did not want to go. He kept lookin' up at Young with a pitiful whine, but at last he started. We never saw him or our horses again.

" 'Waitin' about half an hour, and not hearin' the dog bark, Young said, "By cracky, it's time to vamoose. We're sure surrounded by Apaches, or my name ain't Young. I'm for pullin' our freight back—the sooner the better!"

" 'Reachin' the place where we had last seen Schaeffer's tracks, without findin' any Indian signs, Young said, "By cracky, McGurk I don't believe they'll get us this time, unless they're hidin' in that bunch of quakin' asp over yonder.

" 'At that instant a perfect shower of arrows drove towards us from the thicket, one of them piercin' Young's brain, killin' him instant. I got off without a scratch, reachin' the wood camp about noon. Here another shock was waitin' for me. Those damned Indians had killed all of the wood choppers and two of the troopers, and hed run off all the ridin' and pack animals.

" 'I gathered the men that were left and we pulled freight for Fort Cummings. Captain Tucker after hearin' the bad news, left a small detail to guard the post, takin' the balance of the troops on the trail of the marauders; these troops were to bury the dead, and to find Schaeffer, if possible. Captain Tucker came to the conclusion to stay on the site of the wood camp until the lumber and cut timber could be hauled to Fort Cummings.

" 'After buryin' the wood choppers and troopers, we hit the trail where Young had passed in his chips. When he was buried we followed the Indian signs up to the north end of the Black Range, across the San Augustine plains, and into the Datils. We back-tracked down the west side of this range, cut across the Burros, and on into the San Simon Valley, finally reachin' the line of Mexico.

" 'Not being allowed on foreign soil, there was nothin' for it but to pull back to the wood camp at the headwaters of the Mimbres. Captain Tucker got the wood to the fort that winter as he had planned.

" 'In the meantime soldiers from Fort Craig came to Fort Cummings with news of Schaeffer. He hed roamed for days and wandered at least two hundred miles, before he finally drifted into Fort Craig. The men told us the German came in one day as crazy as a loon, and nearly naked. No gun, feet on the ground, no coat or hat, but holdin' on like grim death to his haversack, which hed in it, I was told by Sergeant Jefferies of Company D of the 5th, nuggets that were almost pure gold, he havin' as near as they could guess well on to ten pounds. He wouldn't let anyone come near him and kept on yellin' the name of Young every little while. On a sudden he started off as if haunted, runnin' like a deer straight for the Rio Grande. He got out of sight before the men at Fort Craig knew what he was about. A detail was started out to find him. They came upon him near a Mexican jacal, or hut, naked as the day he was born, with not a trace of his clothes or haversack.

" 'They took him back to the post, and from there to the hospital, he hangin' between life and death for weeks. All that he could remember was that he had wounded a deer and got lost followin' it. He did not know where he got the nuggets, but he recalled crossin' a wide plain or desert. He saw many wild horses and antelopes, and talked about a mountain with a woman's picture painted on it in bright colors, but where it was he could not tell.

" 'Soon after the visit of the Fort Craig soldiers, Schaeffer pulled freight into Fort Cummings, but he was never like his old self. He would leave camp and be gone for days, always comin' back empty-handed, and as glum as hell.

" 'My enlistment being up, we made up our minds to see if we could find the Schaeffer diggin's. We knew it must be some place between the head of the Mimbres and the headwaters of the Little Colorado. We figured that Schaeffer even for gold would not throw away his rations. He had food enough with him when he lit out from the Mimbres camp to last him for two days, so we surmised he had found the gold on his fourth or fifth day. We believed he would cover at least twenty miles a day, and we felt sure the desert or plain he had crossed was the San Augustine, as both my pal and myself had soldiered up there and knew that section. We reckoned we'd hit the diggin's in a couple of months.

" 'My pal, Jefferies, thought he knew the mountain with the picture on it. He believed it was the Magdalena. On the east slope of this mountain the head of a woman can be made out without any trouble. The shrubs on the mountainside have grown around a rocky outcroppin' and it sure does look like a woman's face. This mountain of many colors in its lonesome settin' stirred up good feelin' in the Spaniards, and they called it our Lady of Magdalena. The mountain is located near the north end of the Black Range, close to the edge of the San Augustine plains.

" 'However, the question was raised as to whether Schaeffer might not in his wanderin's have come within sight of the Santa Rita Mountains. In that case in speakin' of a woman's picture, he might be referrin' to the "Kneelin' Nun". As everyone around Grant County knows, a juttin' needle of rock takes the form of a kneelin' woman on the rim of the Santa Rita basin and can be seen from a long distance. A Mexican half-breed told me the legend about the "Kneelin' Nun." He said in the early days the Spaniards built a monastery for monks and nuns on this mountain. One of the nuns broke her vows, being turned into stone as a punishment. So the story goes, and you can believe it if you want.

" 'But Jeff and I reckoned that the Magdalena was the safer landmark to go by, as it lay in the direction of Fort Craig. Besides, it was the landmark that figured in the tale of the Snively Diggin's.

" 'Me and Jeff soon hed our plans made. We would get our discharges, take our travel pay, go back to God's country on a visit, see our people, and then pull our freight for the German's diggin's. On the first of August we both got our honorables, with our travel pay, and extra clothin' money. Both of us had enlisted from Columbus, Ohio, so we took the stage from Bowie to Los Angeles goin' via boat to New York, arrivin' there O. K. in December. We did not booze nor paint any places red. Just a pair of sensible regulars.

" 'Alas for our plans! Jefferies had gone to St. Louis where he fell in love with a jane. He was jilted by her after she got most of his money in the form of presents. He fell into a morose spell, takin' to John Barleycorn to forget his troubles. His folks wrote to me, but I got to St. Louis too late. He had enlisted in the Seventh Regiment, being sent at once to the Black Hills, where he passed in his chips the followin' summer on the Rosebud Reservation.

" 'I went back to Columbus feelin' down in the mouth. After wanderin' around a month or two, I drifted into State Street, drinkin' beer, and swappin' lies. There I met Sergeant Griffin of the Fourth Regiment who was back recruitin', and I just naturally signed up, so you can see how it was I never got to the Schaeffer Diggin's.'

"So ends McGurk's tale and so ends to-night's session," concluded Baxter.

3. *Baxter's Tale of His Attempt to Find the Snively Diggings*

The next night, as the weather was unsettled, the party of four gathered around the fireplace in my cabin. I had spread a bearskin on the earthen floor, as we would rather sit there before the fire than use the rough bench that took the place of chairs.

"You should learn to smoke, Jimmy," said Baxter to me, as he filled and lighted his cuddy pipe. "Give me my burro, my pipe, and a few good books, and I'll never be lonesome no matter how long I'm on the trail. No, and I'll never miss my jug of corn juice, either, though I'll own up I'd sometimes hanker for a sight of Barbarita."

"Bully for you, Baxter", said Wood Poland, "and now we're rarin' an' plungin' to hear how you made out to find them Snively Diggin's."

"Ay bain havin' another dream about them diggin's," put in Swedish Nelson, "only last night it bain't Apaches. But chust as

Ay was about to hoist up may bag o' nuggets, out steps a silvertip big as an elephant, an' mon, I'd be runnin' yet if Ay hadn't woke up, an' them gould nuggets be still in the gulch."

"I believed," began Baxter, "those lost diggin's were north and east of old Fort West on the Gila, this fort being located where the Mangas empties into the Gila in New Mexico. My reason for thinking this is that Snively when he pulled his freight into Pinos Altos in the sixties with ten thousand dollars in gold nuggets which he showed to Houston, Thomas, and myself, claimed he had come into the fort almost due south of the gulch he got the nuggets out of. He said he had traveled south as the crow flies for a hundred and twenty-five miles before he came into Fort West. 'I'm headin' for the Pacific Coast,' he told us. 'I've got enough dust to last me the rest of my days, and besides its too dangerous amongst them fierce Apaches. They came near gettin' me this time.'

"I thought a lot about Snively's tale and finally got John Adair to hit the trail with me and try to find the diggin's. John was married to a half-breed Mexican woman, which meant he had been keepin' his nose to the grindstone, for he had to divide up as long as there was a bite to eat, with all the primos, or relatives, of his wife. I never knew a white man that didn't go broke in less than three years after tyin' up with one of these women. They don't seem happy until they've sifted him to bed-rock. Then with a house full of children, a few dogs, and a patch of ground to raise chili and beans, her *amigos* and *primos* havin' gotten the rest, she seems content to settle down.

"So I knew that John hed nothin'. But he was on the square, a good shot, and well versed in prospectin' matters. I bought me two good saddle horses and a pair of pack mules with all the, equipment we needed for a long trip. John was glad of the chance, as the placers at Pinos Altos just furnished about enough gold to keep him and the family alive. John had a tale of some rich diggin's which sheep herders told of, havin' seen nuggets in the hands of the Indians, the latter declarin' they had got the nuggets in a small gulch north and west of Socorro, a town on the Rio Grande.

"John made arrangements with the stores to furnish supplies to his family while he was gone, and in case he did not come back he deeded them his minin' claims. While he was arrangin' his affairs, I went over to Santa Rita to spend a few days with Barbarita. After biddin' her good-bye, I went to Silver City where I bought a

Winchester repeatin' rifle, being one of the first in these parts to own such a gun. John had made the packsaddles and we were soon ready to pull our freight.

"Startin' early one mornin' from Silver City, we headed for the government sawmill on the Mimbres River. This was the spot Schaeffer had started from, and the trail led through the Black Range, one of the most important hangouts of Victorio's Apaches. Leavin' the range at the head of Diamond Creek, keepin' north we went around the head of the stream, comin' into the San Augustine Plains near the west end. From there we headed into the Elk Mountains where we camped the third night.

"Deer and elk were plentiful, also grass and water. We concluded to rest up a few days. Durin' this time we found a deserted sheep herder's camp with a stone barricade around it. Lots of empty shells and a good deal of flattened lead showed there had been quite a fight on that spot. We knew the bones of the herders must be lying near-by as we had run across a bunch of goats as wild as deer, at the head of the canyon. We believed they were all that were left of the herder's flock. Indians and wild beasts more than likely had done for the rest. Herders always have a few goats with their sheep to furnish them with milk for drinkin' and cookin'.

"On the mornin' we were to leave, I told John I would go out for a deer, as they came close to camp here and it might be hard to find one later on. A part of the animal could easy be packed on our saddles. Goin' up a canyon I sighted a buck. My shot went home. He ran across the divide and laid down. It was plain he had not seen me. I dropped down and crept into a clump of brush so as not to put him wise to my whereabouts, intendin' to let him stay there until he bled to death. As I sat there on my hunkers I saw somethin' lyin' a short ways ahead that looked like shoes. At that instant the deer gave a long shudder and laid still, so I knew he was dead. I then went closer to the objects which I saw were shoes, sure enough, they being the kind herders wore. On pickin' them up I heard somethin' rattle. By Judas priest! Out tumbled the foot bones, all that was left of the herder's body. Such was the fate of one of the herders who must have got away from the stockade.

"Droppin' the spooky things, I went off and gutted the deer, cuttin' off the hind quarters, and hangin' the balance on a small tree, as the custom was, though it wasn't likely anyone would happen along to make use of it in that lonely spot. Loadin' up the best of the meat, I struck out for camp, also carryin' the shoes to show to John. We buried the bones, but it sure gave us the blues. Too much like an evil omen.

"Adair had the animals ready and we headed towards the Datil Mountains. At the upper end of the Elks, lookin' east, we saw the face on the Magdalenas in its brushy settin'. Adair cheered up for he claimed it was a good sign to be able to see the lady's face from this point. 'Now for the German's diggin's,' I told him.

"Crossin' the Datils the sun almost burned us up. Gettin' into the foothills about two o'clock in the afternoon, and knowin' John Adair had been in them before, I asked him if he hed any idea where we could find water. He said there was a big canyon not very far from where we were, and as a game trail led through it, water couldn't be very far away.

"We headed our stock up the canyon, but the distance sure had us fooled. Not until sundown did we pull into the canyon we were aimin' for, and the horse and mules were sure petered out. As we went up this canyon we were struck by the bright colors in the rocky walls. It seemed the stain of some mineral, which I thought might be copper, the formation being a red and pink shale, here and there streaked with moss green. When I asked John if he thought we were in a copper district, he burst out, 'Oh, hell, I hope not, Jason. A copper mine here would be as good as nothin', two hundred and fifty miles from the nearest railroad, and copper only worth eight cents a pound at that.'

"As night came on we lost the game trail, and we were feelin' pretty glum. If there was water, it was well hidden, but more than likely the game trail led from the Datils to the Negryto or Frisco Rivers, bein' used by deer and antelope from the plains. So there was nothin' for it but to make a dry camp. One of our pack mules appeared to know the section, probably hevin' belonged to sheep men who hed herds in the vicinity. This mule would at times leave the other animals and head for a low range which lay by itself off to the east, a group of mountains standin' as lonely as pyramids in the desert. We picketed the horses and mules that night, knowin' they would strike back to the Elk Mountains lookin' for water, if only hobbled.

"Before lyin' down we ate some of the deer meat, not even cookin' it, and this seemed to quench our thirst, and he'ped save our water supply, which we kept in a keg close to our bed. We built no protection as we had seen no sign of a livin' creature for hours, bein' too far from water to be in danger from wild animals.

"We must hev slept terrible sound, for durin' the night the Mexican mule broke his picket rope and passed close to our heads without wakin' us up. After breakfast we saddled up, dividin' the Mexican mule's load among the other animals. Takin' the loose mule's trail, we found it led us out of the red canyon into another where we picked up the lost game trail. But instead of goin' toward the west, he had struck east, as the crow flies, goin' towards the "Island" mountain we hed noticed the night before. His signs were fresh, we discoverin' he still hed a long piece of the tie rope on him. We were in hopes it would fasten him onto a greasewood or cactus bush tanglin' him up. I havin' the swiftest horse, left Adair and galloped off in the direction of the Island Mountain, not payin' any attention to the trail. I knew the mule must hev been here before and that those mountains must hev in them either a spring of water or a natural rock tank holdin' water.

"The ridin' was good, the surface being almost level, and I was soon out of sight of John. The sun was gettin' hot, the air close and sultry. As I neared the Island Mountain the plants got weird. There were immense sotols and the largest cacti I have ever seen. Bare spots, at times crusted with a coat of alkali, looked like dry lake beds, and were probably filled with water durin' the rainy season. I could see mirages off to the east, and once in a while a salt laguna. I knew I must be in some part of the Great American Desert. Seein' the mule's tracks in one of these lagunas, I scoured the landscape with my field glasses. Then I saw the mule standin' beside a bush not more than a mile away. I came up to him in a few minutes and found him fastened to a mesquite bush where he had stopped to browse. I waited for John at this spot. When he came up we hauled the saddles from the animals and gave them all the water we had left, as we were certain the Mexican mule would soon lead us to a fresh supply. We packed him heavy to relieve the other animals. After restin' we resaddled and turned the mule loose. He struck out on a lope towards the Island Mountain. About four that afternoon the country became rough, with deep arroyos and washed-out gulches. The mule was headed for a ridge which looked like the hub of a crater. The other animals seemed to have scented water and kept close to their leader. The vegetation changed to scrub oak and a few pinon and juniper trees. Many signs of deer and antelope were lying about, a herd of the latter runnin' off the queer-lookin' ridge. To the northwest we could see the White Mountains of Arizona. After a hard climb we found ourselves on the ridge, or hog-back, which we followed to its end, dippin' from there into a wooded box canyon whose sides showed a quartzite formation, then up again at least five hundred yards where a straight face of rock seemed to bring it to a sudden end. The mule kept right on, and when almost against the face of the cliff near an immense boulder, he seemed to pass right through the wall. We followed and came into a small park through a natural gateway, which had been hidden from us by the immense boulder I mentioned a minute ago. The mule still went on, and at the end of the park was another face of rock and another openin', which led us into a much larger park where a deep gulch went up to a small peak. Goin' through this second park we ran across hundreds of elk horns, this bein' one of the places where the males come to be away from the females durin' the moultin' season every year. The elks are usually as grumpy at such times as humans with a sick headache. All the bark had been rubbed from the small trees in this park, showin' how the elks had used them to loosen their old horns, and rub the velvet from their new horns.

"The mule headed straight up the gulch. We now saw signs that proved someone had been here before us. Lyin' close to the roots of a large pinon tree we found a belt marked with a United States brand. We sure got excited. On a sudden the mule stopped and pawed the sand in the gulch, the hole soon fillin' with water. I dismounted, and takin' a shovel from the pack, soon had a pool of water. The animals drank until it's a wonder they didn't bust open. We made up our minds to look for running water a little farther up the gulch. The park widened as we went higher, and we soon found a runnin' stream. The animals had been draggin' along for hours, and they seemed real grateful when we took off the saddles and packs and turned them loose. They were soon feedin' on the rich, dry grass.

"We felt sure the Indians must know of this place, so the first thing we did was to set up a barricade of the rocks that were lyin' around so plentiful. These boulders appeared to have been washed into the spot from a deserted placer, or rolled there by a waterspout at sometime in this canyon; debris and brush were still hangin' on the sides of the canyon and also on trees.

"We dug a hole to build a fire in, as the grass was very dry, and we soon had a good feed of roast venison, chili beans, and hard-tack. We rested after the meal, smokin' our pipes, takin' in the scenery and the cool evenin' air. We must have both been thinkin' the same thoughts, for on a sudden, we got up together. Gettin' our gold pans, without speakin' on the subject, we started up the gulch lookin' for the spot where the German got his nuggets. The water increased as we went up and the canyon walls of white quartz became tinted like a rainbow in the evenin' air. All the clays and rocks looked mineralized. We soon had colors in our pans and horns—ribbon quartz on bed rock, also black sand and pieces of pink quartz, which we believed came from a small hill of that color farther up. The one thought in our minds was, 'How much farther is it to the spot these colors and quartz came from?'

"As we had spent considerable time prospectin' and pannin', night was on us before we knew it. We pulled back to camp and spread our blankets and wagon sheet; and were soon asleep dreamin' of the riches the mornin' would bring us. About two in the mornin' the Mexican mule came to the barricade and stuck his nose into my face, as much as to say, 'Be on the watch.' As they are raised in camps these critters get very lonesome when out in the wilds and will sometimes poke their noses into your face several times in the course of the night. I told the mule to vamoose, but he hung around for nearly an hour, finally pullin' out in a different direction from where the other animals were grazin'.

"I rolled over and discovered that the moon had gone down and slight tinges of gray could be seen in the east. Before I knew it I hed again dropped off to sleep. The next thing I knew some one was holdin' his hand over my mouth. It was John. He whispered me that some one was in the brush above us. It was either an animal or a prowlin' Apache. A whippoorwill call on the air was answered by others in many directions. A turkey gobbled just below us.

"John, grabbin' his rifle, said he never knew a turkey to gobble in August. He wanted to pile up more rocks, for he believed the red devils would rush us as soon as it was daylight. We were in for it and we knew it. We had built our barricade the night before against the canyon wall where we were protected from above by an overhangin' cliff. This was a fine back protection, but our front was only rocks. We soon had enough boulders up to keep our bodies and heads out of sight.

"Not a sound could be heard. Maybe we were both loco. Yet there was a feelin' of danger in the air. Day at last began to break, revealin' low, black clouds scuddin' before a high wind. On a sudden the silence was broken by a swishin' noise that made me think of the lassoin' of cattle. A loud crash. A mule rushed past the barricade with the lariat draggin' from his neck.

"We dropped down inside the barricade as a shower of arrows passed over our heads, followed by hellish, blood-curdlin' yells. It was still too dark to see the savages through the eye holes in our barricade. We waited holdin' our breath, expectin' each moment to be rushed by the red demons. I was lyin' on the left side of the barricade, John bein' in the middle.

"An Apache rose overhead on the cliff throwin' a lance and drawin' fire from Adair. At the same instant eight or ten more of the devils jumped up from their hidin' places just below us and rushed towards the barricade. I pumped my Winchester into them with deadly effect, three of them instantly crumplin' like autumn leaves. Hevin' never before been up against a repeatin' rifle the rest were puzzled and ran back among the boulders. There was a lull in the attack, givin' John time to reload his Sharps.

"I warned John to watch out for the Indian above, as the lance had just missed his leg by a hair's breadth. The Apaches did not rush us again. We had them guessin'. We laid inside our barricade all day, and they kept tryin' to reach us from above. About three o'clock in the afternoon I sighted an Indian on a near-by cliff givin' signals. As John's rifle had the longer range we traded guns, and I drew on the Indian sentinel topplin' him from the cliff. At the same instant the Indian from above again threw his lance, piercin' John's foot, but John got him, and we had no more trouble from that section. John's foot swelled fast, and we had to cut his shoe to get it off. It sure was hell.

"We could still see the signals and figured they were callin' for help. All day long the black clouds hung above us. We longed for the night to come, for our only hope was in darkness. Our getaway must be made up the canyon, for all the Indians seemed to be comin' from below. Night came at last and with it the storm that had held off all day. Lightning flashed, the thunder rolled and cracked as if the mountains were knockin' their heads together, We were in for a night of it and we knew it.

"John was afraid of a cloud burst at that time of the year. Above the screamin' of the wind and the roarin' of the thunder we could hear the calls of the Indians.

"We made up our minds to risk everything to get away through the storm and the dark. The lightnin' was terrible dangerous, for the bright flashes might at any minute give us away to the watchin' Indians. We got together a bit of bacon and flour and our water canteens, and made an openin' in our barricade where the shadow laid thickest against the canyon wall. Soon we were creepin' up the canyon, huggin' the wall and tryin' to shrink out of sight in the glarin' lightnin'. The storm raged like a mad bull—such rain as it was, fallin' in sheets and by the bucketful. The canyon soon became a rushin' torrent.

"John had to stop to put on his shoes, and neither of us could ever figure how he got the shoe over his swollen foot nor how he managed to walk after that, but he did both, whisperin' to me between thunderclaps, that we were between the devil and the deep sea and we would sure drown if we didn't get out of that gulch in a hurry. Hardly had he said this when the lightnin showed us the Mexican mule comin' towards us, still draggin' the lariat rope, probably havin' been driven down by the floodin' waters. He stopped and I caught hold of the rope. John made a halter of it and was soon astraddle. A little farther on we turned into a smaller canyon where the waters were neither so deep nor so swift. The sky became lighter as we went up this gulch which led us finally into quite a valley.

"By the lightnin' flashes we made out an old partly-burned log cabin standin' to one side of the valley. There was no roof and only a few logs were standin'. Close to the ruined cabin we also made out what looked like a sluice box and a pile of lumber; and a short distance away thought we saw two piles of bones. As the Indians, judgin' from their whoops and catcalls, had discovered our escape, we dared not go over to examine the spot. Whippoorwill calls and coyote barks could be heard in all directions except above and to our right.

"The arroyo soon forked again, we choosin' the one goin' west. We splashed along all night, gettin' to the head of the gulch at daybreak. The hill here was very steep and rocky, but we found a game trail which brought us out on the top. Lookin' to the south and east with my field glass, I thought I located the San Mateo Mountains; I also saw the flashes from the lances of a large war-party of Apaches, on their way towards the Rio Grande. Turnin' the glass towards the spot where we had camped, I saw two smoke signals, which might be warnin' the war party of our escape. We reckoned the Indians had come from the south and west, and we made up our minds to head that way, believin' the country would be free of them in those directions, and that we also stood a chance of meetin' United States troopers on the trail of the war party.

"John's foot was givin' him a lot of pain, so he pulled off his shoe and tied it to his canteen. He had used up a lot of water on the foot tryin' to bring down the swellin'. After restin' for a while on a small flat where the mule could graze, we struck a south course, headin' for the north end of the Mogollon Mountains. Water was plentiful on account of the heavy summer rains. We struck the headwaters of the Frisco River, goin' down it to the copper camps of Morenci and Clifton, but we stayed there only long enough to rest up and get John's foot taken care of by a veterinary. I bought John a horse, and he went back to Pinos Altos and his gold pannin'. I heard he died there last year.

"Time flies. I've drifted about from one mine to another, and it's eight years since I left the Island Mountain, but I've never forgotten what the lightnin' showed me that night, and I've always meant to go back there some time. Up till now it has never been safe to make the trip with such devils on the warpath as Nana, Ju, Cochise, and Victorio. It was foolish to venture far away from the settlements until this year. But I'm here now to boil out and hunt and fish during the summer. I'm lookin' around for a couple of pardners, who'll be willin' to go huntin' with me next winter, and be ready to start out next February or March, as soon as grass and water get plentiful, to make one more try for the Lost Diggin's.

"It's time to break up the party for to-night, but I think I've given you plenty to dream about, eh, Nelson?"

4. *We Visit the Gila Cliff Dwellings*

According to Baxter, when he came to the Gila country shortly after the Civil War, the little valley opposite the Hot Springs showed signs of irrigation ditches, its willow thickets being a hide-out for bears. But after the cattle came all these signs were destroyed. I believe these springs were used by the prehistoric people who had their cliff dwellings about six miles above the springs on the West Fork of the Gila. In the summer of 1884 I went through these cliff dwellings with Baxter, who had been around many pueblos and cave houses in New Mexico, and could talk by the hour on what he had seen.

The cliff was reached by a steep hill that rose to a height of about one hundred and seventy-five feet. In the lower part of this canyon wall of sandstone were four caverns with houses built inside them. These cave dwellings are only one story high, but they appear two stories high, owing to the way they stand on the slope. Entering the eastern cave house by crawling through a small, square door, we explored three houses without going outside to enter them, as passageways led behind wide rock pillars; the fourth cave dwelling to the west we had to reach by a separate opening from the outside. We went through more than twenty compartments, some not over five feet square, none above seven feet high.

In the large cliff house on the West Fork, which has since been made a National Monument, we found many partitions built of rock laid in cement. We thought this cement must have been made of lime and sand, crushed in metates, like those still in use among Mexicans and Indians for grinding corn and other grains and seeds; however, some claim the rocks were laid in adobe mud. Whatever it was, it wore well, for these walls are as strong as the day they were built, perhaps five hundred years, perhaps five thousand years ago, since no one can tell their age. All the mortar must have been put on by hand as the masonry still bears many finger prints and hand marks. Even the cracks in the floor were sealed with this mortar, and the floors were still in good shape at the time of our visit. The roofs also were in good condition, being held up by pine beams with the bark peeled off. The pine beams were covered with a network of twigs and grasses, and this again with a plaster of adobe mud. T-shaped air holes gave a dim light.

We found no articles made of metal, but many of stone. The hammers and war axes we took note of were nearly all made of a niggerhead rock not found in the vicinity. A groove was cut through the center in which a split wooden handle was fastened with the sinews of an animal. Other war axes shaped like a mallet were made of a rock called ricolite found near Silver City.

The only ornaments we picked up were of turquoise, generally formed into beads of oblong shape. New Mexico is noted for its high-grade turquoise, but I have never seen any of so fine a quality as that we picked up in the rooms of the cliff dwelling. The beads were strung on animal sinews. Taking in one hand a stone-chipped drill, and in the other a handful of turquoise beads each with a tiny round hole bored through it one could not but wonder at the skill and patience of these workers in stone. How did they do so well? It has always been a mystery to me. Their arrowheads, too, were chipped by the hands of artists.

In the upper cliff dwellings we took note of many ollas, or water jars, made of red and gray clay, not found in this section. The ollas that I saw were all decorated with pictures of bear, elk, and deer, and a number of other designs, but there were no birds, flowers, or trees. In the debris we found many pumpkin seeds and some corn on the cob, with a small amount of the flint variety, though most of it looked like popcorn; we also picked up many pink beans and a few striped ones.

The most interesting thing we found was a perfect mummy with cottonwood fiber woven around it. The sex signs had either decayed or had been removed, but all who saw the mummy believed it to be the remains of a female. The length of the figure was about eighteen inches. It lay with knees drawn up and the palms of the hands covering the face. The features were like those of a Chinese child, with high cheek bones and coarse, dark hair. The age of the child at the time of death was thought to be two years. The body was kept for weeks in the show window of a store in Silver City.

A man happened in to Silver City at that time calling himself Webster. He said he was working for the Smithsonian Institute and showed us some of their letterheads. He borrowed the mummy, promising to give it back in a few months. Not hearing from him at the time set, we wrote to Washington, D.C. We were told that the Smithsonian Institute knew of no one by the name of Webster, and that they had no one doing research in the Gila field. I have always believed that Webster sold the relic to a private collection. Very few mummies have ever been found in the ruins, and we realized too late the value of our relic. A few years ago while I was visiting my nephew, Judge Murdoch of Washington, we looked for my mummy in the Smithsonian Institute, but could not find it. Perhaps through this story it will some day turn up again.

In one of the caves was a large hall, or gathering place, which I have been told was an estuba or kiva. An oblong fireplace took up the center of this room. Lying about were many sandals made of bear grass and yucca fiber. Their small size, the small hand prints on the wall, and the small openings between rooms seemed to tell of a race of short people; however, skeletons found in other ruins do not bear out this idea. Under the floors we found bones and skulls. Perhaps if some one learns to read the pictographs on the canyon walls, other burial places may be discovered. In one room we found a hollow-sounding section, but we had to give up trying to get into it on account of the millions of fleas and mosquitoes we stirred up.

These cliff dwellings have been visited by archaeologists since Baxter and I went through them fifty years ago, and their reports can be read in the public libraries of the State. Many relics had been taken away even before Baxter and I went through the Gila Cliff Dwellings and little remained to carry off. The last time I was in the cliff dwellings, the bats seemed to have staked their claims there. The Apaches never used these caves, saying they had belonged to a people who lived in the Gila country years before they came there.

5. *We Go Hunting*

After going through the Gila Cliff Dwellings, we went back to the Hot Springs for more baths. Then we got our outfit ready for the hunt during the fall and winter. In October we struck north for Snow Creek, crossed over to Iron Creek, and headed through Turkey Feather Pass to the Jerky Mountains on the West Fork of the Gila River, and from there to Old Baldy in the Mogollons.

The game was rolling fat. What loads of deer and turkey we sent to Fort Bayard, Pinos Altos, and Silver City, always getting a fine price! White-tailed and black-tailed, or mule deer, often traveled in bands of thirty or forty animals. The mule deer were more plentiful than the white-tail in the Black and Mogollon Ranges. The white-tail is generally found close to a meadow on the Gila, or along the streams that put into it, as it wants for its home range, scrubby thickets and rough uplands dotted with parks. The mule deer likes the wooded canyons, being fitted by Nature for long, flying leaps in a rocky land. He gets used to almost any mountain footing.

All deer browse on grasses, shrubs, and tender twigs. In the

Gila Forest they feed for the most part on the mast of junipers, pinons, oaks, manzanita, and buck brush. Deer do not live in dens, nor build nests, but choose a brushy spot, hard for the enemy to reach, where their coloring helps to hide them. Nature protects the young by giving them spotted coats with a leafy look. Apart from the gun of the hunter the worst enemies of the deer in the Gila Forest are the coyote, the wildcat, and the mountain lion. I believe the Government should have control of the forests and game animals. Looking back to fifty years ago, I have come to the conclusion I was using up more than my share of the natural resources which belong to all the people of the state, but you cannot put an old head on young shoulders, and at that time no laws had as yet been made to save the treasures of mountain and forest. But I never killed without good reason nor wasted the bounty of our southwestern mountains.

The mule deer of New Mexico is generally heavier than the white-tail, averaging over two hundred pounds, and sometimes weighing from two hundred fifty to three hundred pounds. The hunter can easily pick out the mule deer by its large, hairy ears, and the black tip of its tail which dances like a pompon at the end of a short white rope. The mule deer has a white face with a black patch on the forehead, this being another way of telling it from the white-tail which often has a black band on chin and throat. Both animals wear a buff-colored coat in summer, which is changed by the black-tail in the fall for one of bluish-gray, and by the white-tail for one of yellowish-green.

While hunting in the Black and Mogollon Mountains, in times of deep snow I took note of bucks, and even of does, that would leave the herd and head for a tree near a dwelling, especially a tree in a brushy setting. Hiding himself as well as he could against this background, he would gaze for hours in the direction of the cabin. I have killed many deer not over a hundred feet from my cabin on days when the snow was falling in big flakes.

Hunters who killed deer to furnish a market or to supply a fort with fresh meat soon learned that deer, elk, and moose are affected in their feeding by the light or dark of the moon. During the light of the moon it is very hard to get a deer in the morning, for it feeds at that time in the early part of the night. It is the other way around during the dark of the moon.

The winter of 1883 and 1884 was the best deer season I can remember. Nelson, our Swedish packer, had made three trips;

and as it neared Thanksgiving Day he had orders for a hundred turkeys and a heavy load of deer. Only the hind quarters were in demand, so we jerked the forequarters and other sections of the deer.

To make jerky, or *carne seco*, which we could always sell to the Mexicans, we cut the meat from the bones in long, thin strips and hung it over a line to dry. Jerky generally brought twenty-five cents a pound, for it took seven pounds of fresh meat to make one of jerky. In the fall of the year the flies were often bad, but as a rule the meat dried so fast in the mountain air that no harm was done to the inner part of the strips. Mexicans do not mind eating *carne seco* after the grubs are shaken out of it. To a Mexican or Indian young one a chunk of *carne seco* is as much of a treat as a lollypop to an American child. Jerky dried in winter is a clean food and makes a tasty stew.

When one thinks of the loss in weight in a pound of jerky, it is easy to figure out how a Mexican can travel a long distance with a light outfit. With ten pounds of jerky, a cone of *penoche*, or pressed brown sugar, and a serape, or gray blanket, a Mexican is fitted for a trip of several hundred miles through the mountains. In making the dish known as *chili con carne*, the Mexican puts into a metate, or stone bowl, the right amounts of *carne seco*, red chili, and corn meal and pounds them into a mixture, adding enough water to make the stew.

We found big bunches of deer in a canyon that had heavy banks of snow on its north side. We watched until the deer in their feeding went close to the snow banks; then we ran them into the deep snow where they were soon helpless. The harder they tried to escape, the deeper they sank into the drifts. As Baxter, Poland and I had made it up beforehand, one overshot the bunch of deer, one undershot them, and the third waited for the animals to "freeze" as they do when very much afraid;—he could then drop a half dozen, one after the other. When the deer had been trapped in this manner, we brought down at times every animal in the band.

For several hours after a streak of good luck, we would be very busy cleaning out the entrails and putting in sticks to make openings for air. Sometimes we pitched camp on the spot, hanging the deer meat from trees until it could be taken to the settlements, but more often we packed the deer the same day to our winter diggings. If located near a grove of oaks, we sometimes smoked part of the hind quarters, as meat cured with oak wood has a very sweet taste. From mid-November till the first of the year, we seldom killed a buck, as this is the season of mating and swollen glands. The meat of the buck during this time has a bad taste and does not keep well.

Among the deer of the Southwest is one known to hunters as the cactus buck. Deer are very fond of the young, tender links of the cholla, and in trying to pick them from the thorny bush, often get the silvery spines in nose, head, or other parts of the body. At times the cholla thorns bring on an abcess which ends in sterility for the buck. He sheds his horns as usual the following season, but after that they remain in the velvet even when they harden, and he never sheds them again. The buck fattens and seems in good condition. I have taken note of some very handsome antlered heads on the cactus buck.

Normal deer shed their horns once a year, usually in the early spring. When the bucks want to rid themselves of their dead horns, they generally look for a small park. Here they help Nature by rubbing their horns against tree trunks that are without limbs for at least seven or eight feet above the ground. I have at times seen several car-loads of antlers scattered about in one of these parks. Often we found the skulls of two bucks with the horns still locked, and we knew it had been a fight to the finish. The new antlers form quickly, being closely covered at first with a fine down known as velvet. In the early stage the antlers are tender and bend easily; this accounts for the many odd shapes and queer turns often taken note of in the horns. Some claim that it is not safe to judge a buck's age by the number of points on his antlers, but I hold, like many old hunters, that the number of prongs increases with age. A spiked buck without prongs is one year old, and each year he adds another set of prongs.

When the mast became short close to Old Baldy we moved south to the head of White Creek, near Mogollon Peak, as turkey seemed more plentiful around there. Turkeys brought from two to five dollars apiece, their weight ranging from sixteen to forty pounds each. Merriam turkeys, or bronze turkeys, as we used to call them, are at home in the Gila Forest. Though not as plentiful as in earlier days, they have by no means disappeared in the wooded mountains of New Mexico. In coloring they differ from the Thanksgiving turkey of the Pilgrim Fathers, the coverts and feathers of the lower rump being a tannish white instead of the dark chestnut of the eastern turkey. The Merriam turkey builds her nest on the ground in tall, thick weeds and briars, and lines it with grass, weeds, and leaves. Here she lays from nine to twelve cream-colored eggs, sprinkled with rusty brown specks. The turkeys feed in winter on pinon nuts, acorns, and juniper berries. In summer they eat grass seeds, fruit, berries, and many insects and worms. Turkeys are not often found below an altitude of seven thousand feet, and have at times been seen as high as eleven thousand feet.

By the first of November the nights had grown colder, and the ground in the mornings would be frozen. We had let our supplies run low, expecting to send a couple of extra loads of *carne seco* with our Thanksgiving order, so Nelson would be able to pack on his return trip enough supplies to last the balance of the winter. Our flour and salt had nearly run out, but as the weather stayed clear, we were not worried.

The night before Nelson was to leave for Silver City, we had on hand at least fifty turkeys. During the night we had a real break, for a flock of fifty or sixty more came to roost within three hundred yards of our camp. When they were settled a light rain fell, which seemed to affect their flying. Opening fire, we dropped at least half of them. In the morning those that had fallen on the ground could not fly, and we got quite a few more by clubbing them as they ran by our camp.

When Nelson set out, we figured he was packing at least a hundred and fifty dollars worth of game, more than enough when traded off to stock us up for the winter. It was a big load for nine animals to pack. Baxter gave Nelson a last warning to hurry back.

"Don't you bain worryin' about me," said the Swede. "Ay bain only too glad to come back here because Ay bain expectin' to go along with you to hunt them lost diggin's Ay bain always dreamin' about." We watched the pack train until it was out of sight on the canyon trail.

The day after Nelson left, white clouds drifted overhead, and there were signs of failing weather. We had come to the conclusion to stay where we were until Nelson got back, but it was soon plain that Baxter was worried.

"Boys," he said, "we can't stay here long. We'll have to hit the trail for a lower altitude. The Swede should make the trip in six days, but I think we made a mistake to wait up here, for we bid fair to be snowed under."

In this high altitude the snow often gets seven or eight feet deep, and there are canyons in the Black and Mogollon Ranges where drifts have been known to measure a depth of thirty feet. Gray snow clouds soon pushed out the white ones, and piled up against the mountain slopes. For days the clouds hung over us, but not a single flake of snow drifted down to us. Our hopes kept up, and one or the other of us was always peering down the trail with the field glasses, looking for the packer. Six days went by, seven, eight. Then it began to snow.

Loading our camp outfit and as many deer as we could carry, we struck out for a lower altitude. Poland knew every trail in the mountains, so he led. What snow! Never will I forget it. In a little while we were all soaking wet. We headed for McKenna Park, but never reached it. Big, wet snowflakes stuck to our clothing and piled deeper and deeper around us. We camped in the snow the first night and were kept busy digging ourselves out. The next morning a bitter wind blew up, driving the snow in blinding whirls along the trail.

About three o'clock in the afternoon of the second day, we stumbled on to an old ramshackle cabin. Most of the roof had fallen in, but one corner of it still held up. As luck would have it the cabin was almost buried under a heavy snowdrift, and the fireplace was in good shape. I had never before known how fine a shelter snow made. Our clothes were frozen stiff on our bodies, and the icicles hung from our caps and beards. Poland was the only one who could use his hands, Baxter's and mine being so swollen we were helpless. Poland pulled some timbers from the roof and soon had a fire going. We were wise enough not to warm up too fast. As soon as we got back the use of our hands, we helped Poland to unload the animals. We hung the deer on trees. Baxter next took an ax and cut brush for the mules and burros to browse on. They did not try to eat but crowded up to the fire as close as we would let them, standing around it like humans.

Our clothes soon dried, and when night came on we were warm and safe in our tumble-down shack. We seasoned our turkey stew with the last bit of salt in the bag and washed down our hard-tack with the best hot coffee I ever tasted. Baxter told us a long tale about being lost in a storm and stumbling into an Apache camp where he was treated like a king. We could not help but wonder what had become of our packer and when we would get out of the mountains. Baxter seemed to think we would never hear from Swedish Nelson again, for he was known to be a heavy drinker when he got started, and a gambler who never left the faro table while he had a cent left. At best, we knew he could not get back to us until the weather settled.

The snow fell for three days, so we were kept busy cutting and drying firewood and preparing fodder for the animals. When it quit snowing the weather turned bitter. The trees snapped with the cold until it seemed they would surely burst. By this time all our supplies had run out except meat, which was hard to eat without salt. It tasted like dry wood. Three times a day we ate meat —fried meat, boiled meat, and roasted meat—and at last we all took to raw meat. For three days we lived on raw meat and the stewed inner bark of trees. But we kept alive, and we learned afterwards that we had been lucky, for several cowboys passed in their chips in that snowstorm.

When the snow crusted over, Poland struck out for Grudgins' ranch about five miles away. Towards evening he came back pulling a hand sled with a sack of feed for the animals and some food for ourselves. After feeding the animals and eating a bite ourselves, we loaded up our camp outfit and as many deer as we could carry and pulled out for Grudgins' cabin. Breaking the trail was hard work, but we reached the cabin about midnight. One of the Grudgins boys, who had got back from Silver City just a few hours before the storm broke, had seen Nelson there. The fat was in the fire, sure enough. The Swede had taken to drink and lost everything belonging to us except the pack animals, which were still in the corral. The next day we heard the snowfall had not been heavy at the Hot Springs and was quite light at Silver City. In a few days we pulled out for the Springs, taking along what deer were left. I went on into Silver City with the load of deer meat which I traded off for winter supplies. Having gotten our ten pack animals out of the corral, I followed Baxter and Poland up the river. During the rest of the winter we jerked all the meat we got. In time the weather warmed up. We went back to our old camp site, and packed down the deer meat we had left there to the place that has since been known as Raw Meat Cabin. Here we jerked the meat, tanned the hides, and accomplished a little more hunting.

I never again heard of Swedish Nelson, but I have always believed that he was driven away by shame when he came to himself, for Baxter was the apple of his eye, and in his right senses, he was on the square.

6. *We Head for the Diggings*

It was now February and we were having good weather. In sunny open parks the young grass was pushing through the brown waste of last year's growth. Here and there at the edge of melting snow patches the flowers were springing up. The woods echoed with the songs of birds. The hunt was ended for that season, and many pounds of jerky and hundreds of hides were stacked up in our cabin ready to pack to the settlements as soon as the trails were safe.

The goose hung high but Baxter seemed to have something on his mind. One day he said, "Boys, I believe those red devils are getting ready to leave the reservation as soon as the grass is high enough and the winter broken. I see their letters to one another, and it looks to me as if they're tryin' to get all the Apaches on the warpath at once. They'll never rest easy till they've made a last stand to drive the whites from this section."

He pointed out to Poland and me, piles of triangular rocks, as big as flour barrels, generally built where two or more trails met. "If the top of a rock pile is finished in a circle or has a cross over it, or if it is finished with many pebbles or small rocks, it means a big pow-wow at a certain place. You'll find rock piles built in many strange shapes, some of them like the marks on a Chinese laundry slip. The shape of the pile, its size, and the number of rocks in it, all have a meaning for the Indian scout who passes by. I've been around the Indians a good bit in my day, and I've learned how to read some of their messages in rock piles and pictures. All these pictures that you see scratched on the mountain sides have a meaning for the Indian."

One day after we had moved back to Little Creek, Baxter showed us three rock piles built close to the stream. "Now, here you have messages left only yesterday—one by a Navajo, one by a Mescalero Apache, and a third by a White Mountain Apache. It's plain they're gatherin' to plan a general outbreak, and judgin' from what I've learned of Indian signs, one of their chiefs is against it."

Another time Baxter pointed out and named for me some mountain peaks, warning me to take note of their form and color. "Now, Jimmie," said he, "if anything should happen to me and Poland while we're out on this trip, be sure to stick close to the mountains. It's cooler and you can always find water there, while if you wander out on the plains, the heat may affect your brain, and besides, nearly all the water on the flats is alkali. Now, don' forget what I've told you about these peaks, especially Pinos Altos Peak. You may need to know all about them before we get back from the Lost Diggin's."

Late in March we moved up to White Creek. One day Baxter found some turkey hens setting in the brush. "Boys," said he, "it's time for us to be movin'."

The next day, having packed up our jerkey and hides, we pulled out for Silver City, where we traded off our load for supplies and ammunition. Meeting Tom Woods, hunter, at the Hot Springs when we got back, we gave him some supplies, as he had a large family on a ranch a few miles up the river. I bought from him the burro known as "Old Hog", that had been with us on the trip to Canfield's ranch.

It was early in the season, and there was no one staying at the Hot Springs; but, as we wanted to keep it dark that we were headed for the Lost Diggings, we struck off by night. Our trail led up the West Fork of the Gila, thence over the Zigzag Trail, and up the mesa that lies between the West Fork and the Middle Fork of the Gila River. Keeping upon this mesa with Lily Mountain to our right, we went through Turkey Feather Pass, soon striking Iron Creek. With a ranch to our east which I believe belonged to an Englishman named Graham, we headed due north till we reached the Elk Mountains.

Snow was still on these mountains, and as the mesas were boggy, we camped here a few days, knowing the dry winds would soon make them fit to cross. Quite a few wild horses and thousands of antelopes were feeding in the foothills. We also came across a flock of sheep without a shepherd that must have wintered in these mountains. Had their herder died, or had he been killed by wild beasts or Indians? The sheep were fat and healthy. They seemed glad to have us near, bleating and bedding down beside us at night. We soon took note that these sheep were being herded by dogs. We learned afterwards that the Indians had killed the herders and stampeded the flock, but the dogs had rounded up the sheep and driven them over a hundred miles to their owners.

These Mexican sheep dogs do some wonderful things. Mexicans always keep a few goats with their herd to get milk for themselves and the lambs whose mothers pass out in giving them birth. The pups of the sheep dogs are taken from their mothers before their eyes are open and given to some nanny that has lost her kid. She usually adopts two or more of the pups and suckles them till they are able to shift for themselves. When the dogs grow up the herders teach them to catch a nanny and milk her. One dog holds her while the other sucks her. While there is a nanny left in the herd the dogs will never starve. The dogs get to know every sheep in the herd, and if one or more sheep turn up missing, the dogs will strike out of their own accord and hunt the hills and hollows. They never give up till they have found and driven back the sheep if they are only strayed; if they are dead, killed by wolf or coyote, the dogs will go back to the herder and almost talk to him to get him to come and see where the bodies are.

When we broke camp, we kept close to the mountains, with the San Augustine Plains to the east. The next mountains we struck were the Tularosas, where we crossed the divide. In this section, close to the headwaters of the Negryto, a fork of the San Francisco River, were many springs of fresh water which more than supplied our needs. We slept under immense pines but kept on the alert for bears. We took note of hundreds of beavers at work on their dams. From here we had a fine view of the mountains, lying ridge behind ridge as far as the eye could see.

Some days later, from a mountain that looked northwest, Baxter pointed out our goal, where lay hidden the Lost Diggings of many a prospector's dream. "Those small white streaks in the formation of the ridge are the headwaters of the Little Colorado," said he.

From here on we bore to the right, soon coming down among the foothills. Signs of deer, elk and bear were plentiful, but they all led west to the high mountains. What a change in plant life and air we took note of going down several thousand feet!

We had been high up just below the barren Arctic Zone where heavy snows feed the streams that water desert plants hundreds of miles away. Just below this high cold belt we took note of many fine evergreens, among them the balsam fir and the Engelman spruce. Groves of light-leaved aspen grew along the streams in the higher altitude, and cottonwoods followed the streams from mountain top to plain, often crossing the desert with them. The yellow pine grew everywhere under the timberline but began to be scarce below six thousand feet, where we passed through wooded sections filled with pinons, junipers, live oaks, and walnuts. Among the foothills we took note of many yuccas, century plants, ocotillos, chollas, and manzanita bushes.

At last we were on the San Augustine Plains. All the time we were coming downhill the air got hotter and drier. Every belt of trees has its own animals and birds. The hunter looks for deer, bear, and turkey among the yellow pines and will at times track a grizzly close to the timberline. He knows he will find the wildcat, cougar, fox and coyote preying upon these game animals.

On the San Augustine Plains the weather became hot and sultry and the lagunes were fast drying up. Game was scarcer and waterholes much farther apart. In order to be on the safe side, we kept our four kegs filled with water. One afternoon we followed a mirage and had to make a dry camp. Grass was plentiful, so we picketed the horses and turned the mules and the burro loose. All the next day we crossed a dreary waste. About four o'clock in the afternoon we came into some low hills where we found a water hole. There was water enough for ourselves and the animals after we had cleaned out the hole. We pitched camp near this water hole. There was mighty little sleep for any of us that night, and the stock kept close to camp, for the coyotes began to carry on at sundown. They took note of our camp, and came so close, we could see their eyes shining in the brush like balls of yellow fire. Over and over they began, "Yoo hoo! Yoo hoo hoo hoo!" ending with a string of yaps and barks enough to turn us deaf.

In the morning Baxter warned us to fill all our kegs with water, as we would not have a fresh supply till we got to the diggings. The next day we passed into the canyon with the copper-stained shale. This canyon was about three hundred feet wide and one hundred fifty feet high with a game trail leading through it. A clutter of rocks and debris made very hard going.

Baxter was puzzled. "Boys," said he, "this sure beats hell. I can't make head or tail of this canyon. It looks as if the walls had tumbled in since I was here before. I don't remember any of these boulders or piles of debris on the canyon floor. Those splits in the canyon walls are new to me, too. If you look close you can see a white sandstone formation showing up beneath the copper-stained shale. It's almost as hard as quartz."

"Don't you think there's been an earthquake in here?" I asked him.

"It could hardly have been anything else," he answered, "though I've known a mountain torrent to make almost as many changes."

Some places showed dykes of red shale through the white sandstone. I asked, "Jason, don't you think there may be a big copper deposit here?"

"There may be," said he, "but an ounce of copper will stain an acre, and I want no copper in mine when we can find gold. Besides, it's one hundred and fifty miles to a railroad."

It was hard going, but at last we came out of the desolate canyon. From the top of the next mountain we crossed, Baxter pointed out the one we were headed for. "That's Island Mountain, or Lone Mountain to the northeast. Don't it put you in mind of pictures you've seen of the pyramids of Egypt? After we've passed through the natural gateway I told you about before, we'll soon be in the gulch of the Lost Diggings."

We pushed eastward toward the Island Mountain, which I believe is the one now known as Volcanic Hub. In places on the desert we had to go around deep crevices and fissures. Many of these openings were filled with alkali water unfit to use. There were no signs of animals.

"It sure beats hell," said Jason, "for when we crossed here eight years ago we saw hundreds of antelope."

When we pitched camp, Poland pointed to the Magdalenas. Looking southeast we could see the woman's face on the side of the mountain. "Is she a good or a bad sign?" said Baxter looking solemn. "Did you boys know there has never been a murder done in that mountain? Even an Apache will not kill an enemy if he can get within the shadow of the woman's face. Lady," he ended taking off his battered hat, "we hope you'll lead us to the Lost Diggings. We don't ask to get rich out of 'em, but we would sure like to be the ones to locate 'em. Ain't it so, boys?"

"Why not push on to-night?" asked Poland. "I believe we could make it."

"Well," answered Baxter, "I'd like to make a try for the Island Mountain, myself, but the animals are leg-weary, and I think we'll have to wait till morning."

Grass was good and we were not saving of the water as we expected to find plenty the next day at the diggings. We picketed all the animals except Old Hog, the burro. The moon was nearly full and the night was as bright as day. At daybreak we were on the move. Ten o'clock found us at the Island Mountain.

Baxter rode ahead to look for the opening into the park. When we came up we found him staring around him like one in a daze. And no wonder! The whole mountain looked as if it had been crushed by giant hands, as a child would crush a snowball. Even the ridge was broken in many places. Not a sign of a tree or an animal could be seen in any direction. Immense boulders lay tumbled together as if they had crashed in a mighty battle, scattering splinters in every direction. Following the broken ridge we came to the spot where Baxter expected to find the opening to the park. Instead of the park we came into a barren gulch filled in places almost to the top with rocks and debris. No water. No vegetation. No animals. No mineral.

"This sure beats hell!" was all Baxter could find to say. We went along the sides of the gulch looking for a level stretch to camp, but there was none. "This mountain looks as if it had busted open in a big explosion," said Poland, and it was all that was said by any of us as we climbed over the rocks and the debris. We came back along the ridge the same way.

"Boys," said Baxter, wiping the sweat from his forehead with his red bandana, "this sure beats all. Why, I don't even know the hills. It's plain now why we saw no game. The water has gone, and we cannot stay here. Poland and myself will take two of the horses and look for the Pink Hill. You stay here, Jimmie, and keep an eye on the animals until we come back. Picket them all, for they sure are dry and will pull for water if let loose. From what I see the Lost Diggin's are now in a Lost Canyon, scattered more than likely to the head of the Little Colorado River."

After Baxter and Poland struck off, I unloaded the animals and picketed them. This done, I came to the conclusion to do a little prospecting to the north, being careful to keep in sight of camp. The gulch to the north was deep and rough, and I could not cross as I had planned to do. I found nothing, but on my way back I stopped on a rise to look over the plains we had crossed. In the distance I took note of a cloud of dust which made me think someone was driving stock. I also believed I could see flashes from gun barrels. I did not let the grass grow under me on the height, for I was afraid I would be seen by Indians on the plains. When I got back to camp I put on the coffee to boil and stirred up some flapjacks, for I had it in mind Baxter and Poland would be as hungry as wolves when they got back. After several hours they came back worn-out but not hungry. I did not need to ask if they had found anything, for they were both looking glum.

"At one point," said Poland, "there's a kind of natural bridge thrown across the gulch. We went over, but there's nothing to see on the other side, either, except the end of the world. No water and no mineral."

"There's no sign of the Pink Hill," put in Baxter. "It seems to me that first there came a quake which pretty near shook the mountain to pieces, and then cloudbursts that carried away whatever gold or mineral was in the canyon. Even the rocks look strange, mostly a burnt-out lava and a species of diorite. The Pink Hill may hev been a volcanic vent, producing gold. The mineral zone must hev been small or we'd be able to find extensions nearby, but you can see for yourselves there's nothing here but lava, or malpais. In time some one may locate a valuable copper mine in the canyon with the blue-stained shale, but it's not for us. I'm sorry, boys. It sure is too bad to bring you on this long trip for nothin'."

All day they looked for water and mineral. Around five in the afternoon, worn-out and disgusted, they pulled back to camp.

"We must pull our freight for the Coyote Springs before they dry up, and that means we must get moving pronto," said Baxter.

When I told him what I had seen from the rise earlier in the day, he only laughed at me. "Now, Jimmie," said he, "this thing's gone to your head. All you saw was a dry weather cyclone, and maybe a few lightnin' flashes." But I took note that he got us to build a stone barricade that night. We heard afterwards that Geronimo's band of Apaches had passed close to the Island Mountain. Baxter wanted no fire, so we sat inside our barricade in the moonlight, talking in low voices.

"Boys," said Baxter, "we sure came to Lost Canyon Diggin's. There'll never be any yellow nuggets found here unless there comes another earthquake and cloudburst to throw and wash back into the gulch what they took out of it. It's death from thirst to hang around here, so we'd better pull our freight for the Mogollons and prospect around there this summer. Next spring we can come back to the Island Mountain with a better outfit and see if anything has turned up."

Baxter was restless that night and started up at every sound, but we were not bothered by man or beast. Next morning about eight o'clock we pulled into Coyote Springs. The soft earth around the water hole bore many fresh tracks which we believed had been left by wild horses. After we had watered the stock and filled our kegs, we rested awhile before pulling out for the head of the Negryto River. We stayed only a day on the divide and then headed into the northeast corner of the Mogollons.

Near Snow Creek, Poland killed a young bear which was rolling fat. We camped there to render its fat for frying purposes. What was left of the carcass we hung on a tree for those who might pass by, according to the custom of the times. Later I heard it was found two days later by soldiers out after the Apache marauders. In the vicinity of Snow Creek we took note of many moccasin tracks which we surmised had been made by Mexican charcoal burners as they did considerable burning here for the mines at Alma.

From Snow Creek we crossed to Iron Creek. Here we picked up the trail which led through Turkey Feather Pass to the West Fork of the Gila. The streams were full of trout, and we stopped to go fishing. While going down the West Fork a stray dog took up with us and followed us till we came to White Creek, where we camped close to the cabin of the two McKenzie brothers. This spot is now the site of a fish hatchery and is known as Jenks' Cabin. As water and grass were plentiful and the streams full of speckled trout, we decided to stay some time in the vicinity.

7. *Indians!*

Some one must have told near-by ranchers we were at the McKenzie cabin, for by night eight or ten men had rounded up at our camp. Knowing we had been a long time in the wilderness, most of them brought us newspapers and magazines. Baxter, a Missouri Democrat, was all excited over the election of President Cleveland, which took place while we were hunting in the Mogollons. He and Lily were soon talking politics. Baxter was at his best that night, and before long he was telling the ranchers about our trip. Upon hearing about the moccasin tracks, one of the ranchers said, "It's plain you fellers have been followed by Mexicans. Ten to one, some sheep herders saw you headin' for the Schaeffer Diggings, and now they think you're carryin' nuggets."

"I hardly think it's that," said Baxter, "for we didn't see a livin' soul on our whole trip."

"Well," said Prior, "it might have been Apaches. We heard a few days ago that a bunch has left the reservation."

"I'd be inclined to think it was Apaches myself," put in Lily, "but nothing is known of the whereabouts of the renegades."

We talked about many things and at last about death. "I know when my time will come," said Baxter, "I'll be camped in a small valley with a stream of water runnin' through it. A bunch of cattle will be grazin' on the hillside. Men, women, and children will be rushin' around in excitement, the men with guns in their hands. Everyone will run as if the devil were after him. When this happens I'll know my time has come."

A heavy silence dropped upon the company at the conclusion of Baxter's speech.

"You'll not be goin' across the border in this valley," said Prior brightening up, "for there's never been a cow pastured here yet so far as I know."

Old Papineau, after brooding some time on Baxter's words, burst out, "Now I don't know *how* I'm goin' to die, but I know it will be *sudden*."

The talk went on, but it was tinged with sadness. Stories of death and burial were told one after the other. At last we got to speaking about God.

"Well," said Baxter, "it's a long time since my mother used to lay out my best clothes, see that I had my weekly bath and got off to Sunday School on time. It's many a year, too, since I've had my foot inside a church, but the longer I live in the open the more I believe there's a God. I've never met a man yet who could hold out against the idea above five years after he went in for prospectin', for he comes too close to the works of God in Nature. Think of all the power in water and wind and fire. Where does all this power come from? Why, you can look up this minute and see the moon keepin' her path across the sky, and you know as well as I, that she's goin' by the law laid down for her. And Who is it that keeps the stars in their course and the tides of the sea amovin'? Men like to think they know somethin', but when I want to measure my learnin' all I need to do is to watch the sun comin' up of a mornin'. Pick up a float or a chunk of carbonate of lime and trace it back in all its parts through bygone years; they hed to hev a beginnin', didn't they? Take note of the number of wild animals in this State alone, each siring its own kind—go back as far as you will—there had to be a first pair of each kind, and even if the wise guys get to provin' that one kind grew from the other, there still hed to be a first, didn't there? Call to mind the trees you've bunked under in your lifetime, the wild grasses your stock feeds on in these mountains, and the well-nigh thousand kinds of wild flowers and song birds that gladden a man's heart. How did they all begin? The longer I live the more sure I am there had to be a First One to call these things into being. It's thinkin' on these things when I've been alone on the trail that's kept me believin' in the God I first heard about at my mother's knee."

"Well," said one of the ranchers, ending the long silence that followed Baxter's speech, "I've done a deal of swearin' in my day, and I ain't never been any hand to look up a church, but I agree with you, Baxter, that a man's gotta believe in God when he gets to thinkin' like you say."

"And I'll tell you a few critters the Lord made to pester man with," said another rancher, who like most of us, was slow at giving out his deeper thoughts; "you forgot to say anything about more than fifty kinds of thorny cacti and ten thousand trouble-some varmint and a million tormentin' insects."

"Right you are," agreed Baxter, "but those critters you're so damn hard on are only tryin' to get a livin' same as yourself when you go out for a deer or a turkey."

"Well! Well!" said Lily. "It's a shame to break up this religious meetin', but I must be off, for I've been expectin' a man from Socorro County with some cattle. He should have been here three days ago."

Lily's last words were almost drowned out by the barking of the stray dog that had followed us to McKenzie's. He seemed excited and afraid. As he was just a pup I took him up in my arms and stood with the crowd around Lily's horse while he mounted. It was as light as day, the moon being full. Looking across the valley we saw a bunch of cattle grazing on the hillside. The crowd fell silent. Were the cattle an omen?

Soon all the ranchers had scattered to their homes. I kept the dog near me, but he whined and barked all night. At dawn he broke away from me and disappeared. Later I heard that he came into Alma, thirty miles distant, at noon of that day. Baxter believed the dog must have scented Indians.

The McKenzie brothers set out early that morning for Alma. Baxter, Poland, and I came to the conclusion to take turns staying in camp. At noon it was my turn, but Baxter said, "I'll stay in camp to-day, Jimmie, so I can read the newspapers."

"Come on, Jimmie," said Poland, "we'll get Baxter the biggest mess of trout he ever had."

All of a sudden our stock came running past the camp and crossed to the other side of the river. They were snorting as if afraid and kept looking up White Creek where they had been grazing. Taking up my rifle and a switch, I drove them back. Old Hog balked so hard I finally let him stay near camp. "He acts like a beast that has at some time or another been taken by Apaches, and has had a good whiff of his old enemy," said Baxter.

As I drove the animals back I took note of fresh moccasin tracks. Baxter shrugged his shoulders when I told him about it. "Mexicans or Indians—who can tell?" said he.

About two o'clock as we started for the river, Baxter called after us, "Be sure to bring plenty of trout. I'll hev a bed of hot coals waitin' for you."

"Leave it to us," shouted Poland. "Now, Jimmie," he went on, "I'll go below the box canyon and fish, up the river; you go above the falls and fish down; and when we meet we'll go back to camp. *Adios*, old son, and good luck."

The plan suited me first-rate, for I like to be alone when I fish. I had a long pole and plenty of bait and soon got many bites. In quiet pools I caught several whoppers. Oh, what sport for the man who likes to fish! I almost got another whopper, but he was a smart fellow. Away he went with a big fat worm. When I counted eleven trout on my string, I made up my mind I must have a round dozen. But my luck had turned. After an hour or so of nips and nibbles, I went down below the falls to a deep pool that I knew of, coming to the conclusion to wait there for Poland. Countless nips, but no real bites. It was nearly sundown, and I began to wonder why Poland did not come. The sun goes down early in these canyons, and we generally made it a point to be back to camp before sunset. I was tired of waiting. Hearing some rocks rolling on the side of the hill, I came out from under the falls, hoping I might see Poland. I saw no one, so I thought the rocks must have been loosened by a squirrel.

Just before sundown I came to the conclusion that Poland must have missed me and gone over the hill to the camp. Swinging my pole and the string of fish over my shoulder, I struck out for camp.

Instead of going back the way I had come I headed up through the brush on the side of the river where we were camped. As no trail led up to the McKenzie cabin I went by guess. I had my head up looking for smoke when I stumbled over the body of a dead horse and plunged headlong into the clearing. In an instant thirty or forty Indians were around me. I was pushed along and handed over to two young bucks. I was dazed, but I soon took note of what had happened. Lying dead, close to the ashes of the camp fire, was my friend, Baxter. His body had been mutilated, his face and limbs slashed with the knives of the Indians.

I felt as if I had turned to stone, yet I seemed to see things clearer than ever before. I saw how the bullet that had torn its way through Baxter's body, had bored a neat round hole in the bean pot that stood near the camp fire. The paper he had been reading when attacked by these red devils lay crumpled up a few feet from his body. Soon I woke up to my own danger. The Indians had backed me against the trunk of a large pine tree. I saw five or six bucks dressed like white men, throwing clothes and bedding through the door of the McKenzie cabin. They must have been graduates of the Carlisle Indian School. Some were ripping open the mattresses and throwing the chaff about, while others scattered flour and meal over the ground. All acted as if mad with drink.

The squaws were gathering brush to build fires, and each one as she passed me tried to spit in my face. Oh, how hideous they were, with long stripes of black paint daubed on their faces, and coarse stringy hair flopping against their calicoes and blankets. One of them came close enough to run a mesquite thorn into my leg. Every squaw seemed to belong to a different family, as each one built her own fire except two ugly old women who were working together on an immense pile of brush. Judging from their looks and motions, and the way the young bucks were watching them, I knew that I was to get a good roasting.

A couple of bucks ran the Indians' stock up White River, but in a few minutes the horses came racing wildly back through the camp. Every Indian took part in the stampede and rushed across the river. My guards went, too, and I found myself alone and free, as I had not yet been tied to the tree. I ran by instinct in the direction the horses came from, knowing that no danger could be worse than the one I was getting away from. I saw and heard nothing that could have caused the alarm among the stock, but I surmised the stampede had been started by a silvertip.

It was almost dark. I crept without a sound through the brush, making my way at last to the spot where I had been fishing under the falls. I now felt sure it was not a rock squirrel I had heard, but a prowling Indian. I stayed under the falls until nearly midnight, hidden from sight by an overhanging cliff. As the valley where we were camped might prove a fine trap, I felt sure the Indians would make a hasty getaway. Not a sound could be heard in the little valley. At last I made up my mind to go back to the cabin, hoping to find some of the money we had hidden in our clothes and blankets. I crept back through the brush, often stopping to listen, as I had seen wild animals do.

The Apaches had gone. I found Baxter's body, still lying near the dead ashes of the camp fire, covered by the white moonlight. It was a sight I will never forget. Baxter had crossed his last divide. What had he found on the other side?

I shook out the wagon sheet and spread it over his body. Then I looked about for the money, but every mattress had been slit open and every pocket cut out, so I found nothing. Making my way through the clutter of food and clothing, I entered the cabin. There I found a few raw potatoes, which I ate. Hearing a noise, I peered through the window. Over on the hillside a bunch of cattle grazed in a small valley. Three or four times I had heard Baxter foretell the manner of his death. How had he known?

When I left the McKenzie cabin I again took to the willow thicket along the river, hoping I would find Poland or some signs of him. After passing through the box canyon I found his tracks leading up to the mesa. All at once the air was filled with the hooting of owls and the barking of coyotes. Were the Apaches calling their horses or were they following me? By this time I was on the mesa, which was covered with a thick growth of pine trees. I struck out for the trail that led to the Gila Hot Springs. I moved slowly for the night was as bright as day. Some one moved. I jumped behind the trunk of a big tree just in time to miss a bullet that whistled by. As I went back in the direction of the brushy brakes, I heard the cries of a man and saw him running off to my left with the Indians shooting after him. Then I *did* make tracks for the brush.

It was some time after this that I took note of my feet. My

rawhide moccasins, softened by wading in the river, soon went to pieces on the rough lava bed, or malpais. My feet were almost on the bare ground. I staggered on, but after several hours, I could not stand any more and, I lay down. No sleep. I started up at every sound. I was up again, dragging myself along. Again I lay down and tried to sleep. Again I was too restless. Day broke at last after the longest night of my whole life.

Signs of cattle and clouds of dust warned me to be on the watch, for they meant Indians. How silently I traveled! I passed a herd of deer so close I could have patted a young faun on his spotted back. I was the whole day reaching the Zigzag Trail and followed it down to the river bottom about sundown. I had not had a drop of water since the night before. My throat was parched by this time, and the blisters on my feet were as big as hen eggs. Before I could reach the water a small herd of cattle came running down the valley as if the devil were after them. Keeping quiet in the brush, I saw six or eight Indian bucks ride on down the valley. After they had passed, I went into the river and almost killed myself drinking. I got a severe pain and had to lie down for some time before I had any relief.

I then took off what was left of my moccasins and bathed my feet. After a good sponge bath, I felt better. Not a sound could be heard and I came to the conclusion the settlers had been warned. Once more I headed for the Hot Springs. At the Holmes ranch which was the first one I came to, I found everything looted. I did not know till later that Holmes had left for Boston the week before. There was no food here so I kept on down the valley till I came to the Rodgers ranch. It was plain the family had left in a hurry. The mother cows were gathered around the corrals where the calves were penned. Oh, what pitiful bawling! The first thing I did was to free the calves. In the house the stove was still warm. On the table I found a pan of milk and a part of a loaf of bread. I had left the door open and in walked a big, black dog. How glad he was to see me! Looking about, I found him some meat and bones. I could swallow nothing but milk, as my throat seemed on fire. The Indians had not touched anything in the Rodgers cabin. From here I could see a long way down the valley. Not far from my own cabin a number of small fires were burning, marking the camp site of the bucks who had passed me on the Zigzag Trail.

I could not settle down in the lonely Rodgers cabin, so I struck out for Lesters. The Indians had been at the cabin but had touched nothing except the bedding which they had ripped open looking for money. Pinned on the cabin wall was a notice which read: "Baxter and McKenna killed at McKenzie Cabin. Beware of Apaches. For Safety Come Over to the Wood Place on the East Fork of the Gila River." So they thought I was dead, too! From the Lester place I could plainly see the Indians camped near my cabin. Would I ever again live in peace in my log cabin, with my pet skunk, my pet cubs, my pigs and my potato patch? All at once I felt a great longing for these homely comforts.

In order to get to Tom Wood's ranch, I would have to swim the river and then cross the divide between the Middle Fork and the East Fork of the Gila River, a distance of more than two miles. It seemed a long way, fagged out as I was, but I struck off with the Rodgers' dog still following me. I crossed the river and headed up the canyon towards the divide with the dog between my legs most of the way. On a sudden he bristled with fear and dashed ahead. Presto! Back he came trembling and whining. Thinking he might have scented an Apache, I took up into the brush, the dog following. I heard and saw nothing, and soon struck off again.

In going over a slight hump I heard an angry "Woof!" Up jumped an immense silvertip. Giving another "Woof!" he went by me like a flash, but he did not make any better time than the dog and myself. As nothing was ever seen of the dog again, we came to the conclusion he was killed either by the bear or by the Indians. I kept on up the mountain, but it was a hard climb. When I had almost reached the divide I sat down, and before I knew it I fell asleep. I was at last awakened by the rain dropping on my face. Looking into the heavens I saw it was almost daylight. I heard a noise above me and at the same time I got a whiff of tobacco smoke. I looked up and saw the red glow of a cigarette in the mouth of an Indian, who must have been posted as a lookout on the divide. I did not move. In a few minutes the Indian wrapped his blanket around him and walked on down the hill, passing me at a distance of less than a hundred and fifty feet. I lay quiet and soon dropped off to sleep again.

When I awoke hours later, I was out of my mind. Hell-bent I started downhill swearing and swinging my arms. I knew I was acting like a madman, but I could not help it. Instead of going on to Tom Wood's place, I headed for my own cabin. From the opposite side of the river I shouted at the Indians who had killed a fine steer and were drying the beef near my cabin. They made signs to one another that I was "loco". Gathering up most of the meat, they rode off without harming either me or the cabin. As luck would have it the Indians are superstitious about lunatics and drunken men, and do not often bother them. When they crossed over the ridge, I was still shaking my fist at them. The minute they were out of sight I jumped into the river and swam across.

The cold water brought back my senses, but I kept on till I reached the spot where the bull had been butchered. Seizing a big chunk of meat with the blood still dripping from it, I tore it to pieces like a wolf. Oh, how delicious that blood tasted! The cold swim and the food brought my mind back to normal, but it was many months before I could sleep at night and got to feeling like myself again. I suffered a lot with my feet and my throat. For a while I bid fair to become a regular jingle-brains. Over that part of my life I am glad to drop a curtain.

I knew enough to go into my cabin and look for some clean clothes, as the ones I was wearing had been torn to shreds in the brush. After I had bathed my face and feet and put on clean clothes, I felt better. I thought of staying at my own cabin, believing that the Indians were all on their way south. While I sat there I heard a noise up the river and quickly hid myself in the brush. In a moment two squaws came riding by, one of them with a papoose strapped on her back. Then I came to the conclusion to pull out, so I once more swam the river and went up over the divide, reaching Tom Wood's place about noon.

No one saw me till I pushed open the door. How excited everyone was! They looked at me as though I had risen from the dead, for Poland had given out that he *knew* Baxter was shot, and from the mesa he *thought* he had seen me among the Indians. They told me Poland had gone to Sapello, Georgetown, and Pinos Altos for help to bury Baxter and to go after me if I had been taken by the Indians. I found quite a crowd in Tom Wood's cabin, not much alarmed by the Indians, for they sang and danced nearly all day.

I was out of my mind a good bit of that day. About nine o'clock that evening, Captain Stanton Brannan from Georgetown, came in with Poland and a posse of twenty-five men. I do not mind the names of anyone else in the group. No doubt most of them are now dead. Poland told me that Baxter was buried by a troop of soldiers following the Indians, soon after I left the McKenzie cabin. Finding the body covered with a wagon sheet, they came to the conclusion I had got away. The posse had come out to look for me, believing that I was still hidden along White Creek. As the men were all prepared and armed, they decided to go on to the McKenzie cabin and look around. I went along behind one of the riders. How I ever got there I cannot recall, but Poland told me afterwards that I fell off the horse three times going up to the West Fork. We saw no Indians.

One of the men in the posse told us that Tom Woods, hunter, had been cut off by the Indians; that his wife was about to be confined; and that Tom had been going for a doctor when the Indians saw him and gave him chase. He got away but was barricaded in his cabin and needed help. Tom Woods, hunter, it must be noted, was not young Tom Wood to whose cabin I had gone. Tom Woods, hunter, lived about fifteen miles northeast on the *Middle* Fork of the Gila, while it will be recalled that young Tom Wood lived on the *East* Fork of the Gila. Poland and I offered to go to the aid of Tom Woods, hunter, and the posse supplied us with guns and ammunition. We got there the next morning.

The following day in the barricaded cabin a child was born, without the help of a doctor. Tom said he expected to pull out of the country as soon as his wife was able to travel. There were six children in the family and food was scarce, so Poland and I killed a bull, being careful not to take note of the brand.

In late June things began to quiet down. Wood was packing to leave for Alma, when a company of militia, numbering fifty men, drifted in one morning from Socorro under the command of Colonel Blake. They were on their way to look up a band of Apaches said to be hiding near the head of the Blue River. Poland and Woods, who had hunted in that section, were asked to go along as scouts. Blake left with me, to look after Woods' family, a man named Russell, who was afterwards sheriff of Socorro County.

Woods, Poland, and I each signed a paper under Colonel Blake, and he told us we were enlisted in the Territorial Militia, as members of his company, with the right to salary and pension. Before leaving for the Blue, we helped Tom cut port holes in his cabin. He gave me a last warning, "Be good to my family, Jimmie. Do some scouting every day; and if I don't come back in three weeks, take the family to Silver City."

About a week after they struck out, the meat running short, I said to Russell, "We'll have to kill a beef. These young ones must not go hungry." As Woods had some burros, I told the children to tie them up the next time they came to water. That afternoon the burros came. Next morning we took the burros up the river about a quarter of a mile where I had spotted a bunch of cattle. Seeing a fine, big steer, I fired, dropping him as if I had struck him with a butcher's maul. Having gutted him, we skinned off the two hind quarters and loaded them on the burro. I took the brand also, and turned the hide over the two front quarters. After Russell had left with the burro, I took note of a rustling in the brush, but I thought it was cattle that had been with the steer.

At the cabin we unloaded and showed the children how to cut and salt the meat. After frying ourselves a bit of the fresh meat, we again struck out to bring in the rest of the beef. We had been gone little more than an hour, but every scrap of it had been carried off. Dozens of moccasin tracks showed the thieves to be Apaches. They must have watched me skin the beef, afraid to open fire after taking note of the dead shot that had dropped the steer. We faded out of the landscape in a hurry.

In the course of a few days the militia came back but without any prisoners. Many Indians had been sighted but none were taken. It seems that Colonel Blake wanted the militia to leave their horses in the care of a few good men in a grassy park, the rest to set out afoot through the rough country where they would have to lead the horses. Most of the men would not consent to this, saying they would go just as far as the horses would take them and no farther. "Let the regulars go after the Apache," was the way they put it. They did not get far, as the Indians watched their every move. The company barely missed a trap that had been laid for them by the wily Apaches in a brushy boxed canyon on the Blue. It was only the sharpness of the scouts that saved the company from massacre.

Russell wanted some of the militia to stay at Woods' and go after the band of Apaches that had stolen the beef, but not one of them would do it, Russell himself finally going off with them to Socorro. Only Woods, Poland, and myself were left on the Middle Fork. All the cowmen and ranchers had left the Gila; the nearest whites were at Alma and Sapello, and very few were at either of these settlements.

While hunting and scouting, Poland and I again went to the McKenzie cabin. In the bean pot we found the bullet that had killed Baxter, and hanging on a mesquite bush, not far from the spot where he fell, Poland found his watch. I have heard it said that a wounded man usually grabs his watch if he has one and throws it as he falls. Baxter's watch was in good shape and began to tick as soon as it was wound. A surprise was in store for us at the cabin, for, up came Old Hog, my burro, almost talking, he was so glad to see us. I learned afterwards from the troops that Old Hog had been seen following the Indians at a five-mile distance all the way into Mexico. When Terrazas drove the Indians out of the Sierra Madres, they came back into the Mogollons, and Old Hog came, too. The Indians must have passed through White Creek Valley on their way to their hideout, and there my burro stayed. He followed us back to Woods' place and the children had a big time with him, for I had bought him from their father, and they remembered him well.

By July Indian signs were dim and old. As Woods had a big family to support, I felt that Poland and I added too much to his burden, now that the danger was over; besides, I needed shoes and clothes, so I said good-by to the Woods family. With Old Hog, my faithful burro, I once more headed for Kingston, one hundred miles southeast in the Black Range.

Over the Black Range

THE first night after leaving the Woods place, I bunked with the Hill brothers near the Hot Springs, the next night with Lou Gatten on the Sapello, now the headquarters of the G.O.S. Cattle Company, and the third night at the Mimbres Mill, getting into the outskirts of Kingston the next afternoon. Mrs. Anthony, who had a ranch at the Mimbres Mill, fixed up a package of food for me. She had heard I was taken by the Indians and wanted to do something to show she was sorry for her deer man, as she always called me. I had often sold her fresh meat during our hunting trips.

Near the Georgetown Mill I struck up Noonday Creek for a distance of five or six miles. Coming into a little park, I met an old turkey hen with a brood of young ones. She took no notice of me and went on scratching, so I came to the conclusion that there had not been any Indians in the vicinity. Since it was virtually noon I headed for a shady nook under a cliff, where I opened Mrs. Anthony's package of food and turned Old Hog loose to graze.

I was chewing away on a venison sandwich when I saw the burro stop feeding. Lifting his ears, he gazed for a minute up the creek and then trotted over beside me. I slipped out of the cove and looked in the same direction. What a sight! Crossing the creek where the trail led north over the one I was following were six Indian bucks, each wearing a white stovepipe hat, or castor, as the miners called them. It did not take me long to get back to my hiding place. Old Hog kept close to my side as quiet as a mouse, watching me with big eyes.

For a half hour I lay low. The clatter of horses' hoofs at last died away on the trail leading to Victorio Park. Old Hog and I then lit out for Iron Creek in the Black Range. In a short time I reached a cabin that had been built for the use of travelers and hunters in that section. Smoke rose from the chimney and the door stood open. No one was there, but a pot of beans hung on a hook above the fire. Taking a tin plate, I helped myself.

I was hardly through eating when I heard the sound of voices. In came Webster and McKay, two miners from Kingston, who were hunting on the west side of the Black Range and camping in the vacant cabin. They gave me the glad hand, and I told them about seeing the Indians. But when I said the bucks were wearing plug hats I could see the two men look at each other.

At last Webster said, "Now Jimmie, we know you've been through hell the past six weeks, but take my advice and don't tell this story when you get to Kingston, for they'll sure say you're loony, and you'll not be able to get any work."

"Well, fellows," said I, "I am going to pull out. I may have been blind and imagined what I saw, but my old burro is still acting strange. He wants to get away. He sure has had his troubles with the Indians and can scent one a mile away. So I am going on his judgment. Good-by! I hope you have good luck at your hunting. Let me know if you meet any Indians wearing plug hats."

Away we went. Old Hog needed no punching to get out of Iron Creek Canyon. Crossing over the divide between Iron Creek and the Middle Percha we were soon on the trail that led into Kingston. About four in the afternoon we pulled into Toppy Johnson's place at the foot of the mountains. I saw he was at home, for his horse was tied at the gate. Old Hog and I were both leg-weary, and I was glad when Toppy asked me to stay with him overnight. While we were having a bite to eat I told him about seeing the Indians.

"It's a long time since the old Horace Greeley white-plug hats have been worn," laughed Toppy. "It'll be interestin' to know whose store has been ransacked. But I'm not surprised, for I saw fresh Indian signs on the ranch this morning."

Toppy Johnson may have been a cattle rustler, but he was always ready to do a good turn for a fellow that was down and out. "Now Jimmie," said he when we were through eating, "you throw yourself on that cot and take a rest, for you sure do look all in. You're welcome to a bunk in this cabin until you get yourself a job. You can take forty winks now, while I go out to look after the stock."

He was virtually gone but a minute or two when he called, "Ho, Jimmie, come out here and open the gate. Them damned Apaches have been at it again."

I rushed out and looked up the trail where Toppy was running. One man was staggering along with another thrown over his shoulder. Toppy caught a horse and galloped up to meet them. In a few minutes the wounded man was brought to the cabin. It was no other than Bill McKay, who had been shot in the leg.

"Well, Jimmie," panted Webster, "we know now who the lunatics are. After dinner Bill and I were settin' on the bench in front of the cabin havin' a smoke, and we never seen them damn Indians till they opened fire on us. They got McKay in the leg, but I helped him into the cabin and barricaded the door. The Indians know that place has port holes in it, and they soon rode off. But they sure raised hell enough for one day."

"We'll have to get Bill into town to a doctor," said Toppy. "Man, I don't see how you ever got him this far on your back. He sure ain't no feather. I'll have the horses ready in a jiffy."

McKay got better, but he walked with a limp the rest of his life.

In town Toppy heard that Benivedes' store on the Mimbres River had been raided by the Indians and the owner killed. The store had been overstocked years before with white stovepipe hats, and they had struck the fancy of the Indians.

The next few weeks Kingston virtually buzzed with Indian excitement. The town was jammed with miners and ranchers who had flocked in as soon as they heard the Indians were out. The troops were following the marauders without much luck, though hardly a day passed but some cowboy or rancher brought in news of fresh raids. Three or four men were killed between Lake Valley and Trujillo Creek. Business went to pieces, and it was out of the question to get work.

One day as I went down the Percha Creek from Toppy's cabin I was stopped by John Dwyer, a young Iowan, who was camped near the creek.

"I hear you know these parts pretty well," said he, "and I thought maybe you'd taken note of an open piece of ground with a good spring on it, not too far from Kingston. Some Texans have offered me five hundred dollars for such a piece of ground, and if you can help me out we'll go halves on the deal."

"I know of a fine spring about eight miles out near Cave Creek," I told him, "and if you think it isn't too far we'll go up there tomorrow and find out whether or not it's been located while I was in the Gila section. If not, we'll build our monument and go into Hillsboro to file our claim before some one else beats us to it."

"Well, that's news," said Johnny, "I have a mining claim out there called the Silver Nest, but I didn't know about the spring."

"That's great," said I, "for we can locate it with your mining claim as a mill site. I'll meet you here at daybreak. Be sure your rifle is in good shape, for the spring lies in the direction of Vic's Park."

"Why not camp right here with me?" asked Johnny. "The tent is big enough for two, and there's plenty of grazing here for your burro."

And that is how we became partners.

Soon after sunrise we reached Cave Creek. At Dad Perkins' cabin we stopped to cook a bite of breakfast. There we left the trail that goes over the mesa to the Animas River and struck off down Cave Creek about a mile and a half to a grove of cottonwoods and black oaks. Here the spring seeped through the black soil. The spot was not located. Virtually hundreds of large wood pigeons were feeding on acorns under the trees. We shot three or four to take back to Kingston and came to the conclusion to call the place "Pigeon Springs". By driving stakes into the soil where it showed water seepage I soon saw that we could get a good supply by cribbing, or walling up the spring.

After building our monument we struck out for Hillsboro to file our claim, getting there at three o'clock that afternoon. Luck was with us, for we recorded our claim and caught a freighter wagon back to Kingston that same afternoon.

The Texans looked us up the next morning, finding us still abed in Johnny's tent, for we were fagged out after our long trip of the day before. When they heard we had a place in view for them, they went into town with us, bought us a fine breakfast, and hired horses to take us out to Pigeon Springs. Several cowboys were looking over the ground when we got there. Their faces fell and they rode off when we told them our claim was already recorded.

The Texans were both in high feather and hired us to build a cabin, a corral, and some outhouses, promising to stock us up with food enough to last until the work was done. When the place was ready they expected to pay us five hundred dollars and move their families and cattle from Lake Valley. As I had been promised a job in the mine by Mr. Taylor, it was agreed that if I got a call I could hire a man to take my place at Pigeon Springs.

In a few days Johnny and I moved out to the spring, though the town still buzzed with Indian alarms. As it was late in September and the nights were already getting cold, I thought the Indian trouble would blow over till the next spring. We soon had the logs cut. Several miners from Danville helped with the raising.

One Saturday morning I went into Kingston for more supplies and frames for the door and windows. The town was full of excitement. Women with children in their arms stood in the streets, crying. Mrs. Fitzpatrick took note of me crossing the creek and rushed up, saying, "You will go, won't you, Mr. McKenna, because you know the way?"

"Where?"

"Over to warn our husbands at Upper and Lower Tierra Blanca. We got a heliograph that the Indians are headed that way."

"A burro wouldn't get me there before night," said I.

I had bought a saddle for Old Hog, and I now rode him back and forth between Pigeon Springs and Kingston.

"My husband's race horse is ready for you, and Jim Drummond said he would go along."

I could not say no. By this time a crowd of women and children had gathered around me, while a group of men hung in the background. One of the boys came down the street leading Fitzpatrick's horse. In a trice Jim Drummond and I were off.

We came to the conclusion to go first to Lower Tierra Blanca to warn the men at Log Cabin Mine and those at Monaska, also old man Shaw, who lived near the trail. We met the Monaska miners on their way into Kingston for the weekend. Old man Shaw was working in his garden. He promised to lock himself in his cabin and go into town with the troops when they passed by. At Log Cabin we found the four owners—Sly, Johnston, and the Kinney brothers, Pete and Andy.

"We'll ride along with you, eh, Pete?" said Andy. Their two partners set out at once for Kingston, and the four in our party were soon flying like the wind on the trail to Upper Tierra Blanca. We got there during the lunch hour. Six men sat around the cabin smoking. All had their horses in the corral. Fitzpatrick hauled me over the coals for riding his race horse saying we were out on a wild goose chase, but at last he gave in to go back to town with us. Sykes and Tressel decided to go down the shaft into the drift and stay there till the Indians were gone.

Seeing that the other miners made light of the alarm, the Kinney brothers concluded to go back to the Log Cabin. While we stopped to give out the news, our horses became restless, champing and straining at the bits as if they wanted to be off.

"These animals have surely scented Indians," said I. "We had better not hang around here any longer."

Five of us took the Kingston trail. The Kinney boys were tightening their cinches when we left them not far from the cabin. Not more than six minutes had gone by when we heard a shot. In a twinkle Pete Kinney caught up with us calling out, "I'm shot."

He rushed by with his hat in his hand and with one ear hanging against his cheek. When we came up to him, he cried out, "I was getting on my horse when an Indian opened fire and clipped off my ear. Pull off the damned thing, one of you fellows. It'll never be any good to me now. Andy got away, and I believe he'll make it back to Kingston by the other route."

Hardly had he stopped speaking when we were virtually deafened by the sound of an explosion. "There goes the cabin," said Pete.

The Indians yelled like fiends. Fitzpatrick told us there had been two boxes of dynamite stored in the cabin. The fumes of the powder and the yells of the Indians followed us as we raced like deer along the trail. Among the brakes of Trujillo Creek we slowed up, warned by the actions of our horses. All at once we heard the sound of voices. It turned out to be a rescue party led by Ed Doheny. The noise of the explosion had been heard in Kingston. Andy Kinney had already pulled in with word that he had found old man Shaw lying murdered in his garden. Shaw had not taken our warning in time.

About sundown Sykes and Tressel got into town.

"After blowing up our cabin," Sykes told the crowd, "the Indians gathered around the shaft, calling down, 'John, oh, John!' Getting no answer they began to wind up the windlass and let it and the bucket loose. As the bucket bounced down the shaft they'd give one of their blood-curdlin' whoops. They fired a number of shots down the shaft, but they did not try to come down themselves. At last the windlass jumped out of the standards, and they went off, but not until they had burned or destroyed everything around the mine. Of course they rounded up our horses and took them along. When the boys came out to warn us I thought it was a lot of bunk. You can take it from me, the next time anyone goes to the trouble to tell me the Indians are out I'll give him my ear."

After hearing the story of the two miners I lit out for Pigeon Springs, with Old Hog packing our supplies. Though I was on the alert, I saw no signs of Indians in that direction.

Shortly after this a company of Territorial Militia was made up under Captain Highland. I signed up and went out twice as a scout. Two lieutenants in the company were Maxwell and McKelry. Johnny Moffitt, a friend of Ed Doheny's, who has lived virtually fifty years in Kingston, was also a member of that company. Some white men lost their lives in skirmishes with the Indians, but the Indians themselves always seemed to make a getaway.

Neither Johnny Dwyer nor I had ever seen any Indian signs at Pigeon Springs, though we were less than two miles below the trail to Victorio Park. Our spring by this time was walled up, and door and windows were in place in the cabin. Although our work at the spring was nearly done, the Texans failed to show up as they had promised. We wrote to them at Lake Valley and got word they were on the way back to Texas as fast as the train would take them. Too many Indians. Troops were located at Lake Valley, Hillsboro, and Kingston, and report had it the country was alive with Apaches who had been driven out of Old Mexico.

Johnny went out one morning to get a deer, coming back about noon with the hind quarters. "I had to go all the way up to McCann's Gulch before I got a shot," he told me, "and you know how close it is to Vic's Park. I heard a noise while I was gutting the deer, so I slipped around and peeked through the bushes. 'Twas a squaw I saw washing the wounds of a buck, and wrapping them with rags she was, while a half a dozen Indians stood around watching her. I was that glad to be off that I left my hunting knife behind me."

"And I sure hope you won't be fool enough to go back for it," I warned him.

I might as well have saved my breath, for he went off in the afternoon, and about sundown soon after he got back, I found him cleaning his hunting knife. He never said anything about it, but he was as white as a sheet, and I came to the conclusion he had got a scare he would not soon forget.

Every week I rode into Kingston to ask if there was any chance of getting work in the mines. How Old Hog balked when it was time to light out for Pigeon Springs! It took a lot of punching to get him started. He wanted to stay in town, and we had to picket him to keep him at Pigeon Springs. That burro liked to keep virtually five miles between himself and an Apache.

One morning the brother of Captain Jack Crawford, the poet-scout, dropped in at our cabin warning us that the Indians were near-by. He was pleased to note the port holes in our cabin.

"Here you are safe," said he, "but if you are wise you won't go hunting until this band of red devils clears out."

November had arrived, and the ground was covered with snow before I got word to come into the mine to work. I sent a man named Davenport out to Pigeon Springs with a message to Johnny, telling him I thought he ought to come into Kingston, for the soldiers claimed the Indians were scattered in small bands all through the Black Range. If he came to the conclusion to keep Davenport I agreed to pay for his help, but I warned them both not to go hunting. Report had it that a man had been killed by the Indians near Hachita.

I had not been working more than a week at the Superior Mine when the foreman looked me up one morning at the end line of the Superior, where I was tracing up a float sample at Mr. Taylor's bidding.

"Jimmie," said he, "there's a man here, name of Davenport, looking for you. I am afraid he has bad news about your pardner at Pigeon Springs."

As I rushed away Mr. Taylor's warning of a few days before came back to me. He had been standing near me when the bugles sounded.

"You ought to bring in your partner from Cave Creek," said he.

"If I can get off next Sunday I surely will," I answered.

"I'll see that you have the day free," he promised.

That was the Sunday before and this was Tuesday. God ruled otherwise. As soon as I caught sight of Davenport's face, I knew. "The Indians got Johnny," said I. "Is he dead?"

"No, so I pulled him into the brush until I could get help. He has a wound in his thigh and can't walk.

"Why didn't you carry him to the cabin?"

"Well, we heard a lot of shouting on the mesa where the trail goes to the Animas, and Johnny wanted me to leave before I'd be taken by the Indians. He wanted me to go for help, and I came to you first, because it's a mile nearer than Kingston. I thought maybe I'd meet some of the militia that was ambushed out that way, but I didn't see a soul."

Davenport was in bad shape himself, as white as a sheet and shaking from head to foot.

Taking up my rifle I said to him, "Go into Kingston and see if you can get the Doctor to come out to Dad Perkins' cabin. It can't be more than a couple of hundred yards from where Johnny is lying, and I'll try to get him up there."

I struck out afoot, reaching Johnny about two hours later. I was virtually like an Indian in those days, lean and wiry, and I seldom got tired on the trail. But Johnny was an immense load, and I do not know to this day how I managed to carry him up to Dad Perkins' cabin. He was over six feet tall and weighed about one hundred and seventy-five pounds.

As soon as I got to the cabin Johnny said: "I want you to go back for our guns, Jimmie, and the canteen and anything else we left down there in the brush, before the Indians pick them up. I saw the Indian who shot me, and I know he had a horse, for I could hear the clatter of hoofs for a long time after I crawled into the brush."

After I had brought up our guns and the rest of our things, I fetched a bucket of water from the creek, carried in a few armloads of juniper wood, and locked up the cabin. When the water boiled I took off Johnny's clothes and washed out the wound, which was virtually as big as a teacup with a slit going down from his hip about fourteen inches. I was able to take out quite a few pieces of the exploded cartridges.

While I waited on him Johnny told me what had happened.

"I hope the posse won't be long in getting here, Jimmie. I was that glad to see you, old scout, for 'tis sure I am I wouldn't like to die alone in the brush like a wounded deer. 'Tis myself that is most to blame for this, Jimmie, for Captain Crawford's brother was here again early this morning to tell us they'd had a heliograph from Fort Cummings that a band of Indians was headed for Vic's Park.

"Their horses were about petered out, and everyone was warned to be on the lookout. Captain Crawford told us a posse was going into ambush on the Animas trail among the large rocks that are scattered along there. Big Mack, Bill Reeve, Johnny Moffit, and Charley Wallace, about ten in all, expected to be hiding in there when the Indians came through. As there weren't more than half a dozen Indians in the band Crawford warned us on no account to leave our cabin, for our help would not be needed.

"Well, Jimmie, 'twas only a couple of hours he was gone, when the firing began. Shooting, shouting, more shooting. 'Twas when the firing kept up that I says to Davenport that something had gone wrong, and the posse must sure need our help. He wasn't keen about going, but he was that good he wouldn't be letting me go alone. He advised going directly upon the mesa where we could see, but I had my own way and we followed the regular trail up Cave Creek. 'Twas there I made my mistake.

"Soon it was plain that the Indians had scattered among the rocks. One of them must have heard us talking, as he rode along the edge of the mesa above us. 'Twas Davenport saw him first, and he tried to pull me into the brush. I turned and the bullet hit my cartridge belt, exploding my own shells as well as the Indian's You know the rest. 'Tis suffering a whole lot, I am, Jimmie. Do you think the posse'll soon be here?"

"Well, Johnny, old son, you'll have to buck up, for I didn't see a soul, not even at Danville." This was a small camp about six miles out on the trail from Kingston which we always passed on our way to Pigeon Springs.

I made him some tea and he dropped off to sleep. About two o'clock he woke up suffering terribly. "Johnny," said I, "I'm going to wash out that wound again the best way I can. After that you can have more tea and crackers, and I'll hit the trail for Kingston. You've got to have a doctor. I know you are afraid to let me prod the wound, and there's a lot of copper in it yet."

In less than a half hour I was again on the trail. At Danville's boarding house I found Andy Kinney and Dan McWilliams, who set off at once to stay with Johnny till help came. When I got to Kingston at four o'clock I found the people all excited, putting me in mind of a bunch of cattle that had stampeded. The saloons were full of men, most of them half-seas-over, while the women and children stood in bunches in the street. There is no terror like Indian terror.

I could not get anyone to go back with me to Dad Perkins' cabin. But Harry Calvick loaned me his horse, and the Doctor put up a pack of narcotics and other medicines. He promised to come out about nine o'clock that night.

Once more I struck the trail alone. Johnny was asleep when I reached the cabin. Kinney and McWilliams helped me picket the horse and get a bite to eat. They swore aplenty when I told them that the posse got only one skinny old Indian mare. It seems that a member of the posse had shown the white-feather and fired too soon, giving away the ambush to the wary Indians.

Ten o'clock, and no help had come from town. About midnight

I took the horse and again lit out for Kingston. At Danville I met the Doctor and a party of his friends. Everyone in the crowd was virtually three sheets in the wind, even the Doctor.

Late as it was, we rigged up a stretcher with some boards and Dad Perkins' mattress. Then we carried Johnny three miles to the Danville boarding house and laid him on the mess table. Taking an instrument that looked like a long spoon, the Doctor dug out several more pieces of copper from the wound. After washing it out he filled Johnny with opium and promised to see that he was brought into town in the morning.

It was two o'clock in the morning when the Doctor and his friends set out for town. As they had not had a drink for several hours they were in a big hurry to get away. Besides, none of them were hankering to stay away from town very long when the Indians were out.

By nine o'clock the next morning I had used up all the sedatives left by the Doctor, trying to keep Johnny quiet. We then came to the conclusion to carry him over to the old Solitaire Mine. Two carried the stretcher, one rode the horse with their guns and his own, and I was foot-loose, on the lookout for Indians. When a man at the stretcher grew tired the one on horseback took his place. At the North Percha we stopped to rest. Johnny was asleep. We did not stop again and had virtually reached the Solitaire when we heard wagon wheels. The man on horseback raced ahead and came back with Ed Doheny and several other men. We lifted Johnny into the spring wagon, and Ed Doheny drove him into Kingston to Mrs. Brophy's hotel.

In a few minutes the Doctor came. Ed Doheny, Judge Holt, myself, and several others wanted him to open Johnny's wound, but he was as stubborn as a mule and would not give in to it.

"This is only a flesh wound," said he. "All it needs is a good washing-out. The boy will be well in eight or ten days. He is physically perfect. He's had a shock, and what he needs is a good rest, a little petting, and plenty of food. You may as well go back to work, Jimmie. We'll keep you posted."

The Doctor's orders were carried out, and I went back to work the next morning, though I could hardly believe that Johnny was out of the woods so soon. In the afternoon some one brought me word that Johnny had a chill and wanted to see me. At the hotel Mrs. Donahue told me that Ed Doheny had gone for Dr. Thompson, the Army man, who could be found either at Lake Valley or

Fort Bayard. In a country swarming with Indians it was a trip that took a lot of sand.

I took note of a bad change in Johnny. He was virtually green with the poison in the blood. " 'Tis come to me that I am going to pass out, Jimmie," said he, "and I want you to send word to my sister in Caledonia, Iowa. If you can sell the place, pay our debts, and send the rest of my share to Mary. She'll be that glad to have it, for they haven't much of this world's goods."

Doheny and Dr. Thompson got in about six that evening. The doctor took one look at Johnny and swore. In a twinkling he had lanced the wound, but it was too late. About a gallon of fluid blew up to the ceiling. Johnny fainted. When they had brought him to the doctor said, "My boy, it's time to make your peace with God. You cannot live." He talked very kindly to Johnny for some minutes. I went with him when he left the room.

"You should have opened the wound as you wanted to do," he told me. "That boy should not have to die, but as it is he hasn't even a fighting chance. He's only nineteen years old, and his body is without a blemish, apart from this flesh wound. The lad has been poisoned by the pieces of copper that were not taken from the wound. It is a case of bad judgment on the part of your Kingston doctor. I can do nothing. The boy will be dead in an hour."

Dr. Thompson was right. His sister wired me to bury Johnny in Kingston. After the funeral I went back to work, but I was feeling pretty blue. Within six months I had lost two partners by Indians. Mr. Taylor wanted me to stop working and take a rest.

"How can I?" I asked. "I am head over heels in debt now. I must stay where I am. My luck is bound to turn for the better before long. Besides, when I work hard I don't have time to think." But I was sent away from the mine for the time being.

In December while I was giving a little help in the post office I heard that the S C L Cattle Company had jumped our claim at Pigeon Springs. I went with my troubles to Attorney Harry Elliott, who soon let the Company know he meant to look after our rights. He warned them to buy the place or he would prosecute. The Company officers were as mad as the dickens but they paid me five hundred dollars. I did all that Johnny asked me to and sent his sister about two hundred dollars. My luck had turned for the better. The next week Mr. Taylor sent for me to go back to work in the Superior Mine.

But my health had virtually played out. For two years after

Johnny's death I never slept more than three hours in a night. At the least sound I would be sitting up with my hand on my gun. My brown hair dropped out, and the new hair came in white, though I was virtually a young man.

Danny's Trouble With the Devil

1. *A Midnight Race*

KINGSTON was booming. Early in August, 1882, Jack Sheddon discovered virtually a ton of rich silver float at the spot named by him the "Solitaire" out near Carbonate Creek. There followed a regular old-time rush into the Black Range. In mid-August, A. Barnaby set up a tent and opened the first store on the spot that has ever since been the center of Kingston. By August the 26th, the same year, the surveying of the town was under way; by late fall eighteen hundred people had gathered in the town of Kingston.

Hundreds of people of many nationalities could be seen every day on their way to the silver mecca from the town of Nutt, which at that time was the terminal of the Santa Fe Railroad. At Nutt Station many pilgrims stopped to read the bill posted there:

"HO! FOR THE GOLD AND SILVER MINES
OF NEW MEXICO!

"Fortune hunters, capitalists, poor men,
Sickly folks, all whose hearts are bowed down;
And ye who would live long, be rich, healthy,
And happy: Come to our sunny clime and see
For yourselves!"

Kingston was a tent town all through the first year after it was laid out, but there were plenty of saloons and dance halls there from the beginning. Among the first to come in were gamblers and their friends of the demi-monde. Under the flickering light of a pine knot the first dance was held in Kingston; and thousands of dollars changed hands in the light of the camp fire under the big old pines.

The first winter turned out to be the coldest in the history of the settlement. In spite of the deep snow a wagon road was soon finished and supplies and bedding became plentiful, but the tall prices put things out of reach for most people. Many were poorly housed and clothed; some bunked under the pines rolled in thin blankets, others made out as best they could in a brush shack or tent. Very few made any move to build log cabins, though timber was plentiful. Sawmills were under way and people were anxious to see them finished, as the cost of lumber, hauled by rail and wagon from Texas and Oregon, was over a hundred dollars a thousand feet.

One cold morning in the early winter smallpox broke out in Kingston. The disease had got into the town in the furs and blankets of emigrants from Indian Territory (Oklahoma). An epidemic of black smallpox had almost wiped out an Indian tribe in that country; people had bought the furs and blankets gathered from vacant Indian tents. Two newcomers from Indian Territory were the first to die.

Kingston was better able to deal with the wiles of the Apache than to handle the smallpox. Doctor Guthrie, the only medical man in the settlement, had been there but a few days and was celebrating his coming in his own way. When he got too much nosepaint he would take off his hat and then his wig, to prove that he had been scalped by the Cheyenne Indians. He liked to take a drop and he was as odd as they come, but the people took to him right away, and everyone depended on him to check the disease.

He ordered the largest tent in town to be made a pesthouse, locating it at the west end of the settlement in a grove of juniper trees. Cots, bedding, stoves, and other things were furnished by people in the town. A committee was organized under Doctor Guthrie to help fight the disease. The question of nurses came up. Two old grog-heads who claimed to have had smallpox when they were young offered to take care of the sick on condition that they be supplied every day with a jug of whiskey. "Give them all the liquor they want," ordered the doctor. "It's the most plentiful thing in town. We don't have to worry about either one of them. You couldn't kill them with an axe."

By the time the pest tent was ready, more cases of smallpox had broken out, among them being two big business men of the district. The women of the town cooked the meals for the sick, but it soon became plain that the patients got little food and less care. Doctor Guthrie was wild and ordered the two sots to clear out. Three women from the red-light district then went to him and offered to look after his patients, if the doctor himself promised not to touch another drop until the disease was under control.

WHEN THE GAMBLERS CAME TO KINGSTON

"My dear girls," said he, "if you'll turn in and help me, I'll do anything you want me to—I'll be your slave for life."

The girls quickly changed their fine dresses for calicoes. Seven men had died under the first two nurses, but from the moment these girls went into the pest tent the disease began to die out. Side by side they worked with Doctor Guthrie until the smallpox was a thing of the past. The youngest nurse of the three caught the disease but she pulled through. It was plain to all Kingston that the girl from Shady Lane often had her heart in the right place.

Kingston had no graveyard. It was concluded to bury the dead in the grove of junipers where the pest tent stood. Here the roots of the trees had softened the rocky ground a little. Bed-rock lay below. A shallow hole was blasted in the bed-rock. Even when topsoil had been heaped on the graves, the dead lay within two and one half feet of the surface.

Danny did not die; he did not have the smallpox; he did not bury the dead; he did not nurse the sick; he was not even in Kingston at the time of the epidemic; just the same, he had a part in all this, for the dead did not stay buried. And Danny was an Irishman who believed that the dead sometimes walked. He came from a regular Irish farming community in Illinois where the customs of old Ireland had never been given up. They held wakes, believed in witches and fairies, and kept the brogue. At a funeral or a wedding, so Danny told me, "You could easily believe you were in the Ould Dart."

Danny was of small stature with dark eyes and hair, and was considered very good-looking. He had no bad habits, but he would take a nip of John Barleycorn just for friendship. He was very congenial and kind-hearted, but when he got a few bowls under his belt he was quarrelsome. If he did not like you, this was the time he would let you know it.

I fell out with Danny several times because he gave away our secrets when he was stewed. As soon as he had a drop too much he was sure to spill the beans about some deal we were planning to put through. He always felt sorry for these breaks of his, and at last promised me to let the drink alone if I would keep him for a partner. We worked together for three years. I knew ore better than Danny did, and Danny knew how to handle the hammer better than I did, so it was fifty-fifty between us. The first time I ever saw him was at a foot race. He claimed to be the best heel-

and-toe walker in Illinois. It was probably true, for in Kingston no one was ever found who could beat him on a five-mile stretch.

Danny and I were both underweights, so we naturally drifted together and became partners. An underweight was a man below one hundred seventy-five pounds in weight and less than five feet, eleven inches in height. Mine bosses, who were nearly all men from Grass Valley, California, and the Comstock in Nevada claimed that a man below that weight and height could not handle an eight-pound striking hammer. At this time all mine work was done striking double; that is, one man turned the drill and the other struck the head of it with a double hand, or eight-pound hammer. This was a costly method as no more ground was broken by two men, than by one who turned and struck the drill himself with a four-pound, or single hammer. Danny and I could not get work as drillers. By scheming, contracting, getting assessments—which meant working claims for absent owners according to the law—and prospecting on our own account we managed to get along.

One of these prospects led us past the graves near the South Percha Trail. Danny and I took notice that the bones of the dead had been uncovered by a bad rain-storm during the summer. Every time that we went south we made up our minds to come out some day with tools and powder, blast out a few feet of rock, and put the bones under ground at least four feet. But we kept putting it off. One day Danny said, "Jimmie, have you noticed old man Fanning's burro under those juniper trees? By jove, we've never gone by those graves yet that Bonito hasn't been standin' there like he was on guard."

"I have taken note of Bonito, Danny" said I, "and I've come to the conclusion he has his eye on you. He knows you didn't keep your word about burying those bones."

"I don't see how old Fanning can spare him. I'd think he'd need him to help him pack the wood and trash and do the chores around town."

"The animal has to eat," I reminded him.

"Well then, he's an uncanny beast that likes to do his feeding among the graves of smallpox victims. His looks are against him in the first place. Whoever saw a burro with such long ears, and that's not enough—he wears a regular billy goat goatee. I came up to him the other day with his face grinning at me from the brush, and I had a hard time figuring whether he was a burro or a goat."

"Bonito is a queer-looking burro all right," I agreed. "And have you ever taken note that when he meets the other burros he butts and kicks at them instead of braying and biting as a regular brother burro should? I think myself he must be a half-breed."

"Half-breed," scoffed Danny. "He's bewitched, that's what he is."

"He's friendly and harmless," said I. "Didn't you take note how glad he was to see us as we went by just now?"

Danny snorted. "I hope he don't bring bad luck on our claims. Do you really think we're going to win out, Jimmie?"

The law required a hundred dollars worth of work to be done as an annual assessment. If the work had not been done by midnight, December 31, the claim went back to the Government and anyone on the spot at that time could get the property. By November Danny and I were watching claims on which no work had been done within the year, the parties who owned them being in the East. We made up our minds to keep a close watch on two of these claims, so that no one could afterwards swear away our rights. One lay to the south of Kingston near the South Percha Trail, and the other was north of town close to Pickett's Spring. Once a week we went over the ground on both claims.

The Christmas holidays arrived. Danny and I were counting the days till the claims would belong to us. On the morning of December 31, we made a trip to each of the locations, building a monument and gathering a pile of wood to be ready for the big moment at midnight. No work had yet been started, and no one seemed to have caught on. We went back to the town in high feather.

New Year's Eve in Kingston! Saloons, restaurants, and dance halls were crowded. Orchestras had been brought from El Paso to play for the dances. Big games of faro and poker were going on with coin stacked virtually to the ceiling, especially in the Monarch Saloon and the Brewery. I had followed Danny into the Monarch to keep an eye on him, for he could not stand much liquor, and I was afraid he would not be able to make the trip by midnight. I found him raising Cain with a crowd of hefty miners and blowing that he could teach them all to break rock. The bartender ordered him to quiet down, or he would kick him out. I got him to go with me to the Long Branch where there was less excitement.

When it was time to start, Danny asked, "Who goes out past those bones, Jimmie, me or you?"

"Let's put it up to Knock-Kneed Jim," said I, calling the bartender.

"Sure, boys, I'll settle it for you," agreed Knock-Kneed Jim. "Danny is just *longing* to go by them graves, ain't it so, old son?" he asked, giving me the wink. "Well, here are two broom straws. Whoever gets the short one has the honor of goin' by them poor devils' graves. Draw Danny. You go, old son. I would sure tank up if I was you. I've heard tell the dead get to rovin' around on the last night of the year."

Danny turned pale. "Great Heavens, lads, I'm sure not hankerin' to pass them bones. Let me have a half pint to take along, Jim; and set up the drinks on me. Come on, old sons, drink to the New Year, to the ghosts in the graveyard, and to our new mines. Hurrah!"

About eleven o'clock we set our watches to the second, and once more looked over the location notices we intended to bury in the monuments at the stroke of twelve. Away we went, Danny going south and I north. I reached the claim in good time. At midnight I buried the tin box by the light of the fire I had built. Afterwards I sat before the fire for the hour agreed upon to protect our claim. It was a windy night, and I could hear the old year sighing itself out in the pine trees. The coyotes were yapping close to my fire. At one I lit out for Kingston on the lonely trail, wondering how Danny had made out. He had not yet come into town when I reached the Monarch.

All at once while I stood warming myself before the big goose-egg stove, there was a great clatter and yelling in the street. In a twinkling the door of the Monarch was pushed open. In rushed Danny, shouting, "Save me! It's the devil!" The "devil" followed him. Danny dropped to the floor in a swoon. The jackass, Bonito, upset a table where Dad Perkins and old Colonel Harris were having a game of pitch, and banged his way out through the back door. The bartender threw water on Danny and brought him to. Some of the men playing faro gave him a drink. "The devil sure gave me a run that time, but he didn't get me, and if the Lord lets me live that long I'll sure bury those bones before the sun goes down on another day!" What a commotion and what shrieks of laughter!

While I walked with Danny to the bunk house he told me what happened. "Everything was O. K. on the way out to the claim, but I sure walked light going by them poor devils' graves. I thought once I saw something move under the junipers, but I didn't hang around to make sure. When I got to the claim it was ten minutes to twelve. I lit the fire and loosened a few rocks in the monument to make a safe spot for the tin can where the trade rats couldn't get at it. On the dot of twelve I put the location in the monument and called out, 'I, Danny, have located this mineral land. Anyone that's got anything to say agin it, step forward.' Only a coyote answered me. Then I took a long pull from my bottle and sat down by the fire to wait out the hour as agreed. At the end of the hour I called again, emptied my bottle, and headed for Kingston.

"The moon had gone down, as you'll recall, Jimmie, and a strong wind was blowing. I was terrible sleepy, and I kept wishing I was past the graves. I thought if I'd go fast and keep looking up at the stars I wouldn't see the ghosts. Down I stumble over a broken juniper limb. My hat flies off, and when I reach for it, I looks straight into the devil's own mug, horns and all. I dropped my hat calling out, 'God save me,' like the old folks always said we should when we seen anything from the other world, and then I was off like the wind, but every step I took the devil gained on me. You know that gulch, Jimmie, where you turn off just before you reach town? By gosh, I jumped the whole twelve feet across, the devil doing the same. You know the rest. I don't care what they say, that shenanigan of Fanning's is an uncanny beast, and I believe the devil's in him certain after tonight."

On New Year's afternoon we took our picks, shovels, drills, hammers, and enough ammunition to blast a four-foot hole, and headed for the grove of junipers. At this depth we at last buried safe from beast and cloudburst the bones of the smallpox victims. Danny was sick for a week, but the townsfolk had a good laugh. A crowd went out the next day to the gulch Danny claimed he jumped, to check up on his story. Sure enough! They found his tracks and Bonito's on both sides of the gulch. As we slept in the mine company's bunk house Danny had to listen every night to many wise cracks about the devil.

2. *The White Steer and the Drilling Match*

Shortly after Danny's first experience with the devil we got a contract driving a tunnel from Saw Pit Gulch toward the Comstock Mine. At Saw Pit we put up a shack. All the water we used had to be packed by burro from Pickett's Spring nearly a mile away, costing us twenty-five cents a barrel. Near Saw Pit we built a slack tub for our water supply by cutting a barrel in half. We had to be our own blacksmiths.

One day Danny said, "From now on, Jimmie, I'm going to practice striking with both arms, for I sure believe I can win that five hundred dollars offered as a single-jack prize next Fourth of July. The prize goes to the man who drills the most feet, say, in thirty minutes. I see now I can drill more than most of these crack miners."

"Go to it, Danny," said I. "You'll have plenty of practice in drilling two hundred and fifty feet of tunnel."

Danny went at it heart and soul. Five o'clock in the morning found him striking the head of the drill, and often he was still at it at seven in the evening. We made fine headway on the tunnel, some days going forward over a foot. Our wages averaged six dollars a day, which was good money at that time. Before long Danny was striking just as well in speed and skill with either arm. He had fixed up a canteen with a small syphon hose to feed water from the canteen into the drill hole, so he would not have to stop to pour in the water by hand.

From the day we built our slack tub we had to keep on the lookout, for the stray cattle that browsed in the vicinity soon learned to push the lid from the tub when they wanted water. Among the cattle was a large white steer, which turned out to be a regular thief. He was a heavy animal with horns virtually four feet across. His feet had grown sore on the rough mountain slopes, and he found it hard to travel to a water hole. Many times a day we had to drive him away from the slack tub. He was a real nuisance. In time he made bold enough to go into our cabin, looting it like an Apache. We had often driven him from the tunnel and the dump. His owner paid no attention to our complaints.

By early June we had finished more than two hundred feet of the tunnel. We ran a car on a track hauling rock and debris through the finished part of the tunnel from face to dump. As Danny was keen to get in all the practice he could at drilling, it became my job to fill and empty the car. I always blocked the car after moving it, so it could not be pushed over the dump by the white steer or some other stray animal. When I had emptied the waste I either helped Danny, striking double, or if there was time enough, I put down a hole myself.

One day in June we had both worked extra hard. Not more than a half dozen words had been spoken by either of us during the whole day. By five o'clock in the afternoon we were working our fifth hole. "Get the ammunition, Jimmie, and I'll finish this hole."

When I went to the powder keg I found it empty.

"Suppose you go up to the Comstock and borrow a few sticks of dynamite from Charlie Canfield. He won't say no, for we've got a lease on part of that mine."

As I left the tunnel I took note of the big white steer standing close to the car. I drove him away, but on looking around, saw that he had gone back to the car. It was some time before I located Canfield, and then I stayed to examine a piece of ore he had picked up that day on one of his drifts. He went with me towards the Saw Pit, still talking about his rich find. All at once he said, "Here comes Danny on a dead run. There must be something wrong in the tunnel."

"What's up now?" I wondered.

As he rushed up, excited and out of breath, he yelled, "I got him sure this time, and there ain't been a muff out of him since I struck him!"

"Who?"

"Who else but the devil himself," said Danny, pale and trembling.

"Tell us what happened," said Canfield.

"Well," he began, "I was pounding away on the drill, sitting down to it, as the hole was not high on the face of the tunnel, when I heard the mine car coming. Of course I thought it was Jimmie, though I did wonder why he was pushing it in at that hour. I kept on drilling till the car ran plunk into me. 'Jimmie,' I screams, jumping up, and there staring at me out of the dark, his eyes burning like two coals of fire and his horns straight up, was his majesty himself. I cracked him a good one right between the eyes with my four-pound striking hammer and down he went like a thousand pounds of rock. Over the car I went, and you know the rest."

"Well, Danny, come along, but I can tell you beforehand you're going to have to pay for Kinzie's white steer," said I.

"As if I wouldn't know a steer when I see one," growled Danny.

"Poor Danny," laughed Canfield. "You sure have a deal of trouble with the devil. What has he got on you, Danny, that he's always coming around? But I believe Jimmie's right about the white steer, for he's been around all day, and he's nowhere in sight now. What a boiled-dog we'll have if it really is the devil. Think how glad we'll all be, knowing how much trouble he makes in the world."

Hanging down his head, Danny said, "If I've made an ass of myself, and it's that old ox of Kenzie's, I'll never hear the end of it at the drilling match on the Fourth of July."

"Don't bother your head about what will be said at the drilling match," I advised him. "You're going to win all right, and what do you care what people say, when you can pocket five hundred dollars? Besides, if you really have knocked Kenzie's steer as cold as I think you have, it's all the proof anyone needs of how strong your arm is. Let's go in and see."

Sure enough, there lay the big white steer as dead as a door nail at the foot of the mine car. With Kenzie's help we dragged the body to the mouth of the tunnel, where the butchering took place. Everyone in the neighborhood got a big chunk of beef, and Danny paid Kenzie twenty dollars for his steer. We had a hard time to keep Danny from going into Kingston and painting the town red.

"The prize for the drilling match is all off if you do that," I warned him, "for you know you'll spill the beans if you take a drink."

Of course the news of Danny's second meeting with the devil got around town, causing a lot of hilarity. As yet, no one except Canfield and myself knew that he was planning to enter the drilling match. Big miners from Butte and Grass Valley, who had sent for expert drillers from those districts to enter the contest, were offering big odds on their men. Canfield saw to it that most of the money was covered.

What a crowd was gathered in Kingston on the Fourth of July! People from every mining camp in the United States rounded up in the narrow street where the drilling platform had been set up. There were miners from Butte, Montana; from Grass Valley, California; from Silver City, Idaho; from Georgetown, New Mexico; and from many other camps. Colonel Jack Fleming was there to enter a miner from Silver City. At that time the Colonel was mayor of Silver City, and was known everywhere as a big shot in mining, since he had piled up over half a million dollars from his mining ventures. I knew Jack and told him about Danny, finally getting him not to enter his man.

Danny was as cool as a cucumber. Sizing up the blocks of rock he told me that he could win as easy as pie. The Colorado men were at first backing a powerful-looking Cornishman from Georgetown, Colorado; but some one must have tipped them off, for a gambler from Denver all at once switched about and began to bet on Danny, even offering odds. The bell rang for the appointment of judges. Everyone agreed that the outsiders were given a fair division.

The rocks were sounded, tested, and hoisted to the platforms, some for single contests and some for the double drilling. The names of those to take part in the contest were then called out and the time when each would begin to drill. Those in the contest were next called together to hear the rules read. As most of them had been in contests before, few questions were asked by anyone except Danny, who was taking part for the first time. The arena was roped off. The judges announced that the next time the gong sounded the miners would begin to drill.

An excited crowd pressed against the ropes. The gambler was there, dressed in the latest style, with a girl of the demi-monde hanging to his arm; the miner in his buckskin was there; the miner in his overalls and brogans was there; the miner in his Sunday best was there; the cowboy balancing on his high-topped, high-heeled boots was there, swinging his lariat, a wide sombrero with rattlesnake band shading his lean, brown face. Children from Silver City and other towns clung to their mother's skirts, or rode their father's shoulders, licking peppermint sticks and eating peanuts. Mexican girls in bright calicoes and a few Tornichio Indians were scattered through the crowd. Now and again the people were virtually deafened by a blast of dynamite, and the fumes of powder mixed with the scent of pine and juniper in the blue mountain air.

The gong sounds! Danny starts the first circle without seeming to move. What striking and turning! All make perfect turns and twists, but somehow Danny's drill cuts more and goes deeper. The big boys realize they are dealing with a man who knows what every turn will do. Danny changes with a lightning speed no other can equal.

The time is half up, and Danny is far in the lead. What jeering and cat-calling by the other side! "Hear! Hear, Danny! Here comes the devil! Run, Danny, run! You're going to be hooked!" But the louder the yelling, the harder Danny strikes the head of the drill, the faster he turns it. Seeing they have no chance, the Montana men throw down their hammers and drills.

"Time!" called the judge. Danny asked for a drink of poteen. He knew he had won. The hole was measured and Danny was pronounced the World's Champion Single Jack Driller. Kingston went wild with excitement, and Danny was almost pounded flat with slaps on the back, and hoisted to the shoulders of the big miners he had at last taught how to break rock. He looked like a pygmy among such men as Barbour, who was six feet, six, and weighed three hundred pounds. Colonel Jack Fleming made a speech, praising the men and mines of Kingston, and Danny was the big feather.

With the money we won we paid off all our debts, and each of us sent his mother a postoffice money order. Danny took part in many contests that fall, winning them all. After finishing the tunnel we took a lease on the Brush Heap Mine. Our luck stayed with us. Having sunk a shaft through three hundred feet of shale we struck eight feet of high-grade silver ore. There was a fly in the ointment, though, for only forty-two days were left on our lease, and the owners would not extend our time.

What chances we took! Our credit was good, and the bank loaned us several thousand dollars. The biggest risk was taken by our landlady, as she boarded a day-and-night shift without a penny for weeks. When our lease expired we paid her off with a five-hundred-dollar bonus. After getting rid of all other debts including ten per cent of a considerable amount in usury, Danny and I had about five thousand dollars each to the good.

The Brush Heap became famous, and was a producing mine for many years, as the body of ore discovered by us was continuous. It is claimed that the Brush Heap group was sold for five hundred thousand dollars.

Danny and I felt rich, so we came to the conclusion to go east to God's country to visit our people. At his home in Illinois, Danny and I parted. It was a long time before we met again. Both of us went back to the Black Range after we got rid of our winnings in the Brush Heap, working in many mining camps in the Black Range mining district. Later I heard that Danny's money was fleeced by eastern wildcats. A real estate man in El Paso got me to put all my eggs in one basket, and they soon went to smash.

3. *The Bridal Chamber*

Many times in my wanderings from camp to camp I heard of Danny who was still the World's Champion Driller. One day he appeared at the hotel in Lake Valley, asking for me. We had a lot to say to each other. Danny wanted to change from Kingston, for no one there ever forgot his experiences with the devil.

"Jimmie," he begged, "I know you can put me on to a good bunch of ore if you just think hard enough."

"Danny, old son, I'm sorry I can't take you on for a partner, but I'm in a deal with Charles Gearhart just now. But I think you could probably make some quick money in the roof of the Bridal Chamber. Let's take a walk down there, and I'll show you what I mean."

The Bridal Chamber had been abandoned, though it had been in its day the greatest deposit of silver ever found in the world. Three million ounces of silver were taken from the Bridal Chamber at a time when the ore was worth twelve dollars a pound. A surface thickness of five or six feet had not been touched, in order to form the roof of the chamber and to keep it from falling in.

"I'm sure I could gad off some rich ore from the roof without letting it down," said Danny. The Bridal Chamber was entered through a short tunnel from a level surface, and went down to its greatest depth by two steps, the first being about forty feet across with a drop of seven feet; the second step being about six feet across with a drop of twenty-five feet. I got Danny some lumber and he spent the balance of that day setting up a scaffolding, so he could reach the roof of the chamber from these different steps. I promised to come around the next morning with a canvas which he could spread on the floor of the chamber to catch the ore as it dropped.

On our way back to the hotel, we met old man Kelso, who had lately had his goatee shaved off at the order of Judge Coil. It put me in mind to tell Danny about Kelso and Phillips' goat.

Phillips had a water hole a short distance from Lake Valley and kept a fine herd of Angora goats. Among them was a large billy which at times wandered into town where the miners teased and petted him by turns. But Kelso, with his long stringy, red beard rubbed the billy goat the wrong way, and he would even leave a tin can containing beans to butt Kelso the minute he appeared. It was taken for granted the goat had no use for Kelso on account of his stringy goatee.

One dark night as Kelso was on his way home from Cotton's saloon, singing, "There's a Land that's fairer than this," he got several good biffs from behind. Facing about he grabbed the goat by the horns. In a minute it was hard to tell goat from man. Round and round they went in a dizzy whirl, Kelso still hanging to the goat's horns and screaming for help. A crowd gathered, shrieking with laughter.

"It's a couple of billies having a battle," laughed some one.

"Oh, help the goat," shouted another.

But Kelso and the goat were separated by men in the crowd.

Next day Kelso sued Phillips for assault and battery. The witnesses swore to the *battery*. The court room was crowded, and no amount of rapping with the Judge's mallet could restore order. Judge Coil dismissed the case claiming it had been filed under a misnomer. "Kelso should have sued Phillips for maintaining a nuisance," ruled he, adding with a twinkle in his eye, "One's kith and kin do sometimes become a nuisance." Phillips was ordered to pen up his goat, and Kelso to cut off his beard. The trial had been more fun than a circus.

"How sorry I am I missed the trial," laughed Danny, "but all the same I'm glad that goat is in his pen."

That night a high wind and a rain storm came to Lake Valley. Fences, trees, and outhouses blew about like chaff. Among the debris that went whirling down the valley was the fence that penned in Phillips' goat.

The next morning I made my way through the wreckage to the Bridal Chamber, packing the canvas I had promised Danny. He stood at the mouth of the tunnel, a sight to behold.

"Oh, Danny," I cried, "how did you get hurt?"

"I'm not hurt, but the devil is," said he. "I got his majesty this time sure."

"Well, well, Danny," said I with fear taking hold of my heart, "I certainly hope it was the devil and not a human that you struck."

In the deepest section of the Bridal Chamber lay Phillips' Angora goat as dead as a door nail.

"How did this happen?" I asked.

"Well, Jimmie, I came in about seven this morning and struck a match to light my miner's candle. It's a dangerous thing to use but I thought it would be handy in gadding the ore from the ceiling on account of its sharp scribe. I lighted one match after the other, all the time getting nearer and nearer to the edge of the first step. All of a sudden I stumbled over a snag of rock, dropping the candle down to the next landing. Then I lighted a snuff and leaned over trying to fish up my candle with a crooked stick. Something hit me on the backside knocking me over after my candle. Looking up, I saw the devil on the step above me ready to leap; he had horns, whiskers, and glaring red eyes. I raised the candlestick and drove the short scribe into the heart of the critter. You know the rest."

We soon found out that when the goat's pen was blown away during the storm he set off on a wild run towards town. Passing over the roof of the Bridal Chamber where it had been softened by the flooding rains, he broke through, landing on the first step of the chamber. Through the hole made in the roof by his fall had come the draft to put out Danny's candle.

When we had carried the goat above ground, Danny turned to me, "Can you lend me a few dollars, Jimmie? I'm pulling out of these parts for good, because when this gets out I'll never hear the end of it. I sure am a jackass about the devil. I'm sorry to leave you, Jimmie, because I like you, and I think you're lucky, but you sure are a hoodoo to me with the devil."

Six months later Danny sent me from Arizona the money I had loaned him.

Thirty years went by. Off and on I heard of Danny. He had married in Arizona. One day after I had settled in Deming a little old man knocked at my door. We gazed at each other as two strangers. "I'm looking for Jimmie McKenna," said he. All at once I knew him. We gave each other the glad hand. How the years change us all! Danny and I talked virtually all night. Taking note that he was thinly clad, I gave him an overcoat when he left next morning. He had been prospecting in Kingston and showed me some good specimens of ore he had picked up. I almost promised to go back with him the next spring to our old stamping ground. A month later I learned that he had died with pneumonia.

Danny was always good, and I have never been able to understand his strange fear of the devil. I leave his problem to the wise men, and for myself, I hope that Danny is in Heaven where he cannot be bothered by the devil.

Pilgrims, Burros, and Bears

1. *Pilgrims*

THE Santa Fe and other western railroads, during the early eighties, had advertised far and wide the Black Range and surrounding section, praising the fine climate and great mineral wealth. Almost all the well-known magazines of the time carried articles about new strikes. This led to a rush into these parts from the eastern states.

Among the pilgrims, as all newcomers were called, were two young men from the hard-coal regions of eastern Pennsylvania, near Scranton. They were Joe and Jim Hyatt, typical young men of that part of the state, both having worked in the coal mines. Joe, the elder of the two brothers, was about twenty-six years of age; while Jim could not have been more than nineteen, though he looked younger, being tall, slim, and fair, with boyish ways. Joe was short and stocky, with a serious manner.

They got off the train at Nutt Station, at that time quite a town, being the terminus where freight and passengers were put off for Lake Valley, Hillsboro, and Kingston. Several stage and hack lines ran from there to all points in the Black Range, carrying travelers to and from passenger trains.

The two strangers were still wearing their derbies, or hard-boiled castors, as the miners called them. When they found out the fare was ten dollars, they came to the conclusion to walk the forty miles from Nutt to Kingston. The train got in about four in the afternoon, so they made up their minds to head at once for Lake Valley and stay there overnight. Taking their hand-bags and a couple of blankets, which made up their luggage, they set off. It was the latter part of May and the weather was warm, but in the clear air, at an altitude of four thousand feet, they soon forgot the stuffiness of the train. Both agreed as they went along that the magazines had been right about the climate, but Jim thought the mountains were pretty far away.

They were not long upon their way when a rig overtook them. The driver, seeing they were pilgrims, invited them to get in and make use of the two empty seats. Both young men were pleased by the stranger's kindness and glad to learn that he would take them all the way to Lake Valley.

"Where are you boys from?" he asked.

"Plymouth, Pennsylvania," answered Joe.

"You don't mean it!" said their new friend, "Why, I'm from the Notch myself, just a short distance from there. But it's many years since I saw the place. I'm a regular old timer in these parts now. Do you expect to make a big stake out here?" he asked, smiling at Jim.

"By gollys, sir, we've heard so much about the big strikes in this country, that I wanted to try my luck."

"Well, my good young men, you must remember that silver is not to be picked up on the road, but must be searched for in veins, on ledges, or in deposits called pockets, or vugs. And this means many a weary climb over the mountains, and hardships that beat those of the desert hermits of long ago. You'll have to fight bears, rattlesnakes, and Indians. How will you like that, Jim?"

"By gollys, sir, ever since I read my first story about cowboys and Indians I've wanted to come west, and——"

"I think we are both ready to face danger," put in Joe, "but we have a good deal to learn about ores and how and where to find them."

Their companion, seeing they were honest and deserving young men, went on, "If you boys have any money, I would advise you to do a little prospecting. I can give you some float I picked up about four miles north of Kingston. All that section is still open to location."

"What is float, sir?" asked Joe.

"A float," said their friend, "is a piece of an ore outcropping broken off from a ledge of rock. Such chunks are often washed down into the creeks and gullies, and you might be lucky enough to trace these floats back to the spot they came from. If so, you are in luck, for it will mean a rich stake. The prospector generally takes notice of a float on account of its bright luster and its smooth surface, showing that it has been washed along by a stream of water. At times the prospector finds what looks like 'fool's gold', a pyrite found back east. In the precious mineral country this is seldom pyrite, but very often a sulphide of silver or copper, which can only be proven by a fire assay, or what is known among the old timers as a jack assay. Before using his knife the prospector holds the specimen under a magnifying glass. If the float looks good, he then presses it with the tip of his jack-knife. If the float is soft and malleable when he presses it, and there is no red or rusty tint showing up on the tip of his knife or in the lump of ore, he knows he has found a precious metal."

"I take it, sir, that you are a mining man?" asked Joe.

"Yes, I am. My interests are all in Lake Valley. If you find anything let me know. I will not forget that you are from Pennsylvania. I always like to help out the boys from my home state."

"Thank you, sir," answered both young men.

"I'll be sending the rig up to Kingston, tomorrow," went on their new friend, "and you boys may as well ride along up there with the driver. I'll give him for you, the float specimen that I mentioned, with a little sketch of the section where I found them."

"Oh, sir!" said Jim, leaning forward in his seat, "is that the town ahead of us?"

"That's Lake Valley, and over beyond is Sierra Sombrero, or Hat Mountain, as the Americans call it. You boys will want to climb it some day and see the crater that gives the old volcano its strange shape."

They had been driving nearly three hours over the mesa, the high, grassy plain that stretched away on all sides to distant mountain horizons. "By gollys, ain't this a great country? Look at the sunset colors," said Jim, his eyes full of wonder.

"Yes, Jim, you'll find colors in our morning and evening skies out here that would shame a rainbow."

"The mountains seem to be covered with blue velvet," said Joe.

"You'll find them brown and rough under foot, my boy. And they'll always seem nearer than they really are. That is because in the clear air out here one can see much farther than in the heavier air back home."

Their good companion pointed out a clean place to eat in Lake Valley and took them to a lodging house.

"Well, sir," said Jim as they thanked him for his kindness, "if every day in the Black Range is as lucky for me and Joe as this one has been, we'll have nothin' to complain of."

"By the way," called the stranger as he turned to leave, "here is my card, and I would advise you to give it to Mr. Lindner. He is an honest merchant and will take care of your money for you. So long, boys. I'll have the rig up here to meet you at ten o'clock to-morrow morning."

As both young men were very tired, they turned in early and slept so sound till the next morning, that they did not hear the racket of the dance halls nor any of the saloon brawls, that often went on all night in the new mining camps.

Before leaving Lake Valley they went to the Sierra Grande Mine to watch the surface mining. They were soon to find out that not all metal was as close to the surface as the rich silver ore of the famous Bridal Chamber near Lake Valley. One of the miners pointed out to the boys the spot where the Chinaman had picked up the first float ever found near Lake Valley.

When they got back from the mine the rig with its driver was waiting for them. From him they learned that their friend of the afternoon before was Doc McDonald, that he was not a medical man, but a mining expert, nicknamed Doc by the miners because he knew ore to the queen's taste. He was one of the mine superintendents. The driver told them they had been in luck to meet McDonald on their first day in the Black Range country. The boys were soon taken up with the floats and the rough sketch of the North Percha country, that McDonald had sent with the driver as he promised.

At Hillsboro they left the valley, and from there on, the road for the most part, followed the main fork of the Percha Creek. This creek ran through the town of Hillsboro, and to this day its bed forms the main street there. From Hillsboro on, they took note of many changes in the country. There was little water in the creek at that season of the year, except here and there at bed-rock, but the driver told the boys that later in the season it often became a raging torrent strong enough to root out giant oak trees. The road wound around pine-covered mountains, dipped down through wooded canyons, and passed between high canyon walls.

The town of Kingston was known as the "Gem of the Black Range". It lies in the heart of the Range among pine-covered mountains. Jim and Joe were used to mountain scenery in Pennsylvania, but they were struck by the immensity of these western mountains. Between Hillsboro and Kingston, so the driver told them, the Middle Fork of the Percha Creek is joined by the North and South Forks of the same name.

They got into Kingston about four that afternoon and the driver took them to a large tent lodging house. These tents were probably forty feet long and sixteen feet wide. An aisle about four feet wide, running down the center, separated the two rows of bunks, which were one above the other in tiers of four. At each end of the tent stood a big cast-iron, "goose-egg" stove.

The two lower rows of berths cost the most, as they were safer. The dance halls and gaming saloons kept open all night, and around three o'clock in the morning there was apt to be some wild shooting. Those in the upper bunks generally rolled out on the floor when the first shots came whistling through the tent. It was better not to take chances. As a rule the lower berths were all rented by noon, but Joe and Jim were again in luck, for this day business had been slack and the driver was able to get two lowers for the pilgrims. The price was one dollar and fifty cents each, so they came to the conclusion to do their sleeping in the open from the next night on.

As they were still fagged out from their long trip they again turned in early, but they did not sleep as well as the night before. Towards morning they were aroused by the sound of shots and the thud of falling bodies. Leaping up, they discovered that some of the bullets had passed through the canvas close above them. There was no more sleep that night; in fact, none of the lodgers went back to bed except a few rounders, or gamblers.

Some of the lodgers had rushed out to learn the cause of the shooting. One of those who was left lighted a large brass oil lamp that swung from a rafter, and several others built a fire in one of the big stoves. The crackling of the pine knots was a welcome sound, as the night had been chilly. Soon the boys pulled up rough benches around the stove and settled down to swap lies, some with feet hoisted above their heads. Then cuddy pipes were drawn from hip pockets, filled with Dog Leg tobacco, and lighted with a pine splinter. The talk was on.

"I suppose Tom Tucker has another notch in his gun by this time," said I.

"That's whatever," drawled big Mike Dempsey, "an' I believe that'll make the twenty-first notch on his gun by acshal count. That bird is sure some killer. He's been town marshal in every new camp in these parts."

By this time some of the lodgers had come back, and all waited to hear the news. "Jack Sheddon sure raised hell in this town to-night. Where he made the big haul o' dust is sure some mystery. He set up every house in camp with drinks," said Sheba Hurst.

"That's whatever!" exclaimed Johnny Roach, "one cowboy less to swing the lariat and shoot up the town o' nights. That Tucker'll sure never snub any feller he kin git near enough to reach with a bullet. It's the Texas Kid. He died instant. Some o' them dames from the dance hall took charge o' the body. They was aweepin' and acarryin' on like he was their own brother. Some o' them gals sure have their hearts in the right place in spite of all their fancy clothes and fast ways. They washed his face as tender as if he be a baby. 'We don't know much about him, but he was some mother's son,' was the way Kitty put it."

A deep silence fell after Johnny's speech. Some of the men pulled out red bandanas and blew their noses with a sound like a powder blast. All puffed away at their cuddy pipes. They were a rough-looking crowd. None of them shaved and very few carried combs. All wore overalls and brogans except the two pilgrims. Their faces told of hardship and suffering. Most of them were men with plenty of sand who kept their word at any cost. I hardly ever knew one of them to show the white feather no matter what came up. Some could cuss like a Missouri mule-skinner, but most of them stuck to a few "damns" and "devils" if things went wrong. Too many of them were apt to paint the town red when they came in from a long trip. They were always ready to do a good turn for the fellow that was down and out, but they were quick to pull a gun on the one that was not on the square. A few were regular squaw men, mating with the half-breeds like the birds in the springtime, but many would rather have a good game of faro than the favors of the best-looking girl in the dance hall. Better than anything they liked to sit before a golden camp fire smoking cuddy pipes and swapping lies.

"If you ax me," drawled big Mike Dempsey, "the Texas Kid spent enough on them dizzy dames. There's hardly a one of them that didn't throw a rope on him and hogtie him at one time or another. They can sure afford to drop a few tears over him."

"Did you fellers hear that Senator Tabor is in town tonight?" asked Sheba.

"Great heavens, Kate! What brings him here? He sure must have a hunch o' some kind," said Johnny Roach.

"Mebbe he heard o' the rich silver float I found out near the North Percha," said Sheba. Of course Joe and Jim pricked up their ears at this.

Shorty Hunsaker who was six feet, six, asked, "And wot if he heard o' the rich silver find I made in the Calamity Jane shaft? I sure expect to eat my Christmas turkey at home this year."

"O yeh! And how do you know he ain't here to see me? My hoodoo stick twirled like a top up there on the summit of Old Kentuck," put in Thumby Rogers.

"Wait till you hear from the Comstock," bragged Charcoal Joe; "ask Deaf Jack there. He'll tell you. Why, that mine is goin' ter be even richer than the one it was named fer, the famous Comstock in Virginia City."

"Well! Well!" warned Dad Perkins, "it'll hev ter be a humdinger to beat the Virginia Comstock. Two hundred forty millions is sure some goal to hit, me boys."

"Vell!" said old Dutch Henry, "Vait! Vait! all youse fellers till youse hear from the Goold King!"

"That's whatever!" groaned Johnny Roach. "You fellers ain't tryin' to string these poor innocent pilgrims, is you?" he went on pointing to Joe and Jim, who had not missed a word so far. "Where'd you kids hail from? We seen Doc McDonald's rig bringin' you to town. Are you 'Smoky Jacks'? I know he's one. He's a fine feller an' he sure knows the minin' game. Yer sure lucky to have him fer a friend. Don't let these old jackass punchers fill you up with hot air. Most o' what they told jest now is all O.K., but wait till you hear 'em when they get to swappin' lies in earnest. The biggest bunch o' liars that ever lived. But them 're the only kind I've ever known.

"I was born in Grass Valley, California, an' I don't even know who give me the name o' Roach. I see by them dicers yer wearin' yer from the East. Pennsylvania? I thought so. Two o' my pardners is from there. I'll bring 'em around to see you. Little Jimmy Kinny's from there, too. He's been out west some years now and he's still got pilgrim ways. What's that ahangin' on yer bunk? Rosary beads? *Jimmy Kinny has a pair of 'em, and Ed Doheny sometimes says his prayers. I'll sure let Ed know you boys is Romans. I never was learned any prayers. I wish I knew some. All the edication I got was from the miners and the soldiers around the barracks. I'm kind of a gambler, but sometimes I do a little minin'. Don't worry boys. How are you fixed for dust? Mean money. Twenty dollars? That's not much. Here, take this eagle. Oh, don't thank me. That's O.K. Pay it back when yer flush. So long boys, I'm goin' to turn in now."

*Among the old timers I was always "little Jimmie Kinney."

He made short work of it. The men in those early camps always went to bed with their boots and clothes on. Most of them never had a bath unless they happened to fall in a creek.

After Johnny Roach faded out of the picture the two pilgrims sat without a word. Jim and myself were the only ones in the crowd not smoking, so Mike Dempsey had brought us some pine nuts in his hat and showed Jim how to get out the nut meat. Jim sat with his head bowed over the hatful of nuts, picking out a kernel with his jack-knife. He did not look up. Joe stared as if he could not believe his eyes, at the gold piece in his hand, while all the others peered at the newcomers through the blue clouds of tobacco smoke that filled the tent.

Pike Rogers, seeing the boys did not know what to make of it, said, "By heavens, Kate! You kids keep that dinero. Johnny would prob'ly lose it at the next faro game anyhow. What say? Let's all hit the trail for some eats."

All scrambled to their feet, only stopping long enough to add their advice to his about keeping the eagle, and in a few minutes the crowd was scattered. Soon after breakfast, the boys looked up the business man McDonald had told them about, turning over most of their money to him. As he put away his receipt Joe asked Mr. Lindner if he could point out a safe camping place close to town. He directed them to a clearing across the creek. After looking it over the boys came to the conclusion it would be a fine spot. They went back to town to stock up with supplies and some extra bedding.

Mr. Lindner advised them to buy a good wagon sheet, as it was better than a tent. It could be used both under and over their bed and made fine shade for surface mining. "You will want to pack enough supplies for at least three or four weeks," he told them.

"One of the old prospectors at the tent lodge gave me a good receipt for beans with red chili—frijoles—I think he called them," said Joe. "He says beans are the prospector's staff of life, that they make a man strong and stick to his ribs. He also learned us how to make flapjacks and red sop."

"Yes, and he knows how it's done. But, besides beans, you'll need a few potatoes and onions, and some dried fruit to keep you from getting scurvy."

The bill of merchandise which Mr. Lindner finally handed to Joe was virtually as follows: Two picks and shovels, two hand axes, two magnifying glasses, a coffee pot, a washbasin, a butcher knife, a slab of bacon, twenty-five pounds of flour, a box of yeast powder, two frying pans and a kettle, three pounds of coffee and three of sugar; one sack each of salt, oatmeal, Mexican chili beans, dried fruit, and chili peppers; three boxes of matches and three of Dog Leg tobacco; a few potatoes and onions; a can of lard and one of molasses; fifteen pounds of grain. In the days before the railroad, the boys could not have paid for so ample a supply, but things were much cheaper now.

"The grain is to coax the burro back to camp in the mornings. Used as a bait it may save you miles of walking and a lot of patience," Mr. Lindner told the boys. He promised to have the goods sent over to their camp site, so the boys set off to get a place ready. They cut away all the brush and then lopped off some young pine branches, which they piled together for a bed. By the time the camp was in order it was noon, and they cooked their first meal in the open. They were as hungry as bears after their hard work in the pine-scented air, but they filled up on rye bread, bacon, and coffee.

2. *Burros*

The next move was a trip to town to look for a cheap burro. As they passed the Long Branch Saloon, the door was pushed open, and Jim was almost knocked down by a miner who was half-seas-over.

"Oho!" he cried, "two collier lads, or me name is not Tim Kelly. Jest from Plymouth, eh? Gimme yer fists, me b'ys, and come in and have a drink."

"No thanks," Joe told him, "we're Temperance Leaguers."

"Ah, be ye Father Matthews' b'ys?"

"We are."

"Good fer ye! Shake again. And ye say ye're from Plymouth. Begorra, I worked at the Washington breaker, meself, but it was years ago. Hello there, Jim Delaney!" he shouted through the saloon door. "Come out here and meet a couple o' b'ys from yer ould stampin' ground."

Delaney came out, and the boys saw that he was sober. Kelly exclaimed: "Look at thim tenderfeet, with their derbies and garter shoes. Fresh from Plymouth, Pennsylvania!"

"And what might yer names be?" asked Delaney.

"Jim and Joe Hyatt," said Joe.

"Not sons of Anthony Hyatt from Nanticoke?" They said that was their father's name.

"Well, well, I knew your father, me boys. He was a fine man. Come in and have a nip."

"Ah, be off wid yerself, Delaney. Thim b'ys is Matthew Leaguers," put in Tim.

"Good fer ye, me boys. Far be it from Jim Delaney to tempt ye to break yer pledge. Are your father and mother still alive?"

"Our folks are all dead now," Joe told him.

"Well, well, so old Tony is gone now—it's life, me boys, it's life." In the pause that followed the boys and Delaney took stock of one another. Jim Delaney was an Irishman of medium height, with clear blue eyes and pink skin. He was on the level and he had many friends.

"Ye boys come along to my cabin and cast off them dicers and eastern store clothes, and don't be havin' them Missourians laughin' at ye fer pilgrims. Come along! I'll fit ye both with overalls and brogans, for those clothes ye are wearing won't last any time in the brush and rocks of these mountains. Are ye both lookin' fer work?"

"No," said Joe, "we intend doin' some prospectin'."

"Tim, ye go fer a change o' clothin' fer 'em," said Delaney.

"Wait awhile," put in Joe, "we want to buy a burro now."

"Ye come with me first," said Delaney. "I won't have Tony Hyatt's boys lookin' like two greenhorns."

Delaney was not to be put off, and inside of an hour they were wearing overalls and brogans.

At this time the mining camps of the West were filled with men from the hard-coal regions of Pennsylvania. In fact, about two-thirds of the miners in these camps were either from Cornwall, England, or Luzerne County, Pennsylvania. Delaney told the boys he had been in the West thirty years. "As far as finance is concerned, I am now pretty well fixed. Where do ye boys intend to begin yer prospectin'?"

They showed him the rough map McDonald had given them, Joe saying, "We intend to start up to the North Percha as soon as we can get ready."

"Doc McDonald is a fine feller and a big shot in the mining game. Ye were lucky to meet him. If I can do anything fer ye let me know. If I meet anyone with a good, cheap burro to sell, I'll send fer ye."

At this instant a crowd of miners raced from the saloon, shouting: "The rush is on! The rush is on! Hit the trail fer Carbonate Creek!" There was a big scramble for horses and burros, and the crowd galloped off in a cloud of dust.

"Come on, pilgrims!" said Johnny Roach. "Come along with me to Carbonate Creek if you want to see where a rich stake was made."

Joe and Jim forgot all about buying the burro in the excitement. As they went along Johnny told them as much of Jack Sheddon's story as he had picked up, which was quite a little. "Ed Coffey let the cat out o' the bag," he told them, "when he came into town from Cave Creek with specimens of the ore *Jack Sheddon had discovered. It was easy to figger out where Jack got all his dinero to raise ned in town last night."

"Is Jack Sheddon a reg'lar prospector?" asked Jim.

"Jack Sheddon," began Johnny, grabbing his chance to tell a story, and slowing up for breath, "was one o' the first men to locate in Leadville, Colorado. Cleared over half a million dollars there in a few months, he did. But it was too much for Jack's head. Spent it all on dizzy dames an' faro. At times he'd bet on the high card to the ceilin'. Before long he didn't have much dust left. Then he drifted south to the excitement at Lake Valley, believin' he might find a extension in the neighborhood. But John Barleycorn and the dizzy dames took nearly all he had left. In fact, he become a kind o' nuisance and the town marshal ordered him to vamoose, he hittin' the trail fer Kingston. As there were many prospectors and miners from Leadville in the Black Range at that time he was soon among friends; and as booze was the easiest and cheapest thing to get, Jack never had time to sober up. At times, he was quarrelsome, and the deputies had considable trouble with him, finally makin' him leave town. Jack had a good horse and saddle at one o' the corrals. Gettin' enough money from his friends he settled his debts, and pulled up north fer Chloride, in the northern end of the Black Range, there bein' a excitement up there.

"Bein' about half-seas-over and havin' a bottle o' corn juice, he struck out, takin' the Cave Creek trail. Bein' sleepy an' dozy from the liquor, and seein' a little park close to the trail about two miles out of Kingston, he stopped. There bein' plenty o' good grass he pulled off the saddle and bridle and turned his horse

*Jack Sheddon's rush actually occurred before Kingston was laid out.

loose. He finished his bottle, staggered over to a bunch o' trees an' laid down. Leanin' up against a large boulder he soon fell fast asleep.

"This must a been around nine in the mornin', he sleepin' till three o'clock that afternoon. Then he rubbed his eyes an' seen his horse grazin' nearby. Happenin' to look at the boulder he was leanin' up against, he rubbed his eyes some more, for it sure looked like a chunk o' metal. Pickin' up what he thought was a small rock so he could knock a piece off the big boulder, he sure did get excited, for the stone in his hand was as heavy as lead. If the piece in his hand was a float, he knew the big boulder was one, too. Breakin' apart the small, heavy stone, he found it was almost pure bornite o' silver.

"Takin' out his jackknife, he cut off a pine branch an' whittled a smooth place on it. Then he cut letters into the smooth place, claimin' the land and namin' the claim the 'Solitaire'. As he believed the land was vacant he built a rock monument, about one half o' the stones bein' almost pure silver. He stuck the branch on the monument, first signin' his name with a stub of lead pencil he found in his pocket. Before leavin' he knocked off a piece from the big boulder, and sure enough it was almost pure silver, just as he surmised.

"Saddlin' his horse he rode back to Kingston. Hearin' that Senator Tabor was in town he headed fer Mrs. Brophry's hotel—you know, the place I'm gonna take you to meet Ed Doheny. Some say she'll be his mother-in-law before long, but Ed'll sure have to scratch if he marries Carrie. He's only makin' forty dollars a month now, teachin' school in these parts. He knows a lot about minerals, and has helped more than one Irishman to make a rich stake, but he's never had much luck himself. But let's get back to Jack. Him an' Senator Tabor bein' old friends was soon a shakin' hands an' havin' a great talk. Then Jack ast to see the Senator in private and they both went up to Tabor's room.

"I don't know much more except they both kept mum about the discovery, an' made a trip out to Jack's claim before goin' to Hillsboro to record the papers. I guess the news wouldn't be out yet, but Jack made the Senator give him a partial cash payment, an' when he got too much tarantula juice, he talked. We'll soon be there now, boys. Let's step lively, or we'll miss the show."

Johnny and the two pilgrims were among the last to get there, as most of the men had ridden horses and burros to the spot. The excitement was almost over. "We're too late to get anything good," Johnny told the boys, "but you can see some o' the float ore, an' learn how locations is made. Some o' the old timers can give you the minin' dope—cards and spades—on location laws. You'll have to know what to do when you find mineral on vacant ground. You gotta remember, first: it's dangerous to locate on someone else's property,—that's what we calls jumpin' a claim, an' it leads to lawsuits aplenty and sometimes to killin's,—and second: you must know how to locate so your claim'll be legal."

"What're all them piles of rock? Are they floats?" asked Jim, which Johnny thought a good joke to store away. Jim pointed to piles of rock about three feet in diameter and two feet high, topped with sticks or branches about three feet long, each having on it the name of the claim.

"Them's the claim monuments. Come along, an' I'll show you what they mean." Going up to the nearest monument Johnny pulled out the location stick, and the boys spelled out the words carved on it: "Discovery Monument of Lost Lead Claim. North end center. Location made by John Hill of Kingston. See location certificate in box in monument."

Roach took out some of the rocks. Towards the center of the monument he found the tin box, as he knew he would. Taking off the lid he showed the boys the paper which described the claim. "This paper," said Johnny, "gives the claim locater sixty days to do a certain amount o' work, and measure off his land area, time enough to file the record at the county seat. An' this is important, for you got to play safe in the minin' game."

Having looked over a few more monuments and talked to some regular old timers who were still there, Johnny said: "We might as well hit the trail fer town, fer this section is located from hell to breakfast, an' there'll be lawsuits aplenty, if the camp amounts to anything. Everybody'll vamoose up to Hillsboro now to file their claims, an' they won't be back in Kingston till late tonight, so we'll be in for a boiled-dog time along toward mornin'."

On the way back to town Johnny advised the boys not to head for the North Percha the next morning as they expected to do. "You'd orter stay around town a few days, fer you'll need to know a lot about prospectin', that the old timers'll be glad to tell you free o' charge, things that'll be good fer you to know later on."

But the boys, having found out that Carbonate Creek was in the same direction as the North Percha, decided to carry out their first plan.

Johnny was wearing his best togs and light shoes, and he was limping before they reached town. "You're pretty smart pilgrims, sportin' overalls and brogans so soon. Them brogans ain't much fer looks, but them heavy soles and hobnails is the only thing fer these flinty rocks and rough lava beds. I was all decked out to go over and help bury the Texas Kid this afternoon—I almost missed the rush gettin' ready—but when I see you kids had no way to get out to Carbonate Creek, I thought I'd take care of you instead. Besides, I knowed little Jimmy Kinny and Ed Doheny'd see to the buryin', if nobody else did."

As they came into town a shaggy-looking fellow in front of the Long Branch saloon shouted to them: "Are you the ones that wants to buy a cheap burro? I can sell you one that's a dandy packer and trailer."

"Is this critter easy to manage?" asked Joe.

"Oh, he looks kinda hard, but there ain't a better packer or traveler in the Rockies."

They went off together to see the burro. What a sight! He was covered with cuts and bruises and had a scab on his back as big as a washbasin. His ears looked as if they had been chewed off. But hoofs and legs were in good shape, so Joe asked: "How much do you want for him?"

"Well, he's worth a damn sight more, but you fellers can have the whole outfit for eight dollars cash—burro and saddle to boot. I gotta have the money pronto."

Joe paid out the money, and the boys started with the burro for camp.

Turning down a side street to leave town, they came upon Johnny and Ed Doheny. Both roared when they saw the burro. "Where did you get the menagerie?" shouted Johnny. "Come on over and meet Doheny—and give us a chance to size up the beauty. Great heavens, Kate!" he went on as the boys came up, leading the burro, "You sure got a warrior, judgin' from his looks. Meet Mr. Doheny. Him and me's interested in some wildcats up the gulch. An' don't be gettin' him mixed up with little Jimmy Kinny, like so many does."

"He sure does look like Kinny, at that," said Joe.

Doheny gave them the glad hand. "Johnny tells me you're

Holy Romans. Stick to it and don't let booze and wild women get you, if you want to make good. That jackass, is, I am sure, a regular old-timer; but he'll be a good one to help break you in. Treat him O.K. and he may turn out to be a bargain after all."

"By gollys, he sure *is* a shabby critter," said Jim, "but if he'll just carry our pack for us, we won't mind his looks."

They had a long visit, and it was nearly sundown when the boys once more headed for camp. Both took a liking to Doheny, whose last warning was: "Don't curry the jack too much—it might spoil his looks!"

Ed Doheny, who later became the well-known oil magnate of Los Angeles, was at that time a young man about twenty-eight years of age. Being slim and active, with regular features, ruddy complexion, and blue eyes, he was considered good-looking. He bore no marks of fast living and made one think of the white-collar man rather than the miner. As a matter of fact, he had never done much rough work. He had a good education, and he was a natural-born leader. He was looked up to for advice in mining matters by most of the Irish-Americans in the Black Range country. But somehow in those days he himself managed to come out at the little end of the horn in most of the deals he put through.

When they got back to the camp the boys fed and watered the burro and tied him up to some brush for the night. After filling up on flapjacks, bacon, and coffee, they sat for a spell beside their camp fire, talking over their first day in Kingston. Fagged out with excitement, they came to the conclusion to turn in early. Before slipping between their blankets they stood together looking up into the night sky.

"Never seen such big stars back home," exclaimed Jim. "How white they are, and how they tremble!"

"And they're brighter and seem so close you want to reach up and gather a handful," said Joe. "They almost make me feel like I'm in church with all the candles lit on the altar."

Both got down on their knees for a short prayer and were soon dead to the world in their out-door bunk. Coyotes howled close to camp, and across the creek the town was in a commotion all night, celebrating the Carbonate Creek rush, but both boys said the next morning they had never slept better in their lives.

After breakfast they fed the burro a little corn. He seemed gentle, so Joe went across to town to buy a few more supplies, leaving Jim to saddle and load up. Judging from the way the pack looked he must have put all the bedding under the pack-saddle, tying on the pots and pans with rope.

The burro was one of the kind that can swell up the size of his paunch over half while the cinch is being tightened. Jim had drawn the cinch tight, but by the time he got into the main street, it had come loose, and the whole pack was in a mess. The burro cast a waggish eye at the pack and then at Jim, as much to say, "You're some greenie, and I'm sure goin' to see this town before you learn to pack me right."

All burros have a regular human bump of curiosity. They like to hang around the new mining camps. I have seen as many as twenty burros standing in front of a dance hall or watching a big faro game, just as close to the door as they could get and as silent as ghosts. With ears down and mouths open, they listened either to the music or to the talk of the gamblers. When a new strike was made, I have at times counted virtually a hundred burros in the vicinity of the camp. If there happened to be a warm springs within twenty miles, and the prospector missed his burro when he got awake, he almost knew for certain he would find the animal at the springs. During the rush into the Black Range there were upwards of five hundred wild burros around the warm springs near Hillsboro. How they lived was a mystery, for there was not a blade of grass within miles. I'll venture to say one could still round up a herd of wild burros there even today, and it is the same around all warm springs in the Rockies. Just why the burro likes the warm springs is hard to say, but I believe it is because for hundreds of years these hot springs have been used by Indians and whites. The burro, being a friend to man, goes there to be near him.

By the time Jim got to the store where Joe was to wait for him, the pack had turned clear around, and the burro came to a stand-still. In a twinkling he was rid of his load. Lifting up his hind quarters, he threw the pack over his head, scattering the pans and kettles with a mighty clatter. Of course, the noise drew a crowd. Joe rushed from the store, and the two lads packed the burro again. This time, they did not put so much under the saddle, but when the load was all on, it was top-heavy. Unknown to the boys, of course, the burro had again swelled up his paunch while they tightened the cinch. He trotted up the street as meek as Moses but before long the pack was again as loose as if it had not been fastened.

The burro stopped in front of the Long Branch Saloon, as the pack slid off. By now many of the old timers were watching the circus, and roars of laughter were heard on all sides. Tim Kelly, hearing the commotion, rushed from the saloon. He shot one look at the burro, and shouted, "If there ain't the divil himself, ould Ladrone! Shure, look at the ears of him. Who's the victim?"

The boys said they were the owners.

"Well, ye're shure some packers. Arra, that ould divil could show ye how to make the diamond hitch if he could talk. Musha, I left the ould lad up on Mt. Sneffles, Colorado, at the Virginia Mine, three years ago. Meself an' Dave Burke owned him there. We buyed him off a prospector from the Wasatch Mountains. See! He knows me!" he ended, as the burro came up and rubbed against him.

"He's the best packer and trailer in the Rockies," went on Kelly. "I believe he could walk a tight rope an' never miss a step. But he's the biggest camp robber that ever lived. Come in, ye fellers, and while we pass the drinks, I'll tell ye the story of Ladrone's Christmas dinner. Arra, the ould divil knows I'm tellin' ye his tricks," he ended, as the burro went on rubbing his head against Kelly's shoulder.

Joe tied Ladrone to a post and followed the crowd into the saloon.

"On with the story," said Johnny Roach when drinks had been set up and Kelly had called for hot coffee for the two Leaguers and myself.

"Begad, it was loike this. Me an' Burke hired out to a agent in Silverton to go to woik on the Virginia Mine on Mt. Sneffles, an' as ye know, it's more than 14,000 feet about sea level. This was in August, an' the trail usually closes the first of October on account o' the heavy snows. The agent told us the packers would make only one more trip, an' that we would not be able to get our blankets and clothes hauled up, unless we either hired or bought a burro to pack 'em fer us. 'If ye buy a jack, our company will feed him fer ye until next July,' he told us. 'Ye kin keep him in the underground stables with some more stock that's up there.'

"Begorra, at that time, I knew nothin' o' the Dago lingo, and when lookin' fer a burro we come across ould Ladrone. We got him off a Utah man, as I tould ye before. He sold the critter cheap, and claimed he knowed every trail in the Rockies. Lookin' us over doubtsomely, he says, 'Have ye ever been south?' When we tould him no, he says, 'Ladrone is his name.' Musha, I thought the burro must be named fer some Spanish saint, or noted man of Ould Mexico, fer begad, they're the divil himself, fer namin' their animules after them. Arra, at Christmas we knowed why he was called 'Thief'.

"After buyin' the burro we put him up in one of the Silverton corrals. We wint from there to the agent who empl'yed us, gettin' an order fer feed to hand to the mine foreman. The next mornin' we struck out fer the mine. Puttin' our beddin' an' clothes on the burro we headed up the canyon. Leavin' the canyon about four miles out of town, we hit out on the high mesa. The burro kept quite a piece ahead of us, stoppin' at good bunches o' grass an' nippin' off the heads. Begad, we didn't stop him, fer we knowed a full paunch kept his cinch tight. He sure was a good traveler, an' we arrived at the camp about four o'clock that afternoon.

"The foreman was a big Swede. When we handed him the order fer feed fer ourselves an' Ladrone, he says, 'Mon, I know that critter well. He's been here before. It's Ladrone. He shure is a good burro, but he's better known as a camp robber. That jack kin open every latch in the underground stables. Pull off the pack an' turn him loose. He's well acquainted here.' An' begad, Ladrone set off fer the stable as soon as the pack was off.

"As the fall kept open the packers said they would make another trip, tellin' the miners to send in their orders fer their Christmas supplies. Burke an' meself said we wanted no wet goods, but we seen some fine lookin' corn beef while we was in town, an' we ordered eight or ten pounds of it an' a couple a good heads o' cabbage. We knowed it would keep, as the timperature at that time o' the year was mostly below freezin'. It turned out a mild year, an' as the season kept open the packers did not return until November. Begorra, ye should o' seen the excitement among them miners. Some wanted us to cook the corn beef an' cabbage immejately, but we held out an' kept it fer our Christmas dinner. Winter set in soon after the last trip, an' so before long we was snowed in. But a few days before Christmas the sun come out agin', makin' it real pleasant.

"Christmas Eve the big Swede tould meself an' Burke to take nails an' roofin' paper, an' whenever the ore run showed holes to nail 'em up. He added, 'There is a tripod an' a big camp kittle an' plenty o' wood on that flat above the mouth o' the tunnel. Before ye go up on the roof of the ore run, put down yer meat an' cabbage to cook, an' by noon it'll be done. If ye make a good fire it'll keep the kittle bilin' while ye woik. One of ye kin stay there till it begins to bile, then join the other up on the roof. Then ye kin notify the stableman when ye're ready, as I'll be wantin' to use the ladder to mend some holes on the bunk house roof. I'll send ye back the ladder before noon.'

"We carried out the Swede's orders to the letter, an' were soon at woik on the roof of the ore run, which was built on a hogback o' rock, with steep sides, so we was virchually prisoners there till some one brung the ladder back. It makes me mouth water yet to think o' the odor o' that cabbage. As it was sich a fine day the stableman had turned out the horses an' burros fer air. Arra, how them critters did enj'y theirselves! They made fer nearby flats, an' rolled an' gamboled like kittens in the snow.

"Meself an' Burke were busy nailin' the small holes up, fer we knowed one no bigger'n a head of a pin'd let in a wagonload of snow in a blizzard an' block up the runway. On a suddint I looked towards the cookin' pot. 'By me sowl!' I shouted, 'look at Ladrone!' There be the ould divil, pushin' the handle of the cookin' pot with one foot while he marked time with the other.

"We both yelled at him, but he only pushed an' pulled harder'n ever, an' the kittle was aswingin' loike a bird's nest in a Irish gale. We tried to get the attention o' the Swede, but it were no use. The ould divil finally pushed the kittle with both feet an' it flew clean off the hook. Before the steamin' mess had ary a chanct to cool, the brute was at it, swallowin' big chunks, then barin' all his teeth at us, as much as to say, 'This shure am a good feed, me lads!'

"Och, musha, by the time the ladder was brung to us, that ould baste had et up every morsel of our Christmas dinner, an' when we finally got down, there laid ould Ladrone with a paunch the size of a washtub. The fire was out an' there weren't enough corn beef an' cabbage left to feed a canary.

"Givin' the baste a good kick, the Swede says, 'Let him lie. He desarves to suffer. We may be eatin' burro steaks before next May, an' when we comes to Ladrone's we'll pertend it's corn beef an' cabbage.' We left him, thinkin' he would die, but begorra, the cowld must of helped him digest his load, fer bright an' early

Christmas mornin' he appeared at the bunk house, but he weren't lookin' very merry.

"Begad, fer our Christmas dinner we had plenty o' poteen."

Tim's tale had been hailed again and again with roars of laughter and washed down with plenty of corn juice.

"Great heavens, Kate! What a yarn!" said Mark Fuller, pounding Tim on the back.

"Come on, ye fellers, let's all help these pilgrims pack this burro right," shouted Tim, and the whole crowd headed for the street.

Mark Fuller taught the boys how to make the squaw knot, on the order of a double shoe tie; and Tim showed them how to make the diamond hitch, which is harder to learn. They soon had the burro packed and ready to pull out. Mark's last warning was, "Don't be afraid to tighten the cinch, boys. Ladrone is a smart old codger, and he'll soon learn who's boss."

"Good-by, Mr. Kelly," said Jim, "and thank you for teachin' us to do the diamond and for tellin' us that good story about Ladrone."

"Don't be misterin' me, young man. It's Tim I be to all me friends. Gimme yer fists, me b'ys! But me lads, where's yer guns?"

"Guns!" said Joe, "What do we want with guns fer prospectin'?"

"Begorra, thin, ye may need them. Have ye no arms at all?"

"Why yes," answered Jim, "see this," and he pulled out a small pistol something on the order of an Iver Johnson five-shooter. There was a shout of glee.

"Me lads, don't ye go out into the mountains wid that toy. You'd do jist as well wid a popcorn ball."

Just then Delaney joined the crowd, and at sight of the pistol he said: "Now, me lads, the bears have been bad this year, and ye must not venture into these mountains without guns. The silvertips killed a man over on the Animas about two months ago. Ye must carry either a rifle or a Colt."

"If we see a bear we'll run away," laughed Jim.

"This is no jokin' matter, Jim. Can ye use a rifle if I get ye one?" asked Delaney.

"I never used a rifle in my life," admitted Joe, "but Jim here is a pretty good shot."

At this moment the bartender came to the doorway of the saloon, as mad as the devil. "Get to hell out of here," he roared.

"You fellows have ruined business for the last hour. Get along, you greenhorn pilgrims, and take that devil, Ladrone, along with you."

Kelly did not wait for the boys to answer, but burst out, "You big kangaroo, you overgrown knock-kneed suds-dispenser, take off that apron and get to woik doin' a little drillin'. Come on boys, we'll go to the Forest Home where we'll be treated decent."

Delaney had gone for the rifle, but when the two boys heard this tirade, they would not wait. Kelly tried to hold them back, but they would not listen. "Begad thin, I'll go along wid ye meself as far as Pickett's Springs," said he.

Joe led the burro with a rope, and Jim walked in the rear with a switch. Kelly advised, "Let him loose, he'll soon be leadin' ye both. By the time we reach the springs the cinch'll be loose, an' I'll larn ye how to tighten it widout movin' the pack."

3. *Bears*

When they had crossed the creek and hit the trail, Ladrone took the lead. Kelly told Joe to fasten the leading rope to one of the saddle forks. As soon as the burro was free he struck off and was soon out of sight, but not for long. Having found a good bunch of grass he stopped to feed till the men came up. At Pickett's Springs, they again found Ladrone waiting for them. Kelly showed the boys how to tighten the cinch, as he had promised. He warned them to keep the load well balanced, as it was a help to both pack and burro. After a hearty Irish, "God bless ye, me lads!" he added, "but I shure hate to see ye strike off widout a gun."

"Don't you worry about us, Tim," said Joe, "we'll be coming into town every little while to get our mail, and if we find we need a gun, we'll either borrow or buy one."

Tim Kelly turned away shaking his head, and after filling their canteens at the springs, the boys pushed on for the North Percha, the burro leading.

"You know," said Jim, "one of the old timers told me the reason this creek is called the Percha, is because in the early days when the white men foist came into this country, they found hundreds of turkeys roostin' in the trees along the creek. By gollys, I sure hope we see a few of 'em. He said we prob'ly would, but that many of 'em had been killed or scared away."

"A turkey stew wouldn't be bad after trampin' all day with Ladrone, and we'd sure know more about cleanin' a turkey than we would a deer. I wonder if we could bring down either with this popgun?" he ended, looking at the small pistol he had pulled from his pocket. "Want to carry it, Jim?"

"We sure won't need it if we don't meet any more Indians or wild animals than we have so far," said Jim, as he put the pistol in his pocket.

"There seem to be plenty of birds and flowers, though, and this is sure some rich grass we're goin' through now," said Joe.

They were wading virtually knee-deep through a small park of gramma grass at the time. Here and there were clumps of blue and yellow daisies. They took note of the manzanita bush, with its red brush and small evergreen leaf, and of several other kinds of brush they had never seen before.

"See that cactus, the prickly pear, somebody says they call it," said Jim, "don't those big flat things with the stickers on them put you in mind of hands the way they hold up those yellow and orange flowers on the plant?"

"And did you ever see such a bunch of flowers growing on one stalk before?" said Joe stopping to gaze at an early yucca in bloom.

"By gollys, a fellow would only have to pick one stalk to give his girl the biggest bunch of flowers she ever got, and pretty, too. Don't they look like water lilies just ready to bust open? So white and waxy lookin'!"

"And what do you think of this one for stickers" said Joe, stopping this time beside an immense cholla and trying to push aside the links to look into a bird's nest wedged among the thorns.

"Wow!" he shouted jumping up and down and trying to pull his hand away. But the cholla link came with it, and when Jim finally managed to pull it off between two sticks, Joe's hand was bleeding in a dozen spots.

"How that bird gets out of that nest so fast is a mystery to me," he said, still picking the fine thorns from his fingers. "And I'll bet she didn't even pick up one of these stickers."

The cholla is the worst of all cacti to get mixed up with. Yet cattle and deer learn to eat the thorny cholla links and seem to like them too.

"It is sure all different from anything we seen in our woods and fields back home," he went on. "And did you ever see so many bright-colored hummin' birds in your life? They're dartin' from bush to bush like lightnin'."

Hundreds of nuthatches chattered about in the pine trees, and band-tailed pigeons cooed among their tops. Nearly every manzanita and hackberry bush held nests of young mocking birds, while the songs of the old birds filled the woods and dells.

"There's another bluejay!" said Jim. "Tim Kelly told me as we come along that they are called pinon jays out here. They like the juniper berries, and Tim says when these berries are nipped by the frost they drop and ferment; he says they're the same berries people make into Holland gin, a terrible strong drink; and durin' the fall he claims the jays eat these fermented juniper berries and are half-seas-over most of the time. He says he's seen 'em steppin' high, doin' the turkey dance, and actin' sillier than a cowboy with too much tarantula juice."

"Them junipers're a kind of cedar, ain't they?"

"Yep, that's one just ahead of us at the edge of this park, but Tim says there ain't so many up here as there are in the foothills. We ain't seen any rattlesnakes yet, neither, nor any of them deadly varmints Ed Doheny was tellin' us about."

"You mean them thousand-leggers they call centipedes out here—that grow to be six and eight inches long? I'd just as soon not meet up with any of them things."

"Yes, and them big black spiders, with a body that'd fill a soup bowl, tarant'las, I think Doheny said they was. Mike Dempsey says he found one of them things in his bunk once, and Johnny Roach says he's often wore a centipede under his shirt all day. I sure did like them yarns the old timers told us in Kingston. By gollys, I hope I wake up some mornin' and find myself leanin' up against a forty-thousand-dollar boulder, like that Jack Sheddon done," ended Jim.

For some time after this the boys pushed along in silence, lost in thought. Perhaps they were thinking of other days in Pennsylvania, but like as not they were dreaming of the homes they meant to build when they had made a rich stake by prospecting. One thing is certain: They were a pair of innocents abroad in the wildest section of the Black Range. Little did they realize that they were in the stronghold of Victorio's murderous Apaches. Nor did they know that at any moment a vicious silvertip might step from behind one of the large pine, oak, or juniper trees.

When the burro reached Carbonate Creek he again waited for

the boys to come up. They looked at the pack. "It seems O.K.," said Joe, "the cinch is still tight."

"And no wonder! His paunch is so full of grass it sounds like a drum when you tap it. Good old burro!" said Jim rubbing him behind one of his ragged ears as he had seen Kelly do.

Thence on to the North Percha the country became rougher and more hilly. They passed through many small parks of gramma grass with patches of sacatone as high as their heads, and several times started a black-tailed deer from his feeding. Beyond these parks the brush was heavy and the trees much larger, cutting off the view entirely. In places the boys could not see more than fifty feet ahead. The burro was out of sight virtually all the time.

At last the boys reached one of these parks that lay on a sunny hillside. The trail cut almost through the center of the park. To the right the park climbed the hill. Here large boulders and reefs of rock stood close together near the trail where it again put into the brush, making a fine spot for an ambush. On their left the grassy hill sloped down to a thicket of willows where there was running water.

All of a sudden the burro appeared. He seemed all excited. When he saw the boys he plunged back into the brush among the boulders. Presto! Out he dashed again on the run, soon reaching the boys. They caught him and tried to drive him on, but as soon as he reached the brush he tore loose and rushed back.

The boys did not know much about animals and nothing about a burro, but they came to the conclusion they must get the upper hand of Ladrone. Jim loosened the rope from the saddle fork and went ahead leading him. Joe, having cut a heavy switch, punched him from the back. "If we can force him through the brush he'll learn who's boss, and our troubles will be over. Hang on to that rope, Jim!"

"Woof! Woof!" All of a sudden a large female silvertip stepped from behind a boulder. Jim dropped the rope and snatched out his pistol, firing instantly. He missed, but the bear gave him a vicious slap on the arm that knocked him down and dashed the pistol from his hand.

Joe leaped for the gun and fired a shot into the grizzly, but she did not even flinch. Instead, reaching out, she tore a large piece of flesh from his breast. He went down, but he fired the rest of the shots into her. The shots got her dander up but had no other effect. She stood over Joe waiting for him to move. It was lucky for him that he could not. Ladrone had disappeared. Joe was conscious, but it seemed as if he had been looking into the bear's eyes for hours. Of course, it was but a minute or two, when he heard some terrified cries of "Wee! Wee!" In a twinkling two cubs came tumbling down the hillside, Ladrone pushing them along and worrying them with kicks and bites. The mother bear made off up the hill to them. Ladrone, seeing her, veered off to one side, and kept on pushing the cubs ahead of him. Down towards the willows they all went. When the mother had almost caught up with them, the burro turned and raced away around the hill. He circled back up the hill to the two pilgrims; the mother bear after fondling and washing her cubs, trotted off with them among the willows.

Ladrone was still carrying his pack when he reached the boys. The poor lads lay on the ground shivering in their boots. The burro went from one to the other with an almost human look of pity in his eyes. Finally, he stood over Jim and shook the pack as if he would say, "Hurry up, and unload me for I must carry Joe."

Jim at last aroused himself and unloaded the pack. Ladrone all but knelt down while Jim lifted Joe to his back and strapped him on. The burro set off, carrying the wounded man as gently as a mother her baby, slowing up over rough spots on the hills and through the gullies, and pacing on the flats, without jolting him in the least.

At Pickett's Springs Ladrone stopped to drink. Joe said afterwards the jack really kept him on his back; and he believed the burro would have found some way to hoist him up again, if he had slipped off, as he nearly did several times.

When the burro got into Kingston, he headed straight for the Long Branch Saloon where a big crowd was generally rounded up. Pushing open the door, he virtually reached the bar before the men could stop him.

Joe was almost dead from loss of blood. How he had kept on the burro's back was a mystery. The boys lifted him off and filled him up with liquor. Some one asked if Joe were killed and he shook his head, no. Delaney had the doctor there in a few minutes. When Joe could speak he gasped out that Jim was on his way to town.

Tim Kelly saddled Ladrone and struck out to look for him, others also going out on horseback. The poor boy was found several hours later, just at sundown, stumbling along with his arm dangling. Tim went on looking for the pack. At last Ladrone led him to it. He went over the ground and from what he saw of the tracks, and what the boys were able to tell of the attack, it was plain that Ladrone had saved their lives.

"That clever ould lad was smart enough to know that the she-bear would chase after him and the cubs, and fergit about the boys," he said to the crowd in the saloon. "Ladrone may be a thief, but begorra, I'm ready to fergive him for eatin' me corn beef an' cabbage when I thinks on this day's woik."

After the doctor had set Jim's arm he advised Delaney and others to set up a tent with beds in it, near some warm springs close to town, saying: "The warm water and the fresh air will do Joe's wounds more good than any medicine I can give him. Be sure he doesn't catch cold, as there is reason to fear his lung has been injured, and he might get pneumonia. Otherwise the healing of the wound is only a matter of time."

Delaney and others fixed up a place for the two pilgrims. Ladrone had a corral built for his use, and the miners always brought him an apple or a lump of salt or sugar when they drifted in to see how Joe was getting along.

It was three months before Joe was able to get around, but Jim's arm healed fast. He passed his time hunting, soon becoming a crack shot. Joe's appetite was won back on turkey stews and venison steaks.

When the weather became cooler the boys came to the conclusion to go to a lower altitude. We heard they took a lease on an old mine and made a rich stake. While working this property Ladrone took sick and died. Over his battered remains the two boys shed some honest tears. They buried him on a grassy flat under a lone juniper tree. "Let us bury him deep," said Jim. "We don't want any wild dog or coyote diggin' up his bones."

Shortly after this the Hyatt boys went back to Pennsylvania. When I was in Idaho some years later, I heard that Jim had become a big business man in Seattle. If he has anyone belonging to him there now, they will surely be interested in this tale.

Many times while he lay in bed waiting for his wounds to heal, I heard Joe tell the happenings of his first days in the Black Range country. Some people who lived in Sierra County at that time still remember these incidents.

A Kingston Foot Race

MINERS were flush in Kingston in 1882. A committee had been rounded up to plan a fitting celebration for the Fourth of July. It was decided to make foot races the big attraction on the day. The site chosen for the races lay about a mile below Kingston on a grassy flat surrounded by pine-covered hills. Men of note from Colorado and Texas were put wise and planned to fix the races, agreeing to divide the spoils among themselves.

The schemers had reckoned without Danny and his old friend, Tim Crowley, the big Missourian, who had both been among the first in the rush into the Black Range. Tim was a great runner, but Danny was the only one in Kingston who knew that he could cover a hundred yards in ten seconds. Tim's wife was against having him in the races, but as they were in need of a ham-and-egg stake for their six children, she finally gave in.

Twenty-five dollars was required as an entrance fee, but Tim and Danny got around that by letting several other miners into the secret. Danny was Tim Crowley's trainer, and the miners in the secret promised to keep still. Tim was to be the dark horse. But the news leaked out and many bets were made on Tim and all odds taken.

The Fourth of July found an immense crowd gathered on the flat in the cool mountain air. This park had been a favorite Indian race course in earlier days. It lay between two ridges and was crossed at one end by a third ridge on which stood Toppy Johnson's slaughterhouse. Everyone had been told by the committee to leave firearms at home, an order which was carried out for once. The crowd was in high feather. There were to be a fireman's display and some patriotic speeches, but the foot race was the big event of the day. The affair had been well advertised; miners and prospectors from far and near were scattered through the crowd. The road from Kingston to the park was filled from early morning with rigs, men on horseback, mules and burros, and straggling groups of women and children.

Gamblers were there in droves. At this time all games of chance were permitted by law. The click of the keno's goose, the rolling of the ball, and the whirl of the roulette wheel could be heard in the saloons at all hours of the day and night. The American game of faro always drew the biggest crowd, especially when betting was without limit. The dealer who shuffled the cards for a game of faro had a system of his own. Chinamen often spent months studying the dealer's method. Once a Chinaman caught on to the dealer's secret, word would be dropped among his tong friends. One by one on the night set, the Chinamen slipped in from surrounding camps to watch the big game. Often a Chinaman would win the entire bank roll. At times the players were rich cattlemen and miners who had made a stake, and the limit would be the ceiling. Some one always left the table poor after such a game, the cattlemen sometimes losing thousands of head of stock in a single night. The men who ran these games also had to have big wads of dough.

Among the big gamblers of Kingston were the two Bradley brothers, the two Thurman brothers, and Lou Blanger. Colonel Ed Bradley was, at one time, the owner of some of the finest race horses in the world; his horses won the Kentucky Derby and other great races. Bradley on that Fourth of July must have been about thirty years of age; he was showered with good looks, tall and straight as an Indian brave. His character was without a blemish. No one ever wanted the price of a meal when Colonel Bradley was around. Among other well-known gamblers he headed every donation to charity. No man or woman ever looked to him for help without getting it. Only a square game was ever backed by Colonel Bradley's money.

The opposition had put up Green, a professional runner, and Brown, who was known as their sure-thing man. When these racers had looked Tim over one of them burst out; "Some rube from the woods going in so he can blow about it the rest of his life."

"Say, hayseed, where are the punkins you're goin' to roll?" called another.

It was no wonder that the crowd took note of Crowley. Green and Brown were already on the track decked out in fancy tights and shoes when Crowley appeared in his overalls, carrying a bundle under his arm. Soon the racers were warming up—making little sprints of speed and having their muscles rubbed down by their trainers. After a few easy runs Crowley vanished with Danny into the brush.

When the bell rang calling the racers to position Crowley came

A PROSPECTOR ON THE WAY

out of the brush. What roars of laughter and applause! What jeers and catcalls! Crowley was as cool as a cucumber. He wore only a breech clout fastened about his waist by a gee-string. On his head was a red bandana tied in knots, negro-mammy style. He looked like an immense shaggy bear. What muscles he had! His legs were like columns of iron.

During the uproar caused by Crowley's looks the backers of Green and Brown began to hedge off. The judge, taking note of it, called out in a loud voice that the next time the bell rang the racers must run to scratch, and that if all were in line he would fire a pistol—the race would be on. All went to the scratch perfectly. The pistol barked and they were off! What a race! For twenty-five yards the line was without a break. Then Crowley was seen pushing ahead like a cyclone. Head up, he was leading Brown, the sure-thing man. Realizing they had met their match, Green forged ahead until he had passed Brown. At seventy-five yards Crowley was running like a streak, at least six yards ahead of the professional Green.

Ninety yards! Ninety-three! Ninety-five! Presto! Down dropped a black cub from the rocks above right in Crowley's path. He tried to put on the brakes. It was too late. Over he went. Man and bear whirled to within a foot of the goal.

The crowd went mad. Everyone seemed crazy except Crowley, Green, and the bear. Crowley managed to pull loose from the bear, but Green beat him by six inches. The bear picked himself up and clambered over the hill, snapping and snarling. Crowley pulled himself together and fled into the brush leaving his breech clout on the goal line. The bear had broken Tim's gee-string in the wrestle. It was more fun than a circus for those in the throng who had put up little or no money on the runners. Never was such an uproar.

"Run it over! Pay no money! Make no decision!"

The race was declared off. No bets were to be paid. Crowley's backers wanted the race to be run over, offering big odds on him. The professionals refused, claiming to have won the race, for they knew only too well that the bear's mix-up with Crowley was all that kept them from having to walk out of town.

Everybody was wanting to know how the bear got into the race. Before long Toppy Johnson solved the riddle. He had taken notice for some time that the bears came every day to feed on the offal thrown out from the slaughterhouse. It was thought the young bear had stuffed himself until he was drunk with blood and had then fallen asleep on the ridge. When he awakened the noise of the crowd stirred up his curiosity, and he waddled to the edge of the cliff and toppled off in a rock slide.

As far as Kingston was concerned, Crowley was the winner. Though no bets were paid, Crowley went home that night with a ham-and-egg stake that lasted many a day. Some one had thought to pass the hat.

Christmas in Kingston

CHRISTMAS was coming to Kingston. The Christmas spirit was in the air. Every burro that came into town over mountain trails packed a Christmas tree, a big bunch of mistletoe, or a branch of red berries. A little of the evergreen went to decorate Mrs. O'Boyle's cabin where the Catholics of Kingston would gather on Christmas afternoon to celebrate the birth of Christ; some of the holiday green went to brighten up the eleven saloons of the town; but most of it went to adorn Pretty Sam's new dance hall, the Casino.

An immense crowd was expected in Kingston on Christmas Eve, for in 1882 the town was the metropolis of the Southwest. Nobody knew what the population was—there was no Caesar Augustus to order an enrollment—but it was set at twenty-five hundred. And the great crowd had been invited by Pretty Sam to celebrate the opening of the Casino.

Sam's new dance hall had been under construction for several months and was the finest and biggest in all the southwestern frontier. It was at least one hundred fifty feet long and fifty feet wide, and had a hardwood floor, waxed and polished, until dancing upon it became a feat, especially for a person with new shoes.

Pretty Sam was not the man to do things by halves. To the opening of the new dance hall he invited everybody in the whole countryside and sent special invitations to all the big guns. Everything was to be free, including the big spread at midnight. The elite of Silver City, Lake Valley, Hermosa, and Hillsboro were to be there.

Now level land was at a premium in Kingston, and in order to get a central site for his grand building Pretty Sam had to be content with a location that meant extra work. The front door was on a level with the street, but the back end of the building was supported on a trestle which raised it about thirty feet above the creek. Pretty Sam concluded to run a bridge from his back door to the other side of the canyon, but this had not been finished in time for the opening.

The double door at the back had therefore been bolted and the space just in front of it partitioned off to serve as a cloak room on the opening night. In order to be on the safe side the windows on the end of the building that overlooked the creek had been nailed shut. Some of the guests might sit on the window sill and be careless enough to fall out; or, when the party got into full swing some guests might mistake the window for a door and step out. It was better to play safe.

The big night arrived. It was cool and crisp with a bright moon lighting up the landscape like day. The hall was gay with flags and bunting, and the air was filled with the scent of evergreen. The best orchestra of El Paso had been engaged to furnish the music.

The crowd was a strange one. All were wearing their glad rags. Those who had dress suits had been asked to wear them, and not a few appeared with swallow tails, white shirt fronts, and stove-pipe hats. Officers' uniforms were also to be seen and a few brand-new pairs of overalls and brogans.

Colonel Parker led the grand march. He was a West Point officer who had joined the Confederates on the outbreak of the Civil War. He was now about sixty years of age, but he managed to get his two hundred seventy-five pounds into his old West Point dress uniform. His partner in the grand march was Big Annie, a lady from Missouri. She was corn-fed and the least that can be said about her size is that she was a grand partner for the Colonel. She was dressed to kill.

Four other colonels were there: Colonel Harris, who had gained his title by sitting forty-eight hours in a stud poker game without getting up from his chair; Colonel Crawford, who wore the latest styles and gained the title because he was a regular windjammer and had sold more wildcats than anyone that ever crossed the Rockies; Colonel Jim Finch, who gained the title because he was able to tell by the sound whether it was a 45 or a 45-70 Winchester that was fired; Colonel Bob Hopper, who could tell by the taste whether he drank Old Crow or Sam Thompson. Of course, judges and majors were more or less plentiful. At that time a man without a title was a small potato.

As a special attraction Sergeant "Dog-Face" Connelly, who ran the Orpheum, was to bring all his girls to the dance after the show. All the society women of surrounding towns were present, of course, wearing their best bibs and tuckers, and all the ladies from Shady Lane, including Lousy Lou, Old Hat, Deaf Carrie,

Jew Etta, Big Jennie, and Scotty, the latter being an expert at the "Highland Fling." Bloody Mary was there. She was Cornish and had won her name because she used the word bloody to describe everything from a hairpin to her latest flame. Kate Stewart, the town beauty, came in late, looking like a fashion plate.

There was a sprinkling of many nationalities in the crowd: Greek George, French Joe, Dutch Henry, Hunky Pete, and the Big Turk; also Americans, Irish, Scotch, Blue Noses, Shad Backs, and Cousin Jacks.

Ed Doheny and Neil Boyle were two of the dudes who appeared in dress suits rented from El Paso. Dress suits and castor hats were aired at this dance that were old in Hickory Jackson's time. French Joe wore a white fur hat that he had brought with him from Canada.

It is safe to say that no one present was inclined to put any slight on Pretty Sam's hospitality. There was plenty of liquor for all and sundry—champagne, whiskey, wine, gin, and mescal. The company was in high feather. The girls were looking their best, the music was enough to make a dead man dance, and the old sourdoughs and desert rats were making up for a year of hard and lonely work. It seemed at times as if the floor must surely fall in under the lively dancing.

There had come to town the day before the dance a gay young dame from Denver. John Roach, the gambler, met her at the stage and took her to the hotel. Johnny had been having a run of hard luck, and for several days had been trying to drown his troubles in tarantula juice. Though generally a dandy, he had not shaved for days. Being in no shape to attend the dance, he told his lady friend to stay away from the low-brow affair. Then he went to his cabin and to bed.

The Denver dame heard nothing except the big dance, and the more she heard the more she wanted to attend it. The landlady at the hotel promised to get her an escort. The young man she picked out was Lewis, a Tar Heel from North Carolina, the nephew of Colonel Bob Hopper. Lewis was a smart Aleck and seemed to think that prospectors, miners, gamblers, and all other Westerners were a breed beneath his notice. Lewis and the Denver girl were both good dancers and cut a big swath when they got out on the floor.

By midnight the celebration was going at top-speed. Cornish Mary was calling for a "bloody lunch." John Brockman was shouting for limburger cheese and beer. The Duck, an ex-Episcopal minister, and Sig Lindauer, a merchant, were arguing the difference between a clog and a jig. Judge Bell and other Virginians were singing the strains of "Old Black Joe" to the picking of the banjo. The Georgetown clique—Smith, Hilde, Sternes, and Deemer—had formed a committee to wait upon the orchestra with a request for the "Spanish Cavalier."

With some trouble the different groups were cleared from the floor in order that Lewis and the Denver dame could do one of the latest dances, the two-step valse.

It was while this was going on that Johnny Roach appeared on the scene. Having slept several hours, he had brightened up, and with a drink or two under his belt he had set out to take his lady to the dance. Finding that she had gone without him, he flew into a rage. Arming himself with a Springfield rifle, he headed for the dance hall.

He made himself known by crashing his rifle through the glass in the front door. Then he began to shoot. Luckily he did not see Lewis and his lady, and the shots were directed at the lights. In a twinkling the main light was shot out. Virtually every guest had a gun under his swallow-tail coat, and quite a volley was fired in the general direction of the front door.

The main body of the guests made a wild rush for the double door in the rear of the hall. Over went the partition and crash went the bolted door. Leading the rush was Big Annie, and her weight decided the fate of the door, for she was the first one to land on the dry creek bed thirty feet below, with French Joe a close second. The few others who went over landed in a general heap. Big Annie's screams for help put the gunman at the front door out of mind, and a great scramble took place to get down to her on the creek bottom.

Dan O'Leary ran like mad for Dr. Guthrie, the only medical man in town. The doctor had taken a Christmas toddy and gone to bed. O'Leary, terribly excited, could hardly talk straight, mumbling that the doctor must come at once. Now, Dr. Guthrie had at one time been scalped by the Cheyenne Indians; in his hurry he did not stop to put on his wig, nor even to throw a coat over his nightshirt.

The excitement of the shooting and Annie's accident had had a very sobering effect upon the crowd, and they had reached the stage where a reaction was sure to come. Teeth were chattering and nerves were jangling, when the wild-eyed O'Leary arrived with a creature in a loose white garment, whose face went clear to the back of his neck, and whom they did not remember seeing before. It was the last straw. People fell over one another in trying to get away.

Some, moved by a wholesome fear, scattered to their homes and were among the first to gather for the Christmas services when the bell gave the summons the next afternoon; but most of the crowd came together in the new dance hall. Colonel Parker took this chance to make a speech.

"My friends," he began, "I have been asked to make a few announcements to the crowd gathered here to-night, and this I want to do before you again take the floor to dance.

"To-morrow the postoffice will be open till one o'clock, so you will have time to sleep off this dance and get your mail, besides. There may be a letter you will not want to miss from mother, perhaps, or wife, or sister, or friend, or sweetheart.

"The Catholics of the town are invited to Mrs. O'Boyle's cabin to celebrate this great feast with hymns and prayers. The Protestants of the settlement are invited to gather here in Pretty Sam's Casino. The Episcopal minister, whom you all know better as The Duck, will lead the hymns and prayers for you. The collection taken up at both meetings will go towards building a fence around the graveyard.

"No saloons will be open to-morrow afternoon or evening. Keep sober. Make it a day of memories—memories of Santa Claus and Christmas trees and Christmas toys; memories of mother and the lessons she taught us; memories of those whom we have loved and lost.

"Your mothers will be thinking of you—of the hard life you lead; of the changes you will find at home when you go back; of the children who have grown up since you left. She will be wondering what this life is like that you lead among new friends, new ways, and new strikes. Write her a letter to-morrow, my friends, and send her a few dollars if you can afford it.

"Enjoy the good dinner you may get here or at Mrs. O'Boyle's or in your own cabins, if you would rather do that. I ask God to take care of you and to guide you in this hard life. May He take you to His Heavenly Kingdom at your death. Let us forgive and forget in this season of peace and good will to men.

"And now Sam, I want to thank you in behalf of your guests.

You did not save your best drinks till last, but I congratulate you upon your great act of hospitality. You led your guests into a state of inebriation bordering upon coma, and then furnished an incident which in a few minutes made them so sober they can start all over again with a mighty thirst. A merry Christmas I wish you, Sam, and all the company."

And so it happened that Pretty Sam's dance went into history as the biggest bang-up in the annals of Kingston. Johnny Roach was arrested shortly after leaving the dance hall and put in the jug. No complaint was made against him, and as he promised to pay Big Annie's doctor bill and to stand the damages in Pretty Sam's Casino, he was out in time to eat his Christmas dinner with the dame from Denver.

A Prospector's Dream

I AM an old man now. Looking back through the years, it is not the hilarious Christmas of Kingston that I remember with longing, but the one spent like a hermit in my mountain cabin.

Now when Christmas rolls around I dream that I am far up among pine-covered mountains with the snow drifted almost to the roof of my log cabin. I sit in my homemade rocking chair before a fire of juniper logs with the red sparks flying up the chimney. Above the mantelpiece hangs the deer head bearing my gun in its antlers. My mother looks at me from the picture that stands on the mantel, with evergreen heaped up around it.

To one side of me lies my shaggy gray and brown dog, Tige; curled up on my bed is my big yellow cat; from the corners of the room steal shy, big-eyed mice. Close at hand on a rough table sits the jug of good cheer, and a kettle sings on the hob.

I am alone with my memories and my thoughts. In the silence I ponder again the wonders of that first Christmas Night. The walls of my cabin shine with unearthly light. I am gazing at a Babe in swaddling clothes asleep on a bit of yellow straw. A blue-garbed Mother kneels beside the Babe; a roughly-clad carpenter bends above them. The warm breath of an ox and an ass is carried to me. The door opens, and my cabin fills with frost-bright figures and bleating sheep. Men kneel in reverence to adore the Child.

I awake with a start. Only a bed of red coals is left in the fireplace. Tige stirs and rubs his cold nose against my bearded cheek. I throw a log on the fire and mix another hot toddy. My heart is full of Christmas joy.

The Four Neals

AMONG those who came to Kingston during the big rush of the early eighties were four sons of old Erin, all first-rate miners who had been driven from the hard-coal regions of Pennsylvania because they belonged to the Molly Maguires, an organization of Irish miners who had resolved to get a fair price for mining coal. But the coal barons were too wise for them—they brought in Italians and other foreign workmen who would slave on starvation wages; then they dumped the Irishmen, their families, and their household goods on the roads.

It was the dead of winter. Coal and Iron Police, hired by the company, were ordered to use armed force, if necessary, to get rid of the Irishmen; but the Irishmen, many of whom had been soldiers in the Civil War, knew how to fight and would not get out. In a short time that section of the state was in open warfare. Murder, the burning of tipples, and the stopping of pumps were everyday happenings. Finally the troops were called out to put down the rebellion.

The four sons of old Erin, known as the four Neals, the four Nales, or the four Naleys, according to the brogue of the one who used the name, were among those lucky enough to escape arrest by skipping out.

But they took with them their worst enemy, John Barleycorn. It was due to drink that they came into Kingston without a cent after making good strikes in Colorado and in Tombstone, Arizona.

As there were men in this section from all parts of the world, the four Neals usually met a friend who would buy them a meal when they got hungry; and as whiskey was more plentiful than either food or water they never got thirsty. In time the bartenders complained because they were always in the saloons, and the town marshal ordered them to vamoose, saying he would give them a job breaking stone unless they obeyed orders.

While drinking with the prospectors the Neals had been on the alert and had soon learned where float was to be found. When ordered from town they headed for the North Percha district, about five miles out of Kingston in the very heart of the Black Range. No other section of the Black Range was so well stocked with game, especially deer, bears, and turkeys; no other section had a better supply of timber; and no other section was more often visited by the Apaches when they were out. Victorio's Park, one of their strongholds, lay in the district.

One day the four Neals pulled into the section with all their belongings—a burro loaded with a frying pan, a coffee pot, and an old Dutch oven; a scanty supply of thin blankets; a piece of whiteside, a sack of flour, a can of coffee, and a few packs of tobacco. Soon they had chosen as a camp site the mouth of an old, deserted tunnel that ran into the very heart of a mighty mountain. Who had built the tunnel or for what reason were facts not known even to the old timers of Kingston; the nearest mineral was half a mile away, and the waters of the creek sometimes got into the tunnel in the rainy season. But the four Neals put it to good use, making up their beds just inside the opening and storing their supplies farther in. To keep out skunks and other wild animals they closed the mouth of the tunnel with brush. Not far away they set up a monument, naming the claim Tara Hall.

In a few days the four Neals, bearded and smoke-stained, looked like a crowd of pirates, as they sat before their big fire of pinon logs. Clouds of resin-scented smoke rolled up through the pine trees, helping to keep away wild animals, and at the same time letting the Apaches know they were in the vicinity, but for some reason the Apaches never bothered them.

Each of the four Neals had an Irish surname of which he was very proud. If anyone wanted to insult him all he needed to do was to speak to one of the Neals without putting "O" or "Mc" to the family name. To all who would be their friends they were Neal McGarvey, Neal O'Gallegher, Neal McConway, who claimed to be the only true Celt, and Neal O'Boyle, a true Gael.

Each Neal had a hobby of his own, and though all were devoted to funerals and wakes, it was the special privilege of Neal O'Boyle to be a pallbearer at every funeral, as grand a gentleman as you could wish to see, in his double-breasted black coat with long tails, his stove-pipe hat pushed down on his curly black head in a manner appropriate to the occasion, and his shining new shoes. He wore black gloves and he folded his immense hands on his round paunch like a preacher. Pulling a long face he would go into the house of death and up to the coffin, treading like a camel. Then he would say, "Shure ain't he the fine carpse, ain't he acushla?"

Next, he would snuffle, drop a tear, and get up a dry, hacking cough. "Who would ever have thought he would be the next? May his sowl rest in peace!" If the deceased was a Catholic, Neal O'Boyle always led the prayers for the repose of his soul and never turned down the noggin of potheen given him for his help by the mourners of the dead man.

Neal O'Gallegher could relate Irish history without a slip of the tongue from Brian Boru to Charlie Parnell, and he could describe so well the fights of the Irish chieftains over the pretty colleens that the imagination of his listener was stretched to the breaking point.

Neal McConway specialized in prize fights. He put me in mind of an Irish schoolmaster, being slim and neat with a full round forehead and thoughtful blue eyes. With a twist of his jaw and a smack of his lips he was off, and never would he stop until he had named all the champions including Yankee Sullivan, Mike McCool, Ned O'Baldwin, Jem Mace, and so on, down to our own days. He told the number of rounds, the amount of the stakes, the name of the place, and the name of the referee in each fight. These fighters, he would have you know, did not play around with padded gloves either, but went for one another with bare knuckles.

Neal McGarvey loved to relate tales of fairies and of dog fights in a voice like a burro with a bad cold. What harm that his fairy tale nearly always ran into the story of a dog fight and the account of the dog fight into the praises of whisky as a medicine. "My ould mother," he would wind up, "may her sowl rest in peace, once cured a man of palsy by giving him a bowl of potheen." He went so far as to believe that a noggin of Irish whisky would mend a broken leg.

In a short time the four Neals had picked up some rich float in the North Percha country, and they soon traced it to the ledge it came from. Although the vein was spotted, the rich streaks in it being small and light, it was continuous, and they located several claims on it. These claims they recorded in Hillsboro under the names of the St. Patrick, the Colleen Bawn, the Donegal Slasher, the Home Rule, the Galloway Slugger, the Erin Go Bragh, and the Tara Hall.

When they got back from Hillsboro they stopped in Kingston to buy some sacks, which they soon filled with ore. Their first shipment amounted to three tons, averaging two hundred fifty ounces to the ton in silver. As silver at the time was worth more than a dollar an ounce their net profit was above five hundred dollars.

Oh, what a blow-out they had! In a week's time the gamblers, the tin horns, and the scarlet women got all their money away from them. As soon as it was gone they were ordered out of town.

Back to their mine they went to discover that a rush had taken place in the section while they were away.

The Neals had located everything, as McGarvey put it, "from hell to breakfast" in that district, and the only one to remain there was an Irish Jew named Dean, or as the Neals would say "Daney."

Dean's kind could be found in every mining camp. They were, as a rule, ex-soldiers or ex-policemen, not given to hard work, and they generally got a living by preying on small mine owners and prospectors. These shylocks loaned money at a rate often as high as fifty per cent, always taking care to get a note against the mine or the ore before parting with their money, so they could be sure of their pound of flesh.

Dean had been a policeman in London. After passing the physical examination and other tests Dean was asked by one of the commissioners, "What would you do to break up a mob in a London street?"

"If I were at home in Aberdeen I'd ask one of the Army lassies to pass the hat," came his answer in a broad Harry Lauder accent. He got the job.

Dean told the Neals that he did not want a mining claim but a town site where he could build a saloon. Finally he picked out a grassy flat at the point where the trail to the Neals' locations led off from the main trail to Kingston, which he located, naming it the Vale of Athlone. He soon set up a large tent on the spot, curtaining off one end for his sleeping quarters and building shelves in the other end where he could display his wares; he also set up a bar strong enough to hold up the weight of the four Neals.

A ten-gallon keg of whisky came with the tent; soon a number of bottles stood on the shelves bearing such names as Old Crow, Sam Thompson, Golden Wedding, and Guggenheimer. Of course, all the bottles were filled from the same keg. Several glasses of different sizes stood ready, with a sign, fixing the prices from a short bit to a full two bits per dram. A jar of red beans, a jar of prunes, a string of chili, and a slab of bacon were also on display, and Dean got anything else that was called for, from an onion to a stick of dynamite, out of an immense box under the counter.

Dean was a lover of poetry. He had lived many years in Scotland and could recite Scottish rhymes like a native son. Now, a saloon must have a name, so Dean ordered a large sign painted which read: "Poet's Rest—Everybody Welcome." This he nailed to a post in front of the tent. On the broad blade of a long handled shovel he had two birds painted—one in a hand and the other in a clump of brush. As Dean passed the scoop to his customers he would say, "A bird in the hand is worth a million in the Bush." Then he would quote a line from one of the well-known poets.

The Neals knew from the beginning that Dean had an ax to grind, and when he offered to ship ore for them, the cat was out of the bag. O'Gallegher turned down the offer in no uncertain language, for he was President, Secretary, and Treasurer of the Erin Go Bragh Mining Company; he knew only too well that if Dean handled the returns he would take out the amount of his bill plus a hundred per cent interest—profits would melt like snow in the sun.

The Neals were working hard and seldom went to the Poet's Rest except on Sundays, and then not until the washing was done, a batch of bread turned out of the Dutch oven, and a pile of wood cut for the coming week. Dean had brought out a pair of boxing gloves from Kingston. He had once been handy with the mitts and liked to tell the world about it. On the next Sunday all the Neals had a few rounds with him except O'Gallegher, who had gone to town for the mail. Supposing that the country-born O'Gallegher was an easy mark like the other three, Dean challenged him to fight. O'Gallegher set the date two weeks ahead, so he could invite his friends from town.

"Come out," said he, "and I'll show you Micks a few tricks. I want you to see me knock out that Aberdeen hybrid."

A considerable crowd gathered under the pine trees in the vicinity of the Poet's Rest on the big day. Dean stepped into the ring as sure of winning as Napoleon at Waterloo. For several rounds the boxers sparred and feinted; then O'Gallegher took it on the chin; he took it on the nose; his friends began to lose hope. In the fifth round O'Gallegher turned and gave his cronies the wink. The next instant he struck the unwary Dean a blow behind the ear that would have felled an ox. Everyone went into the tent to drink to Neal's victory, leaving the Aberdeen hero to come to in his own good time. That was the last time Dean was ever seen wearing mitts.

In the course of the next week the Neals made another shipment, spending the returns in Kingston in the usual manner. McGarvey lost his temper during a game of faro. At first his nose was just a little out of joint and he kept saying over and over, "Be me sowl!" Then he shouted, "By the jumping Naley jazes," and his friends knew he was on a rampage. They were not surprised when he leaped upon the faro table, scattering the chips in every direction. The only reason he was not killed was because his partners in the game knew they would get all the money he had sooner or later if they let him live. As usual, when their money was all gone, the four Neals went back to their mine.

Dean had been having a hard time to collect from the Neals, and he finally came to the conclusion not to give them anything without a written order from Neal O'Gallegher, President. As a result his business dropped off, and he spent much of his time in town.

One morning the Neals ran out of candles. Neal O'Boyle was sent post haste to the Poet's Rest to get some. Dean was not there. O'Boyle soon forced an opening into the tent and the candles were as soon forgotten. First he helped himself to a dram of Old Crow and then to a dram of Golden Wedding. Armed with a full bottle he started for Tara Hall. The temptation was too great even for O'Gallegher, President. The Erin Go Bragh Mining Company could not work, for O'Boyle had forgotten to bring the candles. Down to the Poet's Rest went the four Neals, arm in arm. They had to get those candles!

Through some mishap—it was while looking for the candles, they would have you know—they knocked the spigot out of the whisky keg. In the panic which followed pots and pans were filled with whisky, and even the Dutch oven was put to use. Each Neal then carried out a vessel of whisky to the shade of a pine tree. It was O'Gallegher, President, who claimed the Dutch oven for his share. Long before the pots and pans were empty the four Neals were dead to the world. After awhile their burro came up and seeing the sparkling liquid in the Dutch oven, he came to the conclusion to have a good drink. In a short time he lay down near his owners as drunk as a beast could be.

It was in this shape Dean found the group when he got back. He was so blazing mad that for the moment he even forgot his

Scotch poetry. The Poet's Rest looked as though it had been struck by a cyclone. Grabbing a tent pole, Dean beat the burro without mercy till he staggered to his feet in a daze. Dean kept on whacking him, and the burro's wits slowly came back. Lifting his heels he sent the Dutch oven flying. With head up and tail straight out he let go a mighty bray and lit out for the woods like a streak.

"You old waster!" roared Dean after him, now that he had got back the use of his tongue. "Who's going to pay for your drinks, I'd like to know."

The uproar woke up the four Neals. Dean had fastened the spigot into the keg and was busy pouring back the liquor that was left in the pots and pans. McGarvey was the first one to reach the bar.

"Just a wee dram to wet my throttle," he begged of the angry Dean. And Dean handed over the drink. Was he that soft-hearted or did he perhaps call to mind the blow delivered behind his ear by O'Gallegher, President, who had joined McGarvey at the bar? As Dean handed him the dram, he quoted, "A man's a man for a' that."

All the Neals were lined up against the bar by this time, waiting their turns. Dean's bad temper was carried away on a flood of poetry; just the same he gave out the drinks very grudgingly, using the small-bit glasses.

"By me sowl," roared McGarvey, "I never knew a poet worth a damn. What the divil did ould Shakespeare know about chlorides or horn silver? And there is Byron, the club-footed spalpeen—shure he went to Greece and drowned himself; there is Tom Moore, who wrote the Last Rose of Summer—shure he jumped off the porch and kilt himself; there is your friend, Bobby Burns—shure he was a good-for-nothing loafing around the public house; and there was Reilly—shure I knew him well; I worked on the grade with him. He wrote "Jerry Go Ile the Car," and he couldn't git a cartful of dirt in a week. Daney! Daney! I never knew a poet worth a damn."

"What I want to know," came back Dean, "is not what you think about poets, but who is going to pay for this day's devil-ment?"

"When our next returns come in," O'Gallegher told him, "you'll get twenty dollars, no more, no less, law or no law, and that'll include the dram for each one of us right now and the pint to take along for the morrow's morning."

Dean knew they would take it anyway if he refused, so he carried out O'Gallegher's orders. On their way back to the mine O'Gallegher laid down the law to the other Neals. "Ye can go to work now, and not a drop do any of ye get out of this bottle till the morrow's morning." And so it was.

To their big surprise the proprietor of the Poet's Rest appeared at the mine the next afternoon.

"Boys," said he, "I know you must be feeling bad, so I brought you a few swigs of Golden Wedding to cheer you up." He handed over the bottle, saying, "Also, Judge Holt sent me word by Shorty Oakley to tell Neal Boyle—"

"O'Boyle, if you plaze."

"To tell O'Boyle that he's wanted in town to act as pallbearer this afternoon for a Seventh Day Baptist. The Judge says O'Boyle sure understands handling the dead."

As the bottle went the rounds McGarvey said, "You're not such a bad sort after all, Daney."

"Naley O'Boyle," said O'Gallegher, President, "ye can go. We can spare ye, but be shure to be back tonight. We must get out this shipment before the bad weather sets in."

O'Boyle needed no second bidding, but set off at once. At the hotel he had a bath and put on his funeral outfit. Nellie Cashman let him into the house of the dead. Nellie was an angel of mercy in Kingston, always on hand to care for the sick and to watch with the dead. She was the girl who risked her life in the Northwest: she snowshoed into a stranded mining camp with medicines and a bag of dried fruit for the scurvy victims. She used to round up the Catholics of Kingston when Father Edwardo came to say Mass.

Nellie took O'Boyle to the room where the corpse lay. The shades were down and the light was dim. When Neal had gone through his regular performance—remarks, tears, cough, and camel-tread—he was ready for a drink. Nellie pointed to a pitcher on the sideboard, and Neal poured himself a tumblerful. Down it went with a gulp. How he choked and sputtered!

"Nellie," he roared, his funeral manners forgotten entirely, "What kind of poison is this?"

"It's Old Monk spirits."

" 'Tis neither Ould Monk's nor Young Monks; 'tis nothing but belly-wash; 'tis only a concoction to swindle these dry timperance folks, and no ould monk had a hand in its making. 'Tis a tricky Yankee drink made of colored water and sugar. I feel that bad, Nellie, I don't think I can go to the funeral. Can't ye get me a dram of the real stuff, Nellie?"

"Come, Neal," said she, "I'll give you a drop from the sick folks' bottle." She led the way into the kitchen.

"Nellie, ye have saved my life this day," exclaimed the grateful Neal, smacking his lips. "Shure, you're the fine colleen!"

After the burial Neal told Judge Holt, "If any more of those Seventh Day Baptists die, ye needn't send for me for a pallbearer, for such is worthy of his hire, and he needs something stronger than belly-wash to help him carry the dead."

When Neal was leaving Kingston that evening Bill O'Boyle handed him a package to take to McGarvey. The following Sunday all the Neals stayed in camp except O'Gallegher, who went to town for the mail. As soon as he was gone McGarvey opened the package and showed off before the eyes of the other two Neals an American flag, an Irish flag, a painted sign, and a sack of nails.

"Me lads," said he, "follow me, and I'll show ye how to make your names live forever. 'Tis once I'm going to be ahead of O'Gallegher."

He led them toward a high peak on the ridge that separates the North Percha from Carbonate Creek. About half way up he planted a post and nailed up the two flags, flying them toward the peak. Below them he nailed the sign, which read, "This Trail Goes To McGarvey's Peak." A finger painted on the sign pointed out which peak. The other two Neals were smiling like a basket of chips by this time, and they began to look around for peaks to name for themselves.

When O'Gallegher got back from town he was bristling with importance. He called a meeting of the Erin Go Bragh Mining Company. For the moment McGarvey's Peak was forgotten.

"I have that to say to ye now which makes this a red-letter day," he began. "A New Mexico mine is like a young maid who has her eyes on a young man—she shows her best points till she gets him, and when he takes her he finds some points he never thought of. So with the mines of New Mexico—the best ores are on top. Now we have been here for a year and our ore bodies don't improve as we work them. Our next shipment may net us two thousand dollars, and that will round out our salary for the year. I am sure we have skimmed the cream off the ledge, and as water is coming in before long I am in favor of selling an interest, the money to be spent for a pump and an engine. 'Tis shure I am we will need shortly ten thousand dollars to do all this. With the streak so small and the rock so hard, ye'll agree with me, I'm shure, that 'tis wiser to sell out the group. I'm told Bob Hopper, that old Tar Heel, has an eye on it, and I believe after our next returns come in we'll be able to make the deal. Now ye buckos do your talking."

"Mr. President—"

"Mr. Garvey."

"McGarvey, if ye plaze."

"McGarvey it is."

"I move that no one of the Erin Go Bragh Mining Company sells without the consent of the others."

"Do ye second the motion, Mr. Conway?"

"McConway it is."

"It is moved and seconded and passed and so ordered, and will be put on the minutes of this company."

"Mr. President, I move we wait till we get the returns from the next shipment."

" 'Tis seconded and passed. Now we will break up the meeting. I feel it's up to me as President to look out for you omadhauns."

The next week they were busy getting the trails ready and loading the ore. When the cars pulled off they went into Kingston for a little hard-won rest. When they got back to the camp McGarvey took note that some one had set up a painted sign above his on the mountainside. The sign read, "Beyant And Above McGarvey's Peak is Fogarty's Flat, And Beyant And Above Fogarty's Flat On Top Of The Ridge Is Orange Lodge, Where Flies The Flag Of The Prince Of Orange. Signed: A Far Downer."

McGarvey was on his high horse. He blamed the wee Charlie Fogarty, who had no love for him. " 'Twas that little snarlin' dog did it, ye can be sure," he stormed. "Him that be forever showin' his teeth like a bull pup and hissing his words like a snake. I'll give him all the knock-outs as are coming to him for this dirty deed."

"Meself and McConway will look into it in the morning," said O'Gallegher. "Ye left everything as ye found it, didn't ye?"

"That I did."

The next morning the pair went up the trail and examined the tracks. Said McConway, "There are only two men in this section who could make such big tracks—Nigger John who is too lazy to climb the hill, and that big omadhaun who reminds me of a kangaroo with his knock knees and spindle legs, that bartender in the Monarch Saloon; and there is nothing he would like better than to see a fight between Fogarty and McGarvey."

"Right ye are," said O'Gallegher, "Leave the signs just as they are, and we'll soon find out the culprit."

"Mr. President, who will have to take it on the chin for this foul deed?" asked McGarvey when they got back.

"I believe it's that poison-slinger in the Monarch Saloon—I doubt not he's the trickster that's to blame, but it's no Far Downer he is, for I know his father came from Skibbereen near Cork, and as for his mother—may her sowl rest in peace—she was the daughter of one of the best families in Limerick in the County Kerry, a McMahon, none better, that I can tell ye, for shure. But I fear, me lads, their divil of a son'll be a Downer when he dies.

"But, Nale McGarvey, why should ye be carryin' a chip on your shoulder? What the divil's difference is it to ye whether it's Prince Willie's flag or the Pope of Rome's? Shure yourself nor any of us has been inside a church since the day we were christened. I'm that shure if I asked ye this minute to bliss yourself ye'd do it with the left hand.

"Now as I said before, when that little French priest comes around I'm going to bring him out here and make ye all known to him, and ye can see him, one be one, in the little box. I'm that shure your sowls all need a good scrubbing same as my own. Do ye let wee Charlie Fogarty alone, with the mug on him like a Scotch terrier."

Within eight or ten days of the raising of the Orange colors on their property the Neals made the last shipment of the season and went into Kingston to warm up, and at the same time to keep on the lookout for a deal with Hopper and Maxwell. The returns amounted to more than any time before. O'Gallegher, canny Irishman that he was, pretended he did not want to sell, and this whetted the appetite of the two men who were out to make the deal and were inclined to make light of both the skill and the wits of the four Neals.

The Neals went back to their mine, seeming to take no notice of the offers of Hopper and Maxwell. A disappointment was in store for them—the Poet's Rest had changed hands. Dean had sold out to a pair of crooks from Kingston. They were Deafy, a brazen woman who had run a house of shady name, and Yorky, her latest flame. The new sign warned them as they came up to the tent from the Kingston side that it was "The Last Chance"; if they came towards the tent from their mine the sign read: "The First Chance."

"What may this mean?" asked McGarvey darkly, as the four Neals lined up along the bar.

"Only that we bought out Dean," snapped Deafy.

"You're not here to do a good turn for the Erin Go Bragh Mining Company, that we know for shure," put in O'Gallegher.

"It's because we heard you were selling out that we bought the place. Hopper expects to do things on a grand scale in this section."

"Hopper had better wait till he makes the deal before he orders machinery," said O'Boyle.

"Ye'd better be shure you're not out here to blackmail us," growled McGarvey. "Just try to frame the four Neals, and see what happens to yourself and that skunk of a lover you brought out here."

"Be careful how you talk, mister," warned Deafy. "Nobody asked you to come in here, and if you can't hold your tongue you can get out. What will you have to drink?" she asked, turning to O'Gallegher.

"Set us up with Golden Wedding," ordered O'Gallegher. "Remember, we run no whisky bill here. We pay as we drink."

All had a stiff drink except McGarvey, who seemed to be down in the mouth over the change at the Poet's Rest. "What's on you, McGarvey?" asked O'Gallegher on the way to Tara Hall.

"Begob, that ould trull would give ye poison and never blink an eye," he declared. "I'll have none of her drugs or smokes. Not by a jugful!" he declared. "She's a regular buzz-saw and I'll have none of her gob either. She's shure a bad egg if there ever was one, the spalpeen."

The four Neals had asked me and my partner, Danny, to come out and look over their claims. Danny and I were slight of build and for that reason could seldom find work as drillers, so we took to prospecting, soon getting the name of being good judges of ore. When we got there we found the Neals all worked up over the coming of Deafy and Yorky, afraid there might be a plot afoot to get their claims away from them. Such frame-ups were by no means uncommon in the early mining camps.

"Do ye go out and see what ye can find," said O'Gallegher to Danny and me. "Ye might be able to open up some pockets on the ground the company'll be setting buildings on in a few weeks if we sell out. It might mean a little quick money for ye. And don't be minding the troubles of the four Neals."

Just as we were ready to set out who should appear on the scene but Deafy and Yorky. Deafy was smiling like a basket of chips. Each one carried a big apple pie cut in four pieces. Handing her pie to O'Gallegher, Deafy said, "I thought a piece of pie would be a pleasant change for you men."

O'Gallegher, somewhat let down by this neighborly act upon the heels of his unfriendly remarks passed a cut to each of us. Only McGarvey turned it down.

"I'll have none of your pie, and I'm bidding ye and your lover, once and for all, to stay off of these grounds."

"McGarvey has a grouch on. Pay no heed to him," said O'Boyle, putting an end to the silence that followed McGarvey's outbreak.

"Ye country borns can shure make good pies," said McConway. "Shure I'll eat McGarvey's piece, and be glad to have it. What with the skunk flavor on everything we eat here, 'tis a royal treat ye've given us. Some night our old tunnel is going to blow up with skunk odor."

"Ye can bring us a pie or two like this each week," said O'Boyle, "and I'll pay ye for them. I'm sure tired of beans and sow-belly. Oh, for a bowl of slumgullion or a pot of corn beef and cabbage cooked by a colleen from Galway." And he sighed with longing.

"Bring no pie for me," snapped McGarvey, stalking off.

Yorky said nothing, but he looked after McGarvey with a hard eye.

Danny and I spent several days going from claim to claim. The ground had been well covered by the Neals, and we found little ore to reward us for the trip, but I, at least, got a great kick out of it, digging the baking powder cans and yeast boxes from the different monuments to read the names in them. In those days I was something of a wag, and many a trick I played on my Irish friends.

When we got back to the tunnel the four Neals were away. One more monument was left to be looked into—the one which claimed and named the tunnel where they lived. Danny found the box. "What kind of a name is this?" he asked, waving the paper he had pulled out. Danny was slow at reading and thick at grasping a joke.

"That?" said I, peering over his shoulder. "Sure, my lad, what could it be but Terrier Hall?"

As Danny put back the box he said, "They sure named it well. Four terriers living in a tunnel." I knew I would hear of Terrier Hall again.

The next day when we went to the postoffice for our mail we met McGarvey there. While I waited my turn at the window, I kept my ear open to catch what was passing between Danny and McGarvey.

"Well, Danny, me lad," said McGarvey. "Everything is lovely and the goose hangs high. The Erin Go Bragh Mining Company will soon change hands. To-morrow we come back to Kingston to sign up the papers with Hopper and Maxwell. Sorry you and Jimmie didn't have better luck."

"We had good luck finding out the name of your tunnel, though," bragged Danny. "You sure gave it a first-rate name, old son."

"And what may the name be, Danny, me lad?"

"Terrier Hall, of course."

"Terrier Hall! Be me sowl! If I thought ye'd mane that, I would mash ye, Danny. I'd bet the last farthing of the Irish Sweepstakes it was that little divil of a Jimmie told ye that to get ye into trouble. Did he forget so soon how I got even with Knock-kneed Jim for his trick? Did ye know Danny, that I marched him out to McGarvey's Peak at the point of my gun and made him take down those dirty Orange colors? And did ye know I marched him back to Kingston the same way and made him set up the whole saloon with drinks? It's not Terrier Hall, Danny, it's Tara Hall, the place where they crowned the Irish kings."

"Kings! I didn't know the Irish ever had any kings."

"Danny, me lad, they had a bully and a king in every county and two of each in the County Limerick. And they needed them, too, Danny. I'll shake that divil of a Jimmie for this like a terrier shakes a rat. Where is he?"

The door had slammed behind me. I did not stay to get my mail, and I did not stop running till I reached my cabin door. Later in the day I met O'Gallegher.

" 'Tis all settled, Jimmie, ould lad," he told me. "To-morrow when we come in from the mine we make the deal with those Tar-Heels that thinks they knows how to run a mine better than the four Neals. They make their first payment in thirty days."

Alas! A man never knows the future. The four Neals never saw Tara Hall again, nor did the deal come off the next day. On their way out from Kingston they stopped as usual at the Last Chance. Deafy was tending bar. Yorky was in the back part of the tent, cleaning a rabbit. Deafy set out a bottle and four glasses.

"Are ye shure it ain't poison?" growled McGarvey.

"Nobody's asking ye to drink it," came back Deafy, snatching away the bottle. "I'll sell you no more, and see to it that you get out of the Last Chance and stay out, Neal Garvey."

"Ye ould trull," scoffed McGarvey. "All you're here for is to blackmail the four Neals. I made shure of that in town this day."

"You lie!" screamed Deafy.

Yorky then stepped forward with a knife still in his hand. "Neal," said he, as white as a sheet, "we don't want your trade and I won't have you insulting my woman."

"Your woman!" sneered McGarvey. "She's everybody's woman, and you're only sponging on her. You're a low-down cur, that's what ye are!"

"And you're a low-down Irish skunk, that's what you are," shouted Yorky.

With that McGarvey picked up a chair to throw at Yorky. O'Gallegher rushed forward and grabbed the chair, saying, "Have sense, McGarvey, have sense!" Wildly throwing the knife in McGarvey's direction, Yorky had leaped behind the counter. When he took his hand from the box beneath the counter he was clutching a revolver.

"Drop that gun!" roared O'Gallegher. He and McGarvey and Deafy made a rush for Yorky. In the skirmish that followed the gun was turned against Yorky's breast. The pistol barked. There was a flash of blue fire. Yorky toppled over, shot through the heart.

"You've killed him," shrieked Deafy, beating O'Gallegher's broad shoulder with her horny fist.

"Ye pulled the trigger yourself," said O'Gallegher, green in the face. "Shure, ye know I only wanted to knock the divilish thing from his hand."

"O'Gallegher is right. Yorky wanted to do for McGarvey, and

O'Gallegher turned the pistol to save his life," said O'Boyle, who, with McConway had been only an onlooker. "Yorky wouldn't be dead if ye hadn't touched the trigger when you grabbed for the gun yourself. Now you're trying to pass the buck to O'Gallegher."

"Murder has been done and you'll pay the penalty. Oh, my poor Yorky!" cried Deafy.

The four Neals, sobered by the accident, helped to carry Yorky to the bed in the rear of the tent and cover him with a sheet. Then they returned to Kingston and went before Judge Barnes to tell the story.

Judge Barnes put all four of them under arrest. A few hours later Deafy appeared and made charges against them, swearing that O'Gallegher had shot Yorky. The Judge refused to let them out on bail and they were sent to the county jail in Hillsboro. Though their friends did all they could to have them let out, the four Neals were held for trial at the next term of court.

They drew all their money from the bank. Hopper and their attorney had several long talks with the prisoners during their days in jail. It was soon plain that Hopper had taken over their claims, for he installed machinery and put a force of men to work at the Erin Go Bragh Mine.

About a week before the day set for the trial Deafy skipped out. The four Neals must have greased her palm well. The night before the trial was to open the Hillsboro jail was broken into, and the four Neals made their getaway. No effort was made to catch them. Hush money had done its work.

McGarvey and O'Boyle were seen a few days later in Deming. O'Gallegher and McConway made their way to South Africa. Both were killed at Ladysmith, fighting with the Boers. I heard a few years ago that Ed Doheny was taking care of McGarvey in California. No one ever had any luck with the Erin Go Bragh Mine after the Neals left Kingston.

Mandy Lou

1. *The Rawhiders Come to New Mexico*

IN the year 1888 I was a prospector and miner at Lake Valley, in Sierra County, New Mexico. The silver mines here were famous for their rich deposits, most of which were found close to the surface. One of them had produced over three million dollars from what was known as the Bridal Chamber. Its greatest depth was not over forty feet. The shape of the deposit gave it the name.

The mines and the town of Lake Valley lay on the northern edge of the great mesa, or plain, that extends south into Mexico. From all directions and at an immense distance on this plain could be seen an extinct volcano, which from its shape, was called by the Americans, Hat Mountain, and by the Mexicans, Sierra Sombrero. It was about four miles southeast of town, not far north of the old Butterfield road. After the mine was discovered, travelers along this road generally visited the camp, often locating in it. Grass and water were plentiful, but there was no sign of tree or brush within miles of the camp.

The first large deposits had been taken from the mine, and in order to open others the mining company offered leases. The terms were such that both new and old work was done for almost nothing by the leasers. Some new and rich deposits were opened up by the lucky ones among them. The papers, however, were so drawn up that if a leaser found one of these rich bodies of ore, he was allowed only thirty days to work it. Even at that, some managed to clean up fifty thousand dollars. It did not take a first-class miner to work the rock, as the limes contained vugs and slips that at times needed no shooting, but could be worked with pick and shovel. Some of those who made the biggest stakes were goat herders and cowboys who did not know beans from buffaloes in the mining game.

One part of the mine was known as Goat Herders' Heaven, or the Nugget Ground. The formation here was soft limestone containing large cracks and vugs. These cracks were filled with red clay. Scattered through this clay were boulders and chunks of ore, assaying from one hundred to five hundred ounces per ton. This was the section which became by lease the happy hunting ground of sheep herders and rawhiders.

The rawhiders got their name from the many uses they had for cowhide. Cattle were plentiful and cheap in those days. When about to emigrate and even before setting out on a long hunting trip, the rawhiders usually killed three or four large steers, not for food, but for hides. The dried hides were stored in their wagon beds and supplied a hundred and one needs. If they had a breakdown they soaked the hide and cut it into long strips, called whangs, which they wrapped around the broken hub, wheel, or tongue. As the whang dried the edges of the break drew together. I have seen chairs, camp stools, wheel-barrows, and buckets made from hides. Since nails were hard to get, the upright poles around their corrals were fastened by strips of rawhide. Their oxen were shod with it and the *zapatas*, or shoes they wore, were usually made from left-over pieces. I'll venture to say that most of the old timers' corrals in West Texas are still held together by thongs of rawhide.

All rawhiders came from West Texas years before farming and drilling for oil became common there. They were on the move nearly all the time, driving their horses and cattle with them, also numerous large cur, or mongrel dogs. The families traveled in covered wagons, which overflowed with women and children. They were all kinsfolk, continually marrying and intermarrying. Race suicide was unknown. Grandpas and grandmas and babies at the breast were huddled together in almost every wagon. They never carried tents, but there were always a few extra wagon sheets. Everyone over ten used snuff. The rawhider generally looked as if he had a billiard ball under his jaw, and his roll of Pigtail was never long out of sight. This was dry, twisted roll of natural leaf. When they ran out of tobacco the wagon wheels stopped turning. All waited until a John Wesley or a Thomas Jefferson got back with a fresh supply. Sometimes this meant a hundred-mile trip to the nearest government sutler.

Rawhide outfits were usually made up of ten or fifteen wagons strung out for miles. They made it a point, however, to drift together before sun-down. One saw pinto horses, scraggly cattle, and white-haired youngsters, whose heads looked as if they had not been washed or combed for months. All the wagons were either Bain's or Shuttler's, and many a child was born in them.

Sometimes a widow joined the caravan with a brood of children, but as a rule she did not stay single long, as it was against the rawhider's creed. "Increase and multiply" was their maxim. Popular wedding gifts were heifers, sows, fillies, and pullets. Divorces were common. The cast-off wife or husband often stayed in the same outfit with the ex-spouse, perhaps marrying the former husband's brother, or his first wife's sister.

Like gypsies they were ever on the move, sometimes halting but never staying long anywhere, even if they found plenty of water or a fine range with good grass. They were genuine squatters, and if some pilgrim came along and offered them a few cattle or a little cash, they pulled up stakes and migrated the next day, without a thought for the future.

Their food was mostly beef, no matter whose. They never ate their own, claiming that JXT or XLC's had a sweeter taste. I lived amongst them for years and I never saw a piece of roast beef except at a barbecue or a big feast. All meat was boiled or fried. Sometimes they cooked wild greens with the boiled meat. They used suet for frying and cooked everything to a frazzle. Coffee was drunk as black as soot and so strong it could float a bottle. Biscuits, raised with soda or cream of tartar, were apt to be the color of an orange. Some of the old women could cook very well when settled in a shack or a cabin, but the younger element, who never took a bath nor combed their hair, did not know how to boil water.

Who were these people and where did they come from? This has always been a mystery to the other Texans. It is believed they came from the mountain districts of Tennessee or North Carolina. Their Scotch-Irish names suggest this. In the mountain cabins of these states, one may still find chairs, buckets, hoops, and rugs made of rawhide. They lived there by fishing, hunting, and trapping. Pelts and roots were traded off for flour, sugar, and tobacco. Slavery was unknown among them, and they were looked upon by slave-holders as white trash. When the Civil War started, and the South tried to conscript them, they either joined the northern troops or came west to the new lands. Cotton raising did not appeal to them and they drifted to farther western lands. There they found abundant game, plenty of wild horses, and thousands of unbranded cattle. Soon they were joined in this land of milk and honey by many of their kinsfolk.

When the Civil War ended many former slave-owners also came

out to these western lands. They were a wide-awake set of people. Good houses and corrals appeared here and there in the wilderness. Immense herds of wild cattle were branded. The fat ones were driven to the railroad and sold to eastern markets. The rawhiders woke up, and many of them also took up ranges and branded wild mavericks, but the roving fever was still there. Selling often and always moving farther west, they at last reached the banks of the Rio Grande. A spring or a water seepage often invited settlement, but they never built and went on cooking outside. Never in a hurry, they sometimes stayed for months in a wild, grassy valley. No one knew who was President; in fact, they never voted. Without schools or newspapers, there was noththing to interest them except cattle, tobacco, and horse or pony racing. Most of them could neither read nor write, but they could beat the devil himself at swapping. Owners were always trading wagons.

The women even blamed certain makes of wagons for carrying certain diseases. One mother said, "My Georgie Anne is much healthier than Ollie. You know, Mrs. Allison, my Georgie Anne was born in a *Shuttler*. My Zeke traded it for a *Studebaker* to Ike Johnson, and that wagon is sure great for every epidemic or itch, or measles that comes along. Then Zeke traded the *Studebaker* for a *Bain*, and my kids got the mumps in that wagon. Give me a *Shuttler* any day for healthy kids, Arabella."

As soon as the boys could walk they were roping old Lije, the dog, or grandpa. As for roping or branding cattle, the rawhider or border Mexican cowboy could do more with the lariat than any other roper in the world. Most of the boys' legs were so bowed you could throw a barrel between them. In fact, if they went to the spring for water or chopped a little wood they did it on horseback. Some of them could hardly walk. Their highest ambition was to own a bronco, a riding saddle, a pair of spurs and a quirt. Oh, what Biblical names they had! Ike, Zeke, and Luke among the boys while the girls had such names as Patience, Prudence, Ruth, or Martha. But in every family, if they had only one or two children, would be found a John Wesley or an Arabella, or both. They married very young, and before they reached the age of twenty-five they were often the fathers and mothers of five or six children.

A few became rich, taking up ranges and settling down. The later generations who went to school were smart and rather good-looking. Probably, it was having to wash and comb their hair that made the difference. There certainly was a crowd of them with hair of fiery red. A marriage among them was a great event, the dancing and other festivities sometimes lasting for a week.

They were experts at getting around the law. No rawhider was ever found guilty of cattle stealing in a Texas court. They could name every brand from Del Rio to Tucson, and most of them knew the owners and the number of head they had on the range. Some of the women were as handy as the men folk with the rope and branding irons. One and all had a marvelous gift for sighting a maverick or an unbranded calf. They were born cattlemen, but God help the pilgrim who was located near them!

The rawhider, like the buffalo and the Indian, belongs to the past. Wire fences, autos, nesters, and cattle associations put an end to his wanderings.

2. *The Rawhiders' Restaurant*

During the month of April, 1888, a number of rawhiders came to the Lake Valley camp. The mining company gave leases to several of them on a part of the Goat Herders' Heaven. Credit was allowed them for a small supply of groceries and a few tools. The mine foreman gave them some instructions and saw that they worked. The company sampled and shipped all ores and also handled the returns. After taking out costs, royalty, and standing bills, the company paid the leaser what was left, which was often little enough.

In a short time, however, two of the rawhiders struck a good body of ore, cleaning up ten thousand dollars. They or their comrades must have heliographed the news to their friends in West Texas. By August a long string of covered wagons could be seen every day on the old Butterfield road. Most of them came from Tom Green County or the Concho section of Texas. About two miles west of the silver mines at Crystal Springs they made their camp. Other miners and leasers were already living there.

That fall and summer were very hot and dry. The Chinaman, who ran the only eating house in camp, pulled out for a cooler climate, giving as his reason, "Too damn hottee for me cookee." As a result many miners had to batch or else look up another camp for board and lodging. The merchant who owned the restaurant offered it rent free for a year to anyone who would run it, as it meant money in his pocket, as well as a place to eat for the miners. Some of the miners put ads in the El Paso, San Antonio, and Los Angeles papers, offering a cook seventy-five dollars a month, with room and board, but they got no answer.

Along in September there arrived a new rawhide outfit from the Pecos section, numbering about fifteen men, twenty women and children and dogs aplenty. As the mining company was doing considerable building they needed common laborers. When some of this crowd asked for work the foreman ordered them to pull off their spurs and high-heeled boots, and he would give them a try-out. Since they were badly in need of food they gave in. At first, they handled a pick and shovel as if they were about to lasso a steer, but in time, led on by the cuss words of the bosses, they became fairly good hands. On no account would they work underground, as they had come to the conclusion to stay where they could see the sun.

Amongst them was a rather good-looking young woman of twenty. This was Anna Belle, the mother of three-year-old Mandy Lou, whose father was supposed to be taking care of a piece of ground in Texas. The miners, knowing the habits of his kind for gun play, had a good laugh about it, saying the piece must be six feet *under*ground. Anna Belle was kin to everyone in the outfit, and was always visiting from one wagon to the other. She was never seen at work, but everyone in town soon came to know her poke bonnet and the thin gloves that reached to her elbows. She used snuff and the stick very freely. Some of the young miners who took her to a dance gave it out that she was "a red-hot tamale and some doer of the *Bunny Hug* and *Bear Shuffle*, and could throw her hoofs to the queen's taste."

This was the woman who finally took over the restaurant. She told the committee she had never done much cooking and asked for a few days to think it over. The outfit got her to take up the offer, so they could get hold of some badly needed cash, and several of the old grandmas promised to help her. She at last agreed to try it for a month. Ten miners signed up for thirty dollars each. With no rent, cheap help, and the low cost of food this should have made it easy to set a table with the best in the market. But Anna Belle seemed to have made up her mind to stick to rawhide dishes with few exceptions. It was plain she had never seen a range, and she said she would rather cook on a tripod. She never cleaned the stove, and before long the dirty dishes had virtually climbed to the ceiling.

For the first few days the boarders said nothing, being satisfied with a change and hoping she would get the knack. Among the boarders were two Germans. In order to get rid of it, the store clerks told her these men liked sauerkraut. I am sure she had never eaten or heard of it, but the store delivered her a barrelful. She served it raw, just as she took it from the barrel, brine and all. This took for a few times, but when it was put on the table at every meal there were some wry faces. At the end of a week some very sarcastic remarks were going the rounds on kraut. On Sunday one of the grandmas gave us a boiled-pork dinner with white biscuits. The miners brightened up, but the next week it was again, kraut, bully beef, ginger snaps, and coffee that looked like ink. Once in a while we had fried eggs for breakfast, but they always looked as if they had been dragged over the floor. Oh, what disgusted boarders we were! Some paid up and went back to batching.

The restaurant soon became a regular rawhide headquarters, the women gathering there every afternoon. All sat around the range on which they lined up their snuff bottles. Having filled their mouths with snuff, they made a game of squirting the juice at a knot hole in the floor ten feet away, hitting it dead center every time. Then they gossiped and never cleaned a dish or cooked a bite until the men were sighted coming home from work. A quick fire would then be built, the coffee pot set on the range, and presto! the supper was ready.

Mandy Lou had never had much care, but after her mother took over the cooking she was virtually forgotten. She always wore the same dress, and I am sure the poor child would not have known herself with a bonnet or shoes. She was a chubby little thing with big blue eyes and very light hair. Her face was dirty and her hair tangled, but on account of her good-natured ways, she became a general favorite in the camps. Whenever an owner missed his dog, he learned to look for it near the restaurant, where he usually found it tumbling in the dust with Mandy Lou or chasing sticks for her.

Anna Belle herself seemed to have but one dress. She may have washed it after dark, but it surely never looked it. Some of the boarders named her Madam Few Clothes. She had no star boarder. All longed for the month to come to an end. The third week on a Sunday night, some one hung a muslin strip on the front porch, with large black letters on it, reading, "Ginger Hotel,

Rawhide Headquarters, Snappy Service, Kraut and Bully Beef Three Times a Day.—A. B. Few Clothes, Proprietess.—Tom Green, Painter." Next morning the sign could be seen from the stores and saloons. All the town miners read it. It was perhaps ten o'clock before Anna Belle heard of it through some of the grandmas. Her dander was up, and she threatened to leave at once; only her fear of losing the pay that was coming to her kept her from doing so.

She had her revenge otherwise. Things went from bad to worse in the kitchen. Finally two of the grandmas came each day to cook the dinner, which was pretty good. At first they cooked enough for supper, too, but when they found out that the afternoon gossipers made away with all left-overs, they got dinner only. One of these grandmas made Anna Belle a new dress, and the old one which had furnished town talk for so long, was seen no more. She would sit for hours at a time, rubbing snuff, twirling her thumbs round and round, and taking no interest whatever in house or boarders. Poor little Mandy Lou was lost half the time. Her mother said that she was just like her father, always straying. She was usually found asleep in the cupboard or under the bed. It had been well proven by this time that it was bad business to hire a cook on her merits as a dancer.

3. *The Wild Burros and the Lost Rawhide Child*

The last Saturday of that long month of October had arrived. Most of the miners quit at three o'clock on Saturdays, but my partner and I had stayed later than usual at the mine to sample some ores. When we went to the restaurant about sundown we found no one there. Looking up the street, we saw men and women running in every direction. Anna Belle's brother told us Mandy Lou had not been seen for some time, and they were afraid she had strayed up to the mine and fallen down a prospect hole. After a hasty supper of bacon and eggs, which we hustled together for ourselves, we again made for the street. We met a number of miners on their way to drink a few bottles of beer and play a game of auction pitch. One of them thought he had seen the child playing with Nolan's burros. These burros watered at one of the mine troughs, and it was feared she had followed them up there. Nolan came into the saloon shortly afterwards. He said he had not seen the child when he watered the burros at four o'clock, but that he had taken note of a large stray jack with the herd, which was made up of three jacks, four jennies, and two colts. He said they were in the habit of grazing at the south end of Hat Mountain about four miles southeast of town.

Just then Anna Belle rushed up screeching, "O God! I know she is kidnapped! A gypsy told me I would lose a child by a colored person." The miners tried to quiet her, but she hardly listened. By this time the sun was down. Already the air was chilling and a new moon was rising in the east. The whole town was full of excitement. Searchers had found the small footprints of a child among those of the burros in front of the restaurant. Cowboys who rode out to the gulch about a mile west of town found many burro tracks but did not sight the herd.

About one-fourth of the way to the gulch was a large frame house. In this lonely spot with her four children lived a negro wench, known only as Annie. She made a living for herself and the children by washing, baking, and doing chores for the mine bosses and their families. She never mixed with the other Texans, although it was said she came from Fort Worth. From the moment they got there, the rawhiders seemed to have it in for her. When they came back from the gulch, the cowboys said they had seen Annie going into her house with a large clothesbasket as they galloped by.

When the moon went down all the searchers returned to town. They came to the conclusion the burros had either found shelter behind a rock or covered themselves with sand, for no one had caught a glimpse of them. This was probable, as the nights were very cold in those parts even in midsummer. Most of the searchers went home to their cabins, promising to be up at daybreak to help find the child.

Some few still hung around, trying to figure things out. John Robinson, who had just arrived in town, gave them one more clue to work on. While herding his cattle on the Macho that day, he had sighted a pair of lobos, or timber wolves. The animals were eating a large calf when he rode up to the south end of Sierra Sombrero. They had run off towards the Rio Grande. He believed they had come down from the Black Range, seeking a lower altitude for the winter. He had hardly stopped speaking, when the crowd about him was startled by some mournful howls coming from the direction of the big gulch. Some of the men went as white as a sheet, and the women began to cry.

Meanwhile the rawhiders all gathered in the restaurant, motioning, and swearing in loud voices. The women seemed to be after the men, and kept pointing towards the colored woman's house. Some one asked me to go over and see what the trouble was about. On the way I met Anna Belle's father and asked him the cause of the rumpus. He told me the women folks and also some of the men believed the negress was a voodoo doctress, and that she had killed the child for its white blood. They had come to the conclusion to go out to her house to torture her, and to make her tell where she had put its body.

"Have any of you people talked to the wench?" I asked him.

"No," was the answer.

I said to him, "You people must not harm Annie until you have more evidence, as we prospectors and miners don't believe in such bunk, and we won't stand for any nonsense."

On my way back to the saloon I met Mr. Hadley, the superintendent of the mine, who had already been visited by excited rawhiders. Scenting trouble and perhaps a killing, because he knew the miners would not stand for any injustice to Annie, he had rushed into town.

"We'll go out to Annie's house and make a search," he told the miners, explaining to the rawhiders, "Myself and Jimmie, here, will take the lead. You fellows stay in the rear."

There was no light in the wench's house. She called out in answer to Mr. Hadley's knock, and told us we would have to wait till she lit a lamp and put on a dress. Her children woke up and began to cry. There were by this time fifty men and women gathered around the house. In a few minutes Annie threw open the door with a lighted lamp in her hand. When she found out from Mr. Hadley that she was suspected of kidnapping Mandy Lou, she cried out, "Oh, Lordy! Me a voodoo witch and wantin' that child! I have four of my own now, and I know how to get more if I want them. I have aplenty now to support. Them good-fur-nothing rawhiders shouldn't be allowed to have chillun. They don't take no care of them nohow. Come in, Mr. Hadley, and you, too, Mr. Jimmie, but you all no-accounts can stay out."

There being only one large room, we soon satisfied everyone that Mandy Lou was not there. Annie said she had seen the child just shortly before sundown, playing with some burros in front of the restaurant. One of her children put in, "Yes, Mamma, and I saw Mandy Lou pull the burro's tail."

We all left shortly afterwards, Mr. Hadley placing two men with rifles to guard Annie and her children till daylight. Everyone now felt certain Mandy Lou would be found with the burros. As it was long past midnight everyone went home to bed except the rawhiders. They returned to the restaurant and kept up a droning chant until daybreak. These people had no religion, but now and then one of them learned a few verses or parables from the Bible, which he recited every chance he got, the present crisis being one.

Mr. Hadley had supplied their two best trailers with horses and field glasses, and at daybreak the search was on again. When my partner and myself heard the trailers leaving the saloon, after getting a drink to warm them up for the trip, we dressed and struck out for the gulch. We saw the trailers bear off for the peak of Sierra Sombrero.

At sunrise we found the spot in the arroyo where the burros had bedded down. Looking closely we also found the baby's footprints. A careful study of the tracks soon made it plain how Mandy Lou had spent the night. It seemed when the animals bedded down the child also lay down about thirty feet further up the arroyo. It appeared that the herd, startled into flight, had turned back and hustled the child along with them. After that there were many signs of battle, and wolf tracks were mixed with those of the burros. The two big jacks must have done considerable kicking and biting, for at every place where a circle had been formed by the burros, with the child, the colts, and the jennies in the center, we found blood, hair, and bits of flesh.

Following the burros' trail, we soon came out on the mesa. It was plain the burros had headed for the high peak. We had hardly come to this conclusion when we heard two shots from that direction. All at once the two trailers appeared on the ridge, where the wolves had apparently made a last effort to get the child. From there on the stray jack left bloody tracks and signs of limping.

When we looked up from the tracks we saw the two wolves on the crest of a distant ridge. One of them was limping badly. The burros were following the trailers. They were still uneasy and kept looking back towards the ridge where the wolves had disappeared. The trailers were soon sighted by the other searchers, who ran to meet them. Anna Belle was quirting and spurring a borrowed horse and could not get to them fast enough. Grabbing the child from the trailer she hugged and kissed her as if she had always been the best mother in the world to her. Poor Mandy Lou was at last getting a little of the love she had been so long denied. When she could get her breath she lisped, "Oh, Mamma! Mamma! The big black dogs no good. Try to get baby all the time. Big jack, good burro. He bite and kick hard. Big dogs afraid of him. Burros run around me all the time. Oh, Mamma! Mamma! Me afraid. Me no sleep all night. Burros make me walk." With that she fell asleep on her mother's shoulder. Mandy Lou's baby words filled out the story written on five miles of bloody tracks.

The wolves had helped the burros to save Mandy Lou's life, for it had been a night of bitter frost, and if the frightened burros had not kept her moving she would surely have died from exposure. The burros followed the crowd almost all the way to town. All at once, as if knowing their little charge was at last safe, they turned and raced off towards the peak.

That afternoon the rawhide men took their hounds to the ridge where the wolves were last seen. They came back shortly before sundown with two scalps. The first wolf they shot was already badly crippled and his pelt was no good. The second was torn by the dogs, but not before the wolf had killed two of them and wounded four.

As the State paid a bounty of twenty dollars each, the rawhiders were in high feather. Making the most of the general good humor, the boarders sold out and this closed the restaurant. A big gab fest was held among the outfit, and the celebration lasted for a week.

Mandy Lou was an important little somebody for a few days, but before long she was once more growing up with less care than a burro's colt. It was the rawhide way.

Pete

PETE was known in almost every mining camp from Alaska to the border. He was a fairly good mining man. To the pilgrim, or tenderfoot prospector, his knowledge of the different formations of ore seemed marvelous. He had located and owned mining claims in virtually every known district between the years 1880 and 1916. He never worked any of these claims, but sold them to company promoters who knew the future of the different camps.

Pete usually sold his prospects for a small cash sum. Among the first things he bought would always be a few high-class books. But his chief hobby was strumming on the violin, which was generally in need of repairs. After settling up his debts, he was ready with the balance for a "high lonesome", as he called it. This meant trying to buy up all the red eye, or bad whiskey, in the boom towns, which had a way of springing up overnight like mushrooms.

When sober, Pete was quiet and docile, but when loaded with tarantula juice he was noisy and quick to pick a quarrel. His mouth, filled with stumps of teeth, at times caused his voice to start with a coarse roar and to wind up with a shrill whistle. His lion-like roar could be heard above the hee-haw of the jackass, which echoed from end to end of these mining towns every hour of the night.

During the rush into the Burro Mountains, Pete was one of the first on the ground, locating several claims and building a cabin. He lived on beans and bacon, with a few pounds of flour to make what he called red sop. This was a gravy made by browning the flour in strong, salty bacon grease, and adding water. At times he killed a deer or rabbit. This old prospector lived a plain and simple life, being in his sober days, a real hermit. No feather bed nor any luxuries; up at the first break of day and to bed at sunset. Pete's credit was good. The merchants knew he had some locations; and he had the name of being on the square and paying his debts as soon as he made a stake.

None of these new towns had a jail, or calaboose, as it was

called, for it was too well-known that the cowboys and bad men would burn it down. Instead, a snubbing post was set up in the main street. This was used to snub, or hog-tie, any mean or bad man. Having roped him with a lasso, they tied him to the post, gagging him if he were noisy. Here he was kept until he could be turned over to the nearest organized authorities.

In the town of Fierro, thirty miles east of the Burro Mountains, an extra large post of this kind had been set up. It was about ten feet high and at least fifteen inches in diameter. Pete had been in this town and had gone on a rampage there, riling up the people of the settlement who did not know him. He had lately made a sale and he told the bartenders he was going to El Paso to get a set of false teeth. It was the month of October and the nights being cold, he said he would be back soon, as his cabin needed repairs before the winter set in.

"You mean," scoffed a deputy sheriff, "you'll be back when your money is all gone."

Not over a week later Pete notified a neighbor to meet him at Tyrone, naming the day of his return. Thinking that Pete would have a load of groceries, his friend brought along a burro and packsaddle. Pete arrived, in one hand a violin and a six-dollar bow; in the other a large sack of molasses-covered popcorn. Hanging by a strap from his shoulder was a jug of corn juice, which it was plain he had tipped more than once during the journey from El Paso.

The two partners gave each other the glad hand and were soon ready to head for their mountain cabin. Standing beside his burro with fiddle and bow hanging from one fork of the saddle, the bag of popcorn from the other, and the jug of whiskey still swinging against his shoulder, Pete was a striking figure. Dressed in the regular overalls and jumper with a battered-up hat perched on the side of his head, he was the typical prospector. Perhaps, out of respect for his new teeth, his long beard had been cut, and the shaggy hair combed, but the sun-browned look was still there as well as the roguish twinkle of his blue eyes.

Oh, what teeth! That El Paso dentist must have been specializing in beaver molars. The two front teeth stood straight out from his gums, and the whole set was about as much of a misfit as possible. His pal was wise enough "to have eyes and see not."

They headed for Pete's cabin which was about five miles west in the Burro Mountains. As they went along, Pete who was fond of using big words, told the story of his adventures with the dentist.

"What a man that dentist was," he told Tom. "He sure was an aristocratical gent and he had more tools in that office of his than you'd find in a minin' company's supply house. Ach! but when he came chargin' at me with a mean lookin' drill like he was expectin' to strike a rich lode somewhere's near China, I sure let him know I wasn't no gold mine. That wasn't bad enough; he attacted me next with a pair of pliers strong enough to pull the trunk off an elephant, not to speak of the critter's tusks. Then after assurin' me in that soothin' voice of his, that he wouldn't hurt at all, he began to pull off the whole top of my head. I actshally grabbed it with both hands and put it on again. Ach, Man! I told him, 'You ought to get out a patent, for you can sure bring on a blow-up without any dynamite.' I suffered terrible gettin' these molars, Tom, and I don't see as how you care for them a'tall.

"Let's hit the corn," he ended as they reached a bend in the trail. Sitting side by side on a ledge of rock, both took a long pull at the jug, after which Pete opened the bag of popcorn. Popcorn balls and store teeth not geeing very well together, he had to take out the plate in order to get them apart. Then he laid his false teeth to one side, while he went on munching the corn with his gums. When he had finished the ball of popcorn he again hung the plate in his mouth before hitting the trail. But the popcorn made the two old desert rats thirsty, and before long they were again hitting the jug. Of course they had to have another ball of popcorn with the drink. This time in trying to pull the corn away from his teeth he let a big chunk of it fall to the ground within reach of Butcher, the burro. Butcher made a grab for the gob of corn and found it very much to his taste. So the next time the two old sourdoughs stopped for a long pull from the jug and another ball of corn, Butcher reached for the popcorn before Pete could loosen it but got a punch in the nose instead. By the time they had gone four miles in this fashion the jug was virtually empty and the pair were stepping high—in fact, the trail seemed as crooked as a snake.

About a quarter of a mile from the cabin there was a smooth bench of rock. This was, of course, just the right spot to have a last nip and empty the bag of popcorn. This time when the popcorn stuck to his teeth Pete could not pull it away. After letting out a few cuss words that would have done credit to a Missouri mule-skinner he laid the plate to one side on the bench of rock. He then got the violin from the burro's back.

"Tom, I'll give you a few of the latest tunes I learned in El Paso," said he. Butcher followed him back, and while Pete tuned his fiddle he reached over and swallowed plate, teeth, popcorn, and all, without even blinking an eye. Pete meanwhile sawed away on the violin, giving Tom the latest.

"That may be music to some folks, but I'd rather hear an old biddy cackle," said Tom.

"Some people have no ear for music," was Pete's come-back.

He reached for his teeth. Not finding them and seeing Butcher rolling his tongue, he shouted, "Well I be jiggered, if that long-eared jack ain't up and swallowed my store teeth. Well, I be damned. I had intended at first to send that money to Sears and Roebuck for a bill of goods, and now I wish I had. There is sure goin' to be an operation on that jackass by some of the army surgeons at Fort Bayard, or my name is not Peter Van Dusen. Did you see him take them? Well, that sure beats the Dutch."

Tom was full of corn juice by this time and burst out, "Pete, they sure set your face off. You reminded me of one of those seals in the circus."

"Move on," roared Pete, "That jack is liable to have stomach trouble. If I wasn't so close to the cabin I'd pull for the fort to-night."

On reaching the cabin, he hauled the saddle from Butcher and turned him into the corral.

"If he is still alive in the morning I'll sure get an early start," he told Tom.

Pete was as good as his word and daybreak found him on his way to Silver City. When he got there he went to the Old Man Corral and gave the burro a good feed. He asked the genial proprietor, Bob Boulware, what would be the best way to save the jack's life.

"Feed him some balls of dough mixed with Holdfast glue and then watch for results," advised Bob with a hearty laugh.

While the burro was eating, Pete bought a fresh supply of corn juice, and began to comfort himself according to his habit. Finally the pair started for the fort. It is not hard to figure out how Pete missed the trail. He reached the town of Hanover about sundown, and hunted up an old friend, known as Billy Quien Sabe. Quien Sabe gave him the glad hand saying, "Pete, me boy, what's the trouble?"

Pete told him of the loss of his teeth.

"Ah me boy, have you nothin' with you to make you forget your trouble?" asked Quien Sabe.

Pete handed him the jug. After taking a long pull he said, "That sure hits the mark. Maybe if Butcher had a dose of it, it would move the teeth. But Peter, me boy, in the morning go up to McKee's and have him turn his xray on the jack. Perhaps if he can see the teeth he may be able to save them with some of his chemicals."

As both Pete and Butcher were fagged out, Quien Sabe pulled off the jack's saddle and turned him into the G.O.S. pasture. "We will now get some supper," he said.

While they were eating Quien Sabe told Pete that Bill George had invented an electrical forceps with a magnetic attachment. "But I am afraid it won't work on false teeth," he ended sadly. They talked and drank, and drank and talked, till the jug was virtually empty. Pete finally came to the conclusion he would trade Butcher off for a gallon of corn juice to Bob S. who ran the Last Chance Saloon in Fierro. Bob was to have the burro meat for his large pet cougar, Teddy by name, that usually lay in his master's saloon. When the burro was cut open and his stomach taken out Pete was to get his false teeth. Quien Sabe promised to do the butchering. In the middle of their planning they fell asleep over their bug juice.

The mayor of Hanover came by the cabin in his rig early the next morning. He called loudly and got no answer, so he entered the cabin. Before rousing the pair he drank what was left in the jug. Both had a mighty thirst when they woke up. Pete got the mayor to haul them to Fierro to wet their throttles. He took his violin with him, but he left Butcher in the corral.

When they had quenched their thirst with a few bowls Pete began to dicker with Bob S. on the value of the burro meat for his cougar. Quien Sabe and the mayor went back to Hanover, but Pete stayed at the Last Chance, and as he still had money, he kept on imbibing red liquor every few minutes. He soon became hilarious. Taking his fiddle which had now but two strings, he offered to give the crowd in the saloon a few chords from Kreisler.

Having ordered drinks for the house, he began to saw away all the tunes he knew, or thought he knew. When he got through he was foolish enough to ask the crowd how they liked the tunes.

"That kind of music would drive an old tomcat loco," laughed a cowboy.

Pete flew off the handle at this remark, and in the end the cowboy broke the fiddle over his head. Pete howled, he cried, and he preached, until finally a deputy took him to the snubbing post. "I'm a wolf," he cried. "Hear me howl." He kept this up for hours, and very few people slept that night. They turned him loose the next morning and by night he was ready for his old game. The citizens wanted him gagged, but the deputies were unwilling to do it.

"I'm no coyote or grey wolf, but I'm a regular lobo. Hear me! Hear me howl!" And every dog in town howled with him.

The third day he was quiet, saying he was on the edge of the jim-jams. He spent most of the day lying alongside the cougar on the floor of the saloon. Pete did not cut any ice with the cougar. Towards evening Teddy became so cross that he had to be chained in the back yard. When it grew dark Pete again took to howling. The deputy snubbed him early, threatening to quirt him if he kept up his noise. But Pete howled louder than any other night. Finally the deputy got ready to gag him. Pete, seeing this, promised if they would give him a bottle and lead him down the canyon a short way he would leave. The deputies gave in and led him quite a distance down the gulch.

The night was dark and cloudy. Pete must have sat down to take a nip and ended with a nap. When he awoke he returned to town like a cat over a back trail. We never learned how he got over the fence, but he did. It must have been after midnight, for no one ever heard or saw him. He ended up in the shed behind the Last Chance. The lion made the best of it and did not bother him. Pete woke up at daylight, face to face with the cougar. He must have crawled close to Teddy to keep warm, for his arms were around the animal. His heart must have been in his mouth, for he left his hat and a drink in the bottle. Coming into the yard just after sunrise, Bob found this evidence. What had become of Pete? Had Teddy eaten him? If so, he must have liked his meal, for he was in good humor and smacking his lips.

Pete went through Hanover aflying, telling Quien Sabe that the town of Fierro "had treated him rough," and thrown him to the cougar to get rid of him. "I'm lightin' out of these parts for good," said he.

Quien Sabe told him the burro had died, and that he and the mayor of Hanover had cut open his stomach and found in it a queer ball of stuff that looked like resin.

"But Peter, me boy," he said, "have a pull at this mescal; it will revive your spirits."

Quien Sabe must have made a good trade on that burro, for he had mescal for three months, and poor old Pete was never any the wiser.

The next spring Bob sold his pet cougar to Sells Brothers' Circus. When the circus tents were pitched in Deming, Teddy found himself in a cage close to the main entrance. Pete got into town the same day. Following the circus-going crowds, he bought a ticket. What a surprise! At the first cage he came face to face with Teddy. The cougar rolled its eyes and seemed in great glee, trying very hard to reach his former bedfellow. Pete gazed at him.

"I feel sorry for you old pal, you're sure a friendly brute, but I am leavin' this town pronto. No more Daniel in the Lions' Den for Peter Van Dusen. I was tempted to get on a high lonesome and do some howlin' to-night. But seein' you, Teddy, I'm cured! I bid this town *adios*. Good-by old sleepin' mate. I am hittin' the trail for the west. *Adios, companero. No mas tigre* for me."

The last I heard of Pete, he was hunting for the Lost Dutch Oven diggings, somewhere near Mojave, California.

ONE OF THE DANGERS OF THE TRAIL

The Apache Passes By

1. *Silver City Punishes Marauders*

ABOUT the year 1870 wandering tribes of Apaches in southwestern New Mexico hit the trail intending to drive out the miners and prospectors who had come into their mountain fastnesses. Not satisfied with attacking lone prospectors and burning their cabins, they went to the very edge of the towns, often driving away the cattle and horses that grazed within a few hundred yards of the settlements.

Silver City, a small town among the foothills of the Mimbres Range, became a rendezvous for the Indians. In those days it was not safe for anyone to venture outside the town limits unless he was well armed. The stretch of country lying between Silver City and Fort Bayard was just right for the kind of warfare used by the Indians. They knew how to hide their half-naked bodies with the cunning of lizards, snakes, and other desert varmint. They hid among the oak, juniper, and pinon trees; they crept from rock to rock; they crawled like snakes from one bunch of sacatone to another; they even took on the shape of the yucca plants where they were hiding.

The settlers resolved to teach the Indians a needed lesson when they got so daring as to break into the corral where the stock had been rounded up for safety. The Indians drove off all the animals in the middle of the night. With a rawhide lariat the Indians sawed a hole in the adobe wall of the corral big enough to let out a horse. In order to speed up the sawing one Indian poured a steady stream of water on the wall, while two others drew the lariat back and forth.

The next day a meeting was held in the town to decide what punishment should be given the thieves. It was planned to follow them into their winter camp among the San Francisco Mountains near Clifton, Arizona, and to show them no mercy. John Bullard, one of the founders of Silver City, a man loved for his bravery and kindness, was elected the leader of the party. Sam Eckles, Ed Moulton, Amos Clark, Jason Baxter, and a dozen other famous Indian fighters made up the little company.

The trail led along Bear Creek from Pinos Altos, westward to the Gila River through rough mountains, up Duck Creek Valley, across Cactus Flats, over the divide, and on to the Gila Hot Springs, where the party stopped the second night out from Silver City. The next morning they headed up the West Fork of the Gila for a high peak in the Frisco Range. Snow had begun to fall, and it was hard to see the tracks on the trail. All of a sudden the leaders wheeled about and signaled for John Bullard. They had sighted the Indians' camp. Within five minutes Bullard had divided his company into three groups—one to guard the pack train, a second to attack the camp from the south end, and a third to attack from the north.

The Indians, taken by surprise, dropped like pine cones in a high wind. In a few minutes fourteen red men were stretched in the snow. Bullard went forward to help strip them of their arms. As he stooped over a wounded sub-chief the Indian grabbed Bullard's gun from his holster. Bullard called for help, and three guns went off at once—Clark's, Moulton's, and the Indian's. The Indian fell back with the top of his head blown off; Bullard staggered and sank to the ground. Tearing open his shirt he gazed at the bleeding wound in his chest and then fell back without a word.

His sorrowful comrades made a litter which they fastened to the saddles between two gentle horses. In this manner they made their way back to the Hot Springs. At the Hot Springs the company waited until Clark and Moulton could bring a wagon from Silver City. They made the trip in two days, but how they did it was a mystery. Bullard's body was lifted into the wagon; it was a sad party that headed back to Silver City, where Bullard was buried with military honors.

The day after the fight a cowboy who was looking for stray horses passed the battlefield. Hearing the cry of a child he looked about in the brush and soon came upon a dead squaw with a child still hanging to her back. How it had lived through the night was a mystery. It was the only Indian that had missed death at the hands of Bullard's men. In keeping with the bitter saying of the times that "nits make lice" the whites had spared no one in the Indian camp. Patton, the cowboy, felt sorry for the nino and took it to Silver City where he gave it to a man named Benevides. But it had the blood of a savage in its veins. It is said that a few years later Mrs. Benevides left the Indian lad to rock the baby while she did some work in another room. When she returned she found the boy with an ax raised, ready to crush the head of the babe. Benevides had some of the Army officers take the boy to the San Carlos Reservation. It was an incident that helped to increase bad feeling towards the Indians.

2. *Victorio*

When the Bosque Redondo was abandoned in 1868 the Chiricahua Indians were moved to Ojo Caliente in Grant County near the north end of the Black Range. In spite of the watchfulness of reservation officials small bands of marauders at times slipped away from the reservation carrying death and ruin to lone prospectors and ranchers. For this reason settlers complained to the Government, asking that the Indians be moved to the San Carlos Reservation in Arizona. Against the wishes of the Indians and the advice of Army officers the Government ordered the change to be made. Under military guard, the unhappy Indians were marched to the San Carlos Reservation under the command of General Howard, who had lost an arm in the battle of Gettysburg.

It happened that I was in camp near the trail the Indians passed over. They spent a night in the old Catholic cemetery of Silver City. They were a sad group, leg-weary, cold, and half-naked. Victorio's son, a lad about seventeen years of age, could speak English very well. He told me that his people did not want to move from Ojo Caliente. "The old braves and the squaws, they like not this change."

Victorio, one of the greatest Indian warriors of the Southwest in the long war with the white man, was the leader of the Chiricahuas at the time of the removal to San Carlos. Brooding over the wrongs of his people, he fled twice from the San Carlos Reservation, only to be driven back by the militia. In April, 1879, he again skipped out, this time from the Fort Stanton Reservation where he had taken refuge several months before. With less than thirty Mescaleros he headed for Ojo Caliente, killed six of Captain Hooker's men at that post, and lit out with forty-five horses. One morning soon afterwards a hundred and fifty Chiricahuas were missing from the San Carlos Reservation. They had joined Victorio, who had come to the conclusion never to give up.

At that time Victorio was a lean, medium-sized Indian past fifty years of age, easy to pick out among his warriors on his fine big horse. With his small band of bucks Victorio proved a real enemy to the powerful nation he was fighting against.

At times he directed the movements of three hundred warriors, and though the American forces often outnumbered him ten to one, he always made a getaway. One time Colonel Buel with a thousand cavalry and three hundred Indian scouts pressing him from the north, Colonel Carr with six hundred cavalry on the west, and General Grierson with the 10th Cavalry on the east, after hard fighting, only drove him into the fastnesses of the Sierra Madres, where he was willing to go anyway. Victorio was assisted by the wily chiefs, Nana, Loco, and Chappo.

It is claimed that Victorio vowed to wipe out the settlers in the San Francisco Valley to avenge the death of Toribio, his son-in-law, who was killed by a party from Alma. In 1878 several families staked their claims on the Frisco River and built their cabins close together for safety. They were a group of earnest pioneers and soon had the fields plowed and seeded. The Indians watched the little settlement but did not bother anyone for many months. One day, however, Keller, a member of the new community, returned to his ranch to find five head of cattle slashed to pieces. Getting several of his neighbors to go with him, he set out to punish the marauders.

Tying a horse to a tree along the Indian trail in order to trap the raiders, the five white men hid in the brush. Supposing the horse to belong to a lone owner, the Indians tried to untie him. The five white men opened fire, and Toribio was one of the three Indians who dropped dead.

The last Indian war in the Southwest was opened shortly after this in 1879 and closed with the capture of Geronimo in Skeleton Canyon, Arizona, in 1886. During this time of bloodshed and terror, the lives of three hundred Mexicans and of more than two hundred American citizens were taken by the Indians.

With the troops hot on his trail, Victorio, daring and desperate, would stop to kill, to rape, and to burn. Countless wagon trains, mining camps, ranches, and isolated cabins were left in ruins by his marauders. Millions of dollars were spent by the Government trying to capture this wily chief and his bucks.

Though thousands of Apaches stayed peacefully on their reservations, they shared the hatred of the whites. Virtually all the settlers agreed with the old Mexican saying that "the only good Indian is a dead Indian."

3. *Dust*

August 21, 1881, word reached Hillsboro that the Indians were in the vicinity. Captain Schmitt, in charge of a negro troop, was hot on their trail. The trail led south to the Rio Grande River, which the Indians expected to ford near the border, but owing to high water they were forced to turn back. Striking north into the mountains, they followed the Palomas Creek for awhile, then veered west, and crossed the Animas River at the spot since bridged for the Hillsboro wagon road. About noon they reached the placer region.

George Wells had a gang of thirty men at work in Flap Jack Gulch. Some of them had moved their families into tents on a mesa about a half a mile south of the gulch, where the town of Gold Dust now stands. As the heliograph was not yet in use by the Government no one at the placers knew that the Indians were out.

However, everyone knew enough to keep on the lookout for clouds of dust, even in times of peace. It might be a sand spout twisting along before the wind; it might be the dust of a herd of cattle or sheep; but it could be the dust of a band of marauders.

So, when the women and children resting in the shade of the tents saw a cloud of dust loom into sight on the horizon and roll steadily nearer, they were filled with alarm. Mrs. Allen, calmer than the rest, hustled everyone into the tents, saw that the flaps were tied shut, and got the terrified women and children to lie flat on the ground.

In a few minutes the air was full of Apache yells, and the warriors galloped by, fairly riddling the upper part of the tent with bullets. Luckily the Indians did not dismount. Hearing the shots and the yells, the miners grabbed their rifles and rushed up from the gulch. As they ran like mad across the mesa in the direction of the tents they sighted the Indians on the crest of a ridge near Hillsboro and fully expected to find their families murdered or captured. When they unfastened the tent flaps they found everyone safe, though still as white as sheets from the scare they had had.

4. *Victorio Punishes a Liar*

The Indians took a trail going east, making their next stop at the Trujillo ranch about five miles south of Hillsboro on the road to Lake Valley. Trujillo, a half-breed, had been suspected of furnishing the Indians with arms and ammunition, for the raiders had never bothered his stock when they were out and were known to have stopped at his ranch off and on. Trujillo was the father of twin lads about fifteen years of age. Their chum was Homer Tarbill, a boy from Hillsboro who spent a lot of his time at the Trujillo ranch.

The boys had just got back from Hillsboro with their chum. Having unsaddled their horses, they were leaving the corrals, when Victorio rode into the yard with nearly ninety braves. The boys stood in a huddle staring at the great chief and his half-naked braves while Victorio spoke to their mother. In a few minutes Trujillo came in sight driving a herd of fat steers. When he saw the Indians he turned pale.

Victorio spoke to Trujillo, asking him if he had seen any troops that day and seemed pleased to get no for an answer. Some of Victorio's bucks rode forward and headed the cattle into the corral with the horses, sizing them up with knowing looks at one another. The wife invited Victorio to have dinner with the family, but he did not answer her. Trujillo did not say anything, for he had heard that morning that the Indians were again on the warpath. In the meantime the boys had disappeared behind the house.

"Call your sons," ordered Victorio. When the boys came back the chief pointed to Homer Tarbill, saying, "He not your son!"

"Yes! Yes! He is my son," lied the frightened woman, thinking to save the boy's life.

"You lie!" shouted Victorio. Rushing towards the poor woman, he grabbed her by the hair and boxed her ears right and left, before Trujillo could come between them.

Victorio then spoke to a buck who grabbed Homer and stripped him of all his duds. Several other bucks, at Victorio's bidding, cut some long switches from the willow trees growing beside the Trujillo Creek.

"We now have a race to Hillsboro," said Victorio, and the bucks shouted with glee.

Homer was allowed a start of fifty yards before the bucks set off behind him with their switches. For three miles the terrified lad kept ahead of the bucks, but finally they caught up with him. During the last two miles of the race the Indians slashed the poor boy with their switches, running him to the edge of the town of Hillsboro. On the hill where the courthouse now stands the bucks wheeled about and fled back over the trail the way they had come. Homer ran into town, stark-naked and streaming with blood. In front of Perrault and Galles' store he fell in a swoon.

After Homer Tarbill had been run off, Victorio ordered his bucks to ham-string several of Trujillo's fat steers. Then they loaded a few of the hind quarters on Trujillo's best horses and rode off. Victorio had punished a lie, but he had also cleared the Trujillo family of suspicion among their neighbors.

Homer Tarbill got well. He afterwards lived on the Mimbres and Sapello Rivers. For many years he was sheriff at Dwyer. During Geronimo's uprising in 1885, Tarbill again got away with his life by riding his horse over a steep cliff in the Gila country.

5. *Victorio Punishes Two Drunkards*

After leaving the Trujillo ranch, Victorio and his braves followed the wagon road leading to Lake Valley. At Tierra Blanca Creek they came upon two men asleep in the brush, with partly-filled bottles lying beside them. Picking up the bottles, Victorio smashed them against a rock. The miners woke up at the sound of the splintering glass and reached for their guns, only to see them pointed towards them in the hands of two of the bucks.

"Kill them!" shouted the bucks.

"No," exclaimed Victorio, "let them live. Drunkards are the white man's scourge."

Then he ordered his warriors to take turns kicking the two men along the road. For over a mile the bucks amused themselves in this way. Finally the miners were all fagged out and lay down in the middle of the road, refusing to go another step. The Indians kicked them till they were senseless, and rode on. Victorio's punishment kept the two miners on the water wagon for four or five months at least.

6. *Gavilan Canyon*

The Apaches kept on towards Lake Valley, but Victorio and the main band soon struck off to the right in the direction of Gavilan Canyon. Five or six bucks, headed by Nana, a squaw among the number, pushed on towards Lake Valley. Irwin's ranch was about three miles above the town on the Lake Valley road. Irwin was out rounding up his cattle. When his wife Sally saw the big cloud of dust she picked up her child and hid in the brush. As soon as she saw by the dust that the Indians were bearing off towards Gavilan Canyon she went back to the house, leaving the door open. All of a sudden Nana stood in the doorway with his bucks right behind him. Sally had the child in her arms. Nana grabbed it and was about to dash its brains out when Sally cried out in Spanish, "Don't kill my child, and I'll make you a fine present of a twenty-dollar gold piece and some gewgaws."

"Bueno!" said Nana, handing back the child.

Sally led the Indians into the front room and opened the trunk, saying "The gold piece is in the bottom of the trunk." The eyes of the Indians almost popped out of their heads at sight of the bright ribbons and ornaments. Nana, the squaw, and the rest were soon taken up with the finery and bent over the trunk, forgetting all about Sally. The instant she saw this, she hastened out of the house and again hid in the near-by brush.

After the Indians had found the gold piece they ransacked the house. Then they set fire to it. Sally saw them going towards Gavilan Canyon, but she was afraid to go back to the house. Irwin seeing the dust and the smoke of the burning house felt sure it was Indians and made off like the wind for his home. First he put out the fire, and then he searched the brush, but he could not find Sally. Believing the Indians had taken her away, he rode into Lake Valley. In the meantime Sally herself headed for Lake Valley with the child. Irwin was almost crazed and accused Schmitt and Daly of hanging around the town while people were being massacred. While he was talking Sally came into town footsore and weary.

In Lake Valley Irwin had found a big crowd of excited men. Captain Schmitt was there with part of the 10th Regiment, made up of both negroes and whites; a posse of citizens had arrived from Hillsboro under J. B. McPhearson; Superintendent Daly of the Lake Valley Mining Company and twenty-five men, had reported armed and mounted.

Many of these men were gathered at Cotton's saloon, and most of them were half-seas-over. Daly accused Schmitt of not trying to find the Indians, and hot words flew between the pair. The arrival of a scout with word that the Indians had gone into Gavilan Canyon put an end to the dispute.

Gavilan Canyon is rough and narrow. A wagon road led through it connecting the Mimbres settlement with Lake Valley. It was an ideal spot for an ambush. Daly and Schmitt started for their horses, and soon a hundred men were on their way to the canyon. Following the troops was a string of pack animals heavily loaded with pans, kettles, bedding, ammunition, and other supplies. It was a disorderly mob that straggled along the trail, not an organized army. Some of the men were so much the worse for tarantula juice they could hardly keep their saddles. As they rode along a few of the old timers came up to Daly and Schmitt, begging them to send scouts ahead into the canyon, but no heed was taken of the warning.

Superintendent Daly and Captain Schmitt rode straight into the ambush laid for them by the wily Indians. All of a sudden came the crack of rifles, and the two leaders fell dead. In the volley of shots that followed, four troopers were killed and several wounded. A fight took place in the narrow canyon. Although equally matched in numbers, it was a one-sided affair, for the Apaches had the better position, ambushed as they were on both sides of the canyon. Besides, many of the whites were tenderfeet with no experience whatever in Indian warfare. Most of the men deserted their horses and hid among the rocks. Some of those in the rear got away on their horses into the open. Others had their horses shot from under them. John Deemer, wounded when his horse fell, got away by leaping behind another rider. Their flight was so swift that a bullet passed through Deemer's streaming coat without touching his body. The pack animals, deserted by their drivers, caused a blockade in the canyon. Soon the mules, screaming and kicking, were all killed by the Indians.

The coming of fresh troops from Lake Valley under General Hatch was all that saved the lives of the men hidden among the rocks. Warned by their scouts of the coming of more troops, the Apaches split into small bands and lit out across the border. They took with them all of the horses of the party from Lake Valley.

After more than fifty years, bones, cots, camp kettles, and canteens can still be found in Gavilan Canyon.

7. *The New Shovel*

Jim Blaine came to the conclusion that he needed a new shovel, so he climbed out of his ten-foot hole and struck out for Hillsboro to buy one. Jim was a regular old desert rat and the ten-foot hole was a prospect shaft that he had sunk near the placers on the Animas River. He found the town of Hillsboro full of excitement.

Victorio with his marauding Apaches was reported in the neighborhood.

Jim went about his business as cool as a cucumber. Though he had a hard time getting a clerk to wait on him, he finally got a long-handled shovel with a shiny new blade and headed back to his diggings.

The next day he got along fine in the prospect hole, and a big cloud of dust rose like smoke above the opening where he was at work. In the late afternoon he straightened up to rest a bit and take note of the amount of rock and gravel he had moved with the new shovel. His quick ear caught the clatter of horses' hoofs. In a twinkling he climbed up the notched pole and peered across the flat.

Racing in the direction of his hole was a band of Indians, attracted, no doubt, by the cloud of dust above it. Jim had no weapon at hand, but he reached down and picked up the long-handled shiny shovel. The Apaches were now near enough to see Jim's head and shoulders above the prospect hole. With a bloodcurdling war whoop they came on. Jim threw his shovel over his shoulder, with the blade resting against his neck in perfect firing position. The Indians halted instantly, stared, and fled.

In an instant Jim clambered out of the hole and started on a dead run for his dug-out where he had left his gun. The Indians discovering him in flight, turned to run him down. Again Jim threw his shovel to his shoulder, ready to fire. The Indians apparently came to the conclusion that they were faced by a new kind of rifle and gave up the chase. They rode off without again looking back.

In a few minutes Jim got to his dug-out, where he was safe, as it was surrounded by a rock barricade and he had plenty of ammunition. The Indians did not bother him. The new shovel had made him the winner.

8. *A Georgetown Scare*

The placers near Hillsboro later closed down, because the Indians were always in the vicinity. Most of the miners went across the Black Range to Georgetown, which was still booming, in spite of the rumors that flew about. It was reported that the Indians had attacked Silver City and other near-by towns.

Everyone in Georgetown went about well-armed. Some carried

Winchesters; others packed six-shooters with two belts of cartridges and a long knife. No one took time to shave or to wash up, too afraid of being caught in the act. At the end of a month of this fear the men of Georgetown had a wild and woolly look.

The ten saloons of Georgetown were crowded all night, and every chair at the twenty gaming tables was in use, though it cost more than the best seat at a horse race. As the mines were running full blast and full time the town was virtually deserted during the day.

Some time after the arrival of the Hillsboro refugees a badly frightened goat herder dashed into town saying he had seen fifty Indians in the near-by brush close to the graveyard. The town went mad with excitement. Business was at a standstill. Stores, saloons, and all public houses were quickly locked and even barricaded. A crowd of Georgetown men forced the trembling goat herder to lead them to the spot where he had seen the Indians. Hardly had they reached the place when John Bragaw shouted, "There they are!" Instantly lifting their guns to their shoulders, the miners peered into the woods, but they could see nothing.

Sig Lindauer, for many years a well-known merchant in southern New Mexico, lifted his double-barreled shot gun, which was loaded for bear. In his excitement, instead of touching the trigger he threw his hand on the lever, forcing out both cartridges. "Vell! Vell! Vot kind of a goose gun is this?" he shouted. "Give me that six-shooter, Helde. I'm not used to this damn blunderbuss."

By the time they had traded guns the goat herder had disappeared, making his getaway during the commotion. It then dawned on the posse that it was a false alarm. The "Indians" had been all in the eye of the timid herder.

I expect that when *Sig Lindauer reads this account he will invite me to Sunday dinner, so he can explain once more over a bottle of *cerveza* how he made that mistake with the gun. I have known Sig Lindauer for 56 years. Sig came into this section during the diamond boom in 1872. He soon discovered it was a fake and went to some of his friends at Clifton, Arizona, who owned a big copper mine and wholesale store there. He got in with them, and thereafter was one of the finest merchants of the Southwest. No old sourdough or desert rat ever leaves his store empty-handed.

*Sig Lindauer has crossed his last divide since I set down the above.

9. *Victorio Camps in the Floridas*

In 1882 Victorio and his warriors, driven into Chihuahua by General Hatch, had another streak of hard luck. Terrazas, the governor of Chihuahua at the time, was virtually its king. He owned hundreds of acres of land and thousands of cattle and sheep. His land was patrolled by his well-trained bands of Tornichia and Yaqui Indians. Equipped with the latest rifles, these fearless riders drove off the thieves and killed the wild animals that infested the country. They were trailing the Apaches at all times, and the Indians had no chance to run down the cattle and sheep that had replaced the deer and other game in their old haunts. All the water holes were well watched by Terrazas' men, and the Indians had a hard time to get water.

Notified by his rurales of the return of Victorio, Terrazas called the chief to his headquarters near Ascension and warned him not to bother his patrols nor to steal his cattle, saying that any Apache caught among his flocks would be killed on the spot. Victorio promised to leave the grassy foothills at once. The squaws wanted him to go back to the United States and be moved to the San Carlos Reservation. For awhile the chief thought of doing so, but the young bucks of the tribe were against it, so he finally led his people into the High Sierras.

It was still warm in the foothills, but the High Sierras were covered with snow. For a few weeks, though, the Indians still found plenty of game and water; then in late September a blizzard drove them again into the foothills. Game, wood, and water being scarce, it was but a short time till the hungry Apaches were filling up on beef.

Again Victorio and his people were ordered to move. Rounding up some of Terrazas' horses, a band of young bucks crossed the border into the United States. A few days later two of Victorio's favorite bucks were found shot to death under a juniper tree, and the war was on. In a blinding snowstorm Victorio and his people were again driven into the High Sierras. To remain there meant starvation, and he decided to return to the United States.

Meanwhile the prospectors in New Mexico came to the conclusion that the Indians would stay in Old Mexico, perhaps never to return, and they scattered again among the mountains. It was believed that Victorio and his bucks would be wiped out by the rurales of Terrazas, for Terrazas believed that "nits make lice," and his men never took a prisoner. But in order to be on the safe side, the prospectors generally traveled in groups numbering from fifteen to twenty-five men. A train of horses, mules, and burros carried supplies and bedding for the group. Every man in the outfit promised to obey the leader chosen before setting forth.

Rumor had it in Pinos Altos that rich float had of late been picked up in the Florida Mountains, about fifteen miles south of Deming in what is now Luna County. At a distance they look like a large battleship with its smokestacks and turrets. They were named by the early Spaniards on account of the flora in their small parks. The north side can be approached by low ridges and hogbacks covered with scrubby brush, but the south side is very steep, and the ridges are like knife blades, their sides being almost impossible to climb. It is said that at one time there were many mountain goats in these rough mountains, but a few black-tail deer and an occasional stray antelope seem to be the only game in them now. Water is scarce, and these mountains have never been very well settled. Only a few goat ranches are on them now.

Some mining has been done, but most of the ores are base of a very low grade, complex ores of lead and zinc. Like most isolated mountains of the Southwest the Floridas seem to be what is left of a long-past extinct volcano. They are cut with ribbons, or faultings, of limes and shales, and have high buttes of hard porphyry. Through erosion the long pipes or what look like smoke-stacks have been left standing high above the rest of the formation. At the far east end there is a low hogback called the Little Floridas. Here has been found one of the largest deposits of manganese of iron in the United States. This has been mined for years at a profit, but on account of the depression, high freights, and low tariffs, the mine is now closed.

As far as I know, these mountains have no historical past. A few small caves exist which show that some early race lived in them. The mountains are rugged and bleak, but at a distance, especially in the early morning and evening, they take on colors that would shame a rainbow, this being brought about by the rays of the sun passing through the film of dust that covers them. No one who has seen these blue mountains of the south will ever forget them.

Many people visit the Floridas to see the perfect bow and arrow in nature at the east end of the mountains. The rocks that form it are about seventy-five feet from one end of the arc to the other and the arrow crossing to the center of the arc is about thirty feet across.

But the seventeen prospectors who met in the Bell and Stevens' store in Pinos Altos were not taken up with the beauty of the Florida Mountains but with their formation, which was turned topsy-turvy by volcanic action in past centuries, large sections of the mountains being composed of malpais. The western end of the mountains is solid granite, and close under the peaks they are cut with veins of silver and gold.

Among the well-known sharpshooters in the group bound for the Floridas under Jason Baxter were John Adair, Frank Bell, Lon Ironton, and William Coleman, Each of them carried a 45-90, a Sharp's rifle, or buffalo gun of such long range that a bullet from it hitting a vital spot in a victim a mile off meant certain death.

It so happened that Jason Baxter and his band of prospectors, having crossed the plains from Faywood Hot Springs, went into dry camp in the Florida Mountains at the point known as Capitol Dome the same evening that Victorio and his bucks pitched camp at Bear Spring in these mountains. Between Capitol Dome and Bear Spring is a pass about a mile and a half wide; each camp was unknown to the other.

The prospectors were up at dawn, cooking their breakfast and changing their animals to new bunches of grass. Having emptied their canteens into the kegs for their stock, they struck out for Bear Spring to get a fresh supply for the day with Baxter leading the way through a heavy fog. In no mood for talk at that early hour, the prospectors passed as silent as the grave over the divide and down the southern slope. The spring lies in a cove, well-hidden from view, until the opening is reached. The bucks were cooking their breakfast when Baxter went into the cove.

"Indians!" he shouted. "Run, boys, run!"

The prospectors needed no second warning but ran pell-mell for a reef of rocks about four hundred yards above the cove. The first ones had reached the rocks before the Indians opened fire. One of the prospectors dropped dead and two others fell wounded in the volley of shots. The prospectors cracked down their man every time they fired, and the Indians soon dropped back under cover. They seemed to know they were up against a band of men who wasted no shot. One of the wounded prospectors then got up and ran for the shelter of the rocks, but the other one lost his nerve and lay where he had fallen, shouting and crying.

Again and again his comrades begged him to get up and run, but he only wept harder than ever. Realizing that this would have a bad effect on his men, Baxter leaped from behind the rocks and rushed to the fallen man, who had become the target for every hidden Indian. Throwing him over his shoulder Baxter fled back to the rock protection through a shower of bullets. The prospectors were on the alert. Zip! A bullet spit dirt a few feet ahead of Victorio's white horse. Zip! A second bullet from Coleman's rifle raised the dust a few feet to the rear of Victorio's horse.

The chief wheeled and galloped off, not stopping till he reached the mesa nearly a mile away. A lull followed his flight, and the prospectors made the most of it to throw up a barricade of the loose rocks lying about. The ledge where the prospectors were gathered had its good points, for it lay under an overhanging cliff. Victorio in the meantime returned and took up his position on a ridge where he could watch the movements of both parties. Most of his ninety warriors stayed in ambush, but a few gathered around him to get orders. It was soon plain that one group had orders to enfilade, or rake lengthwise with shot, the ledge where the prospectors were crowded.

Two bucks climbed up above the ledge and crawled forward on their bellies like snakes, so the prospectors could not see them. All of a sudden one of these Indians leaned over the cliff and fired his gun, injuring a prospector in the foot. Almost at the same instant the Indian who had fired the shot rolled off the cliff in plain sight of every hidden Indian, hit by a prospector's ball, his arms and legs working like a spider's as he dropped into the gulch below. The Indians who were getting ready to enfilade disappeared like the mist that had clouded the peaks.

The sun had grown hot, and the prospectors were suffering with thirst, but Baxter would not let anyone leave the ledge for water, as he felt sure the Indians would soon make their getaway. Though Victorio kept at them, the bucks stopped firing. They seemed to be afraid of the dead shots.

About four-thirty in the afternoon Baxter suggested to Coleman that they both raise the sights on their long-range guns and aim for Victorio and his horse. Two rifles cracked at the same instant. The white horse reared on his hind legs and plunged forward dead. Terror took hold of the bucks and they fled in every direction.

Not long afterwards a group of Indians was seen going south carrying a wounded man on a horse. The great white horse lay where he had fallen. A second band of Indians was sighted near the Little Floridas. The prospectors who were not wounded now went across the ridge for their horses, which luckily had not been found by the Indians. Some of the men watered the animals, while others dug a hole in which to bury the dead prospector.

At sunset the prospectors hurriedly gathered with uncovered heads while the body of their comrade was lowered into his high and lonely grave. A pile of rocks was heaped on the shallow grave to get ahead of the coyotes that were already howling on the hill below. A young prospector, much moved by the scenes of this terrible day, pulled up a clump of blue daisies in a sheltered nook and laid it on the pile of stones.

Four men, none of them badly hurt, were helped into their saddles, and the party headed for Fort Cummings thirty-five miles northeast. Soon the plain was white with moonlight. At the point where Florida Station now stands the prospectors, looking northeast towards the Macho saw the band of Indians moving slowly, for they had many wounded. About midnight the prospectors reached the fort, and the Army surgeon dressed the wounds of the injured men. A troop of cavalry was ordered out at once to follow the band of Indians going north. The bucks quickly discovered they were being followed, and scattered like quail through the Black Range. During the next two months they kept coming in, a few at a time, to the San Carlos Reservation to give up. Many were suffering from their wounds, and two had been been buried in Victorio's Park above Kingston. It was reported at the post that eight Indians had been killed in the Florida fight and ten wounded. Eventually some of the squaws left behind in Mexico came back to the reservation. According to them, all the bucks who went south after the Florida fight, were killed shortly afterwards in a battle with the Mexican rurales at Tres Castillos. The Mexican and American soldiers, by a special arrangement between their governments, had, during this period, the right to cross the border at any time without passports in pursuit of marauding Apaches. Mexican troops returning into their own country at Tres Castillos came upon a Chiricahua camp numbering about four hundred women and children and a hundred warriors.

The battle began instantly and lasted all night. The Indians hidden among the rocks kept up the firing until daybreak. The Mexicans claim to have seen Victorio on a ridge directing his warriors. A little later he dropped dead, shot through the heart, and his people soon gave up. A number of squaws and children were killed during this fight.

The squaws who told the story at San Carlos had a different tale about the death of their great chief. Victorio had been wounded, they said, in the fight with the Florida prospectors. He was taken south in the hope that his squaw whom he had left in the Sierra Madres could nurse him back to health. At Palomas Lake where they stopped to rest, Victorio died, and they buried him at the south end of the lake. One of the sub-chiefs had taken Victorio's war trophies, and it was he who had been killed at Tres Castillos.

A few years after the battle of Tres Castillos I was prospecting with Baxter in the White Mountains of Arizona. The Apaches for the time being were at peace with the whites. Baxter knew several Indian dialects and could talk freely with the Indians we met. One day two young bucks came to our camp. We fed them and gave them a good supply of tobacco. As they belonged to the Chiricahua tribe from which Victorio also came, Baxter asked them where their great chief had been killed, and by whom. They said the squaws claimed he had got a death wound from some prospectors in the Florida Mountains, and that he was buried at the south end of Palomas Lake near the border. I have always thought Baxter made a bad break when he told them he was in that fight. Though they still acted friendly I took note that they looked him over from head to foot. When these bucks later fled from the reservation with Geronimo, Baxter was one of their first victims, as I related in the tale called Lost Canyon Diggings.

Whether Victorio was killed by the prospectors in the Florida Mountains in the United States, or met his death at the hands of the Mexicans at Tres Castillos, would be a point worth looking into among the descendants of the squaws mentioned. At any rate it is certain that Victorio was never again seen in the United States after the Florida fight.

During the World War I went with some officers from the Deming encampment on a trip to the Florida Mountains. The rocks thrown up by the prospectors for their protection were still standing on the ledge. Goat herders used them at times when rounding up their flocks, and they often took shelter there during bad weather.

10. *The Apaches Go to Kingston*

After the depredations of May and June, 1885, Geronimo and his band fled into Mexico. The sections around Silver City, Lake Valley, and Kingston little by little put aside the fear that had brought business to a standstill. General Crook, however, thought it best to be prepared for still more trouble and asked for more troops. Lieutenant Pershing, later the leader of the American troops in the World War, with a sergeant of the signal corps from Fort Sumner, was making experiments with the heliograph at Fort Bayard.

The heliograph saved many lives in the Southwest and thousands of dollars to the United States Government in the days before telegraph lines had been strung over the mountains. In heliographing, sunlight is flashed by mirrors to stations at different points, often a hundred miles away. Many people learned enough of the code in use by Army officials to pick up the danger signals by counting the flashes.

One day in September, 1885, when most people had come to the conclusion that the Apaches would stay in Mexico, a flash was sent by Lieutenant Gatewood, stationed close to the national boundary line, that a band from the Sierra Madres had crossed the border. General Crook ordered flashes sent out to warn the settlers. Hardly had the word been flashed when news came from Lake Valley that a man had been murdered by the Apaches on Berenda Creek. Fort Cummings flashed Kingston and Hillsboro that two bands were headed that way. Riders were sent post haste to outlying mines and ranches to bring in women and children to the nearest posts and towns.

By the time the flashes had been read and the news sent out, it was nearing sundown. Tom Paige, who had a contract to furnish wood for the Kingston smelter, knew nothing of the recent alarm. The section where Paige cut this wood was about two miles east of town near Toppy Johnson's slaughter house. As his day's work was ended, Paige loaded the wood on his wagon and hitched up his mules. When he turned to climb into his wagon seat he noticed that one of the lead mules showed excitement, looking off towards the south. Gazing in that direction, Paige saw at least ten Indian bucks dashing toward him on their fast buckskin ponies. Not more than five hundred yards were between him and certain death. In a jiffy he unhitched a mule and leaped to its back. Away he went! By this time the Indians had opened fire and Paige fled along the trail in a shower of bullets.

Paige pulled his rifle from the scabbard, but the mule was going so fast, it was not until he reached the main road that he dared to turn and fire at the Indians. After reaching a bend in the road he saw no more of the Apaches. In a few minutes he galloped into Kingston, shouting, "Indians!" and at every few leaps of the mule he turned and fired.

Kingston was stampeded by the spectacle. The men rushed into the stores and saloons and barricaded the doors with the nearest furniture. But the women ran into the middle of Main Street carrying or dragging their children with them!

Some of the men with cooler heads caught the mule, and Paige told his story. One by one the men came sneaking from the buildings to join the crowd in the street. The women stopped shaking and crying, while the children looked on, still whimpering. In a few minutes the bugle sounded the call for the militia, but in the thick dusk of a mountain evening it was out of the question to do anything until the next morning. Word was sent to Hillsboro, however, and Captain Fechet with a detachment of cavalry galloped over to Kingston to encamp for the night and be ready to take the trail early in the morning.

In a day or so Kingston got over the scare and held its sides laughing over some of the strange stories afoot concerning escape from the Apaches.

An Italian as vain as a peacock, a regular dandy, owned a fancy grocery store and bakeshop on Main Street. While standing in his favorite place in front of his show window he saw Paige gallop into town. The shooting and yelling made the excited Italian think that a whole tribe of Apaches was right at his heels. His dignity and his fine clothes were forgotten in a trice. He raced into the back of the bakery and dove headfirst into the open oven. Darkness fell shortly afterwards.

Several hours later Joe Askew and Johnny Roach, seeing the door open and the store in darkness, went in to look about. Moans and groans came from the rear of the store. Striking matches, they made their way to the back room and in the flickering light soon made out two well-shod feet sticking out of the oven. Smothered cries of "Mercy! Mercy!" reached their ears. Each taking a foot, they pulled the frightened Italian from his hiding place. He surely felt cheap when he came face to face with two white men instead of Indians ready to scalp him. He begged them to say nothing about it, giving each one a box of the finest cigars in stock. The two men took the bribe, but the secret was too good to keep. The Italian was a proud fellow and could not laugh off the jibes when the story got around, so he sold out and moved to Colorado.

Another story, which helped the men of Kingston to forget their own foolish part in the general stampede, had to do with a little sawed-off German named Gus who owned some prospects in Saw Pit Gulch and at times came into town to stock up with supplies. He was also fond of his beer. It happened that Gus came into Kingston the day that the Apaches arrived in the neighborhood.

Being very orderly, like most Germans, Gus first bought and paid for his supplies, making arrangements to have them delivered the next day at Saw Pit Gulch. Gus was rather stingy, so he hied him to the brewery where a schooner of beer could be had for a short bit. Planking down a dollar, he began as usual on his first schooner, allowing himself just one more each hour as long as the dollar lasted. He always drank by himself, singing German songs and yodelling to pass away the time between schooners.

On this particular day, according to custom, he set out in the late afternoon for Saw Pit Gulch armed with a bottle of red eye. Word of the Apaches' coming had not yet reached Kingston, but Gus must have had a hunch, for he moved along as silent as the grave, neither singing nor yodelling. His good angel was surely watching over him, for it was learned the next day from the tracks and the time, that the Apaches must have passed Gus on the Saw Pit Trail.

The Apaches' tracks showed that they had followed Paige to the bend in the road; then seeing the danger of following him any further, they had gone back to his wagon, killed the mules, and fired both wagon and cord wood. Afterwards they struck off for Pickett's Spring, where they watered their horses, going from there across a small divide into Saw Pit Gulch.

A number of prospectors' tunnels opened into this gulch along each side. The mouth of one of the tunnels was picked by the

Indians for a camp. A fire was soon built and they sat around it waiting for the stew to get done. At the opposite side of this tunnel Gus came to the conclusion to halt for a swallow of red eye. As he raised the bottle to his lips he looked straight into the eyes of a buck who was standing apart from the circle. Throwing his bottle towards the head of the surprised Indian, the frightened Gus set off at great speed, considering the shortness of his legs and the size of his paunch. In a trice the whole band of bucks was in pursuit. How the stones flew under the feet of the racing German!

He rounded a bend in the gulch with a tunnel at either side. He was sober by this time, though gasping for breath, and he thought quickly. Throwing his hat and his lunch bucket into the tunnel on the right hand side, he scurried like a rabbit into the one on the left. After running a few feet, he stopped to listen. He knew by the sounds the Indians stopped to look into the tunnels. When they found his hat and lunch bucket, they fired several shots into that tunnel, not daring to go into it for fear of being ambushed from a side drift.

Soon the Indians had built another fire. Some of the bucks went back for their horses to their first camp site, and poor Gus knew by that they meant to stay all night at the mouth of the tunnel opposite the one he was in. He dared not move for fear his hiding place would be discovered by the alert Indians. It was a long night full of thought for the stolid German.

At daybreak the Apaches heard the bugle sounding the reveille and scattered quickly over a ridge near the Iron King Mine.

Gus reached Kingston before the troops set out, and told them the direction taken by the Indians. Some of the men wanted Gus to come into the brewery for a drink, but he refused. "Ach! No! Dis Dutchman has joined the temperance gang. No more schooners for little Gus!" No amount of coaxing could break down his resolution. The Apaches had made a sober man of Gus.

Not everyone was as lucky as Gus, for the marauding band cut across the Black Range to the Mimbres River, where they killed a man named Horn and one of John McKim's boys. Two of McKim's sons, aged eleven and fifteen, were herding sheep among the hills. The younger lad was throwing stones into the river and watching the circles ride to the banks when he heard a rifle shot. Whirling about he saw his brother drop dead among the sheep. The frightened lad tried to hide himself in the brush, but the Indians dug him out, and asked how many people were in the near-by cabin. When the bucks heard that the cabin was empty they tied the boy to a pony. They took him along and drove McKim's stock into their stronghold higher up in the Black Range.

Later in the day the sorrowful father found his son's mutilated body. Months later, when Geronimo gave up, the captured lad was returned to his father at Deming. He had almost forgotten how to speak both English and Spanish.

11. *Deming Takes Alarm*

In the fore part of the year 1886 a small band of Apaches left the Sierra Madres to return to their old stamping ground near Kingston. Crossing the border near the Tres Hermanas Mountains they began at once to kill and to destory. A family named Yates lived near Florida Gap, about twenty miles south of Deming. It was Saturday afternoon, and the family had driven in their mountain buckboard to Deming to do some shopping.

Mrs. Yates went to the millinery store owned by a woman named Keeler. There she learned that the Apaches were reported in the vicinity. Mrs. Keeler tried to get her to stay in town until the Apaches had passed by. While the two women were talking Mr. Yates came in. He scoffed at the idea of remaining in town, saying he had never yet "lost an Indian." Late in the afternoon the Yates left Deming; they had almost reached their home when the Apaches rode towards them, firing and yelling. Mr. and Mrs. Yates were both massacred and their mules driven off by the Indians.

The shooting took place not far from the home of the Shy family. Realizing their danger, the Shys barricaded their cabin none too soon, for the Indians raced up. When they could not break into the cabin, they set it afire. As it was dark the Shys made their getaway into the near-by rocks, not, however before their son Larry had been shot in the leg. Mrs. Shy half carried, half dragged the injured lad into hiding. As soon as the Indians had left the vicinity she set out afoot for Deming.

Some distance ahead of her a cowboy loped along on his way to a dance in Deming. He found the bodies of the Yates and raced to town to sound the alarm. Andy Laird, a prominent citizen, wired Governor Ross the news of the raid. Ross wired back to organize a company of militia and to take the field at once. Laird called a meeting at which he was elected captain, Holgate, first lieutenant, and Walt Wilkinson, second lieutenant. About forty men signed up. Among them were Loeffler and Frank Preusser, the latter a scout who knew every water-hole in this section.

As soon as the party was organized they set forth to rescue the Shy family and to bury the Yateses. They met Mrs. Shy on the road. She led them to the place where her husband and son were hiding among the rocks in Florida Gap. A detail went back with the Shy family into Deming. A second detail was sent to bury the bodies of Yates and his wife. Frank Preusser and a gambler named Keel were ordered to warn the miners who were at work in the Florida Mountains at the Silver Cave and Cincinnati mines. They reached the mines at daybreak, but the Indians had not molested them.

After leaving the Shy's cabin in flames, the Indians took the path to the steam pump some distance in the Floridas. A lone woman lived near-by in a cabin. They forced the woman to go to the well and draw up a bucket of water, promising not to hurt her if she did as she was told. When she had drawn up the water they told her to take out a gourdful and drink it. Apparently they were afraid of being poisoned. After the woman had drunk they passed the gourd among them, and rode off without harming her or her cabin.

Not far from this steam pump a company of United States cavalry was located. They had heard the shooting and had seen the Shy's cabin burning, but they did not make any move to help, for at that time no soldier could go against the Indians without orders from Washington. This caused much hard feeling among the settlers in the Southwest. So much had been said and written about the unjust treatment of the Indians by the whites that the sympathy of the people in the eastern United States all went to the Indian, and small heed was given to the prospectors and ranchers who appealed for help.

The marauders headed into the Black Range where they stayed but a few days. In April of that year they surrendered to Lawton and Miles in Skeleton Canyon. Many of them were transported to Florida.

Tales of a Western Judge

1. **The Ways of God*

MINERAL was first found on Cook's Peak in 1876 by Edward Orr, but the discovery did not amount to much until 1882. This well-known mountain, twenty miles north of Deming, lies in the rugged Mimbres Range, which runs north to join the Black Range. For centuries this high mountain, commanding a wide view of the alluvial plains from which it rises, was a favorite haunt of the Apache.

Several springs furnished a good water supply, a fact taken note of by whites as well as Indians, for the old Butterfield trail left a shorter and easier course over the plains to climb the steep side of this granite mountain. From its bare peak at an elevation of 9000 feet the Indian sentinel would take note of distant enemies and send up smoke signals for watching friends.

At the present time Cook's Peak is a weather-man for aviators. If no cloud drifts over the peak the flyer knows the sign to be a good one. When the clouds are whirling about its snowy head this mountain might be called the Matterhorn of southern New Mexico.

As the Indians still went often to the spot in 1882, an escort of soldiers from Fort Cummings was detailed to stay on guard while a road was graded up the main canyon of the mountain. The camp site chosen by George Brooks lay on the divide close to a fine spring. Down this wagon road Brooks in time hauled twenty-seven hundred tons of lead-silver ore.

During the five years after the opening of the first mine on Cook's Peak several million dollars was earned by various mines. At times immense caves were discovered filled with high-grade carbonate of lead, averaging more than fifty per cent lead and four ounces of silver to the ton. After a few years of such production the lead not only dropped in price but became harder to reach; as a result, the owners, about the year 1890, offered long leases with liberal terms.

* Real names are not given in this tale.

Oxide of lead is very dusty and bad for the health of the miner. Though the miner wears a mask, he swallows a lot of the poisonous dust. This sometimes forms a ball in the stomach, and brings on a colic. The lead can only be dissolved by an acid so strong that it often eats away the membrane; the dust also clogs the lungs, at times causing miner's consumption. Now and then a miner is poisoned by his first day of work. For this reason not many miners cared to take up the generous offers made by the owners of the lead mines.

Among those who did get leases was Tim O'Keefe, who took over three claims for a two-year period. Tim lived in a cabin on one of the claims, and though he worked hard, he seemed down on his luck and was making "a side leap at a rind of bacon". In order to make ends meet his wife cooked for a crowd of miners and sometimes kept a boarder or two.

One day Adolph Sweitzer, a German bookkeeper, dragged into the camp, looking for a job. As he could not get work in his own line, he had left his wife and child in Deming and set out with his mind made up to take the first job that came along. Observing that the stranger was down to bed-rock, Tim offered to sub-lease a piece of ground to him. He also supplied the German with tools and ammunition, and offered him credit for room and board until his luck should turn for the better.

Adolph went to work in a tunnel where Tim had already located a low-grade ore. As the tunnel was filled with caves and vugs, it needed little shooting or drilling, a man being able to work the rock with a pick and crowbar. Tim agreed to let Adolph work two weeks to see how he stood the lead dust, before signing a contract.

After a few days the rock got harder, and Adolph hired a Mexican to put down a few holes for him. All of a sudden Adolph's luck turned for the better—he broke into an immense chamber filled with high-grade lead. Little as he knew of mining, he realized it was a rich find. Sending away the Mexican, who had not caught on, Adolph covered the hole with debris and quit work till he could make up his mind what to do next. The almighty dollar was too much for him, for he came to the conclusion to fleece the Irishman who had been his friend on a rainy day.

When Adolph next met Tim he told him he was thinking of going back to Deming, which was true enough. After hanging around for a few more days as though he had lost interest in the mine he again went to Tim, telling him he thought better of the matter and would like to sign the necessary papers to take over the lease.

"How much vill you take to transfer your lease to me? Mine brothers, I think they help me with money ven I go back to Deming."

"I'll transfer my lease to you for five hundred dollars," said Tim, nettled by this change of front, "but I want a hundred dollars down and the balance within six months. And you can put this down too, Adolph—I didn't crowd you to make this step, and you can't blame me if you lose your dough. Everyone around here knows I'm down on my luck."

"It is mine own risk," said the German. "You put down in writing vot you vant me to sign, and ve go today to Judge McKenna. I bring you the hundred dollars ven I come back from Deming."

Adolph not only brought the hundred dollars from Deming, but also his wife and child, his two brothers, and a half dozen miners. Within ten days he was shipping two carloads of rich ore every day, averaging more than a thousand dollars a day in net profit. Tim O'Keefe was kicked out of camp by the German.

In order to keep his mine running, Adolph wormed his way into the good graces of certain sheriffs in neighboring counties; and soon thieves, cutthroats, and outlaws were crossing the counties to Cook's Peak from Old Mexico. The officials were all blind. In the course of a few weeks more than fifty of these men had to be dealt with in Cook's Peak District. Adolph's brothers were soon installed in the store, the saloon, and the dance hall, which had been hastily thrown up with a score of cabins to take care of the newcomers.

By the end of a month Adolph had seventy-five men at work. Instead of paying them by the day he put them to work on a percentage basis, which meant big wages for those who produced ore averaging fifty per cent pure lead, or more, per ton. Many lived in clover, but others worked like slaves on starvation wages, for a knock-down was made in salary for each one per cent of lead yield below the fifty per cent mark.

The dance hall and saloon were kept open day and night, and every week-end was marked by at least one killing. As justice of the peace I had a hot time of it, and my sheriff was always busy. I asked the priest on the Mimbres River to come up and talk to the men, hoping he might be able to do something with them.

After a few visits he gave up, saying they were the hardest lot he had ever met.

There were men working in that camp who had killed a dozen men each, and the women who followed them were just as bad. Amongst the renegades were two powerful Mexicans, leaders in all the cuttings and shootings, whose faces and heads were covered with knife marks. Many a game of twenty-one they broke up if the cards were against them, generally cracking the dealer over the head with a gun. It goes without saying that everyone in camp was well-heeled.

As the time of his lease got shorter, Adolph drove his men harder and harder; I heard many complaints and even threats. Finally I went to the German to warn him, but it was waste of air.

"Plenty more men; if they don't like my vay of doing, let them quit," snapped he.

The miners worked in shifts of ten hours each, the night shift coming off about four o'clock in the morning. The men on this shift ate their lunch around midnight after firing the holes they had drilled. In order to get away from the dust and the bad air following the explosion of the dynamite, they took their lunches to a drift where there was a strong current of air. There they sat filling up on tortillas and jerky, and ripping Adolph up one side and down the other.

Manuel also worked on the night shift, but he was like a sheep among the wolves. He had worked quite a spell for my partner and me, and we were sorry to send him away when the ore vein played out. As Manuel was apparently immune to lead poisoning and as honest as the sun, I put in a good word for him to the German, and he would stand on his head for me.

Manuel lived near my office with his family and often stopped in to give me the camp news or to tell me how the ore body looked. One day when he came in I took note that he was down in the mouth.

"You are worried, Manuel," said I.

"Yes, Judge," said he. "Trouble she is brewing in the mine. They sure are a bunch of hard-boiled hombres that Adolph has brought to Cook's Peak. Soon all the miners strike. I like not the way they talk about the German. Alexandro and Juan—those two with the scars all over their bodies—sit every day to eat their lunch on a shelf under that big ledge of rock that hangs over the drift. They act like kings on their throne, and they sure hate that

Adolph Sweitzer. And all the miners sit around in the drift below them, and they listen to those two killers, and they all the time agree with them. And every night the talk gets worse against the German. He a damn fool not to know he can't drive men like beasts."

Soon after this Manuel stopped coming in to see me. At once I smelt a rat. When he did not come in for several days I sent my partner to look him up and bring him to my office. One glance at his face was enough. I pulled him into the room and locked the door.

"Now Manuel, what's the trouble?"

"Oh, Judge," he groaned, "to-night them devils blow up Adolph Sweitzer and his house and his wife and his child. And if they know I come here they blow me up, too." The poor fellow was shaking like a leaf.

"They will not know you've been here," I told him. "When do they plan to do this devilment?"

"To-night, after they eat their lunch as usual in the drift. The dynamite, Alexandro and Juan have put it already under the German's cabin. The fuse is ready to light. You know it is easy to get under his house the way it stands on them posts. To-night while the whole family is asleep them two devils will crawl on their bellies under the cabin to light the fuse. That little German girl she a nice little nina and the wife is good woman. Judge, you won't let it happen, will you?"

"No, Manuel," said I, "not by a jugful. They'll never get that far. You go to work now the same as usual, and don't you dare to tell Adolph what you know. Keep with the crowd, and no one will be any the wiser."

I made up my mind to take the bull by the horns. When he had gone I called my partner, my constable, and two American neighbors and made known the plot to them. All agreed to help me.

An hour before midnight, well-armed and carrying bulls-eye lanterns, we headed for Adolph's mine, getting there as we had planned while every miner was busy finishing his hole and filling it with powder. It was a quiet night, dark as Erebus, with black clouds flying across the sky. We found the battery and disconnected it, but we did not take away the dynamite for fear of waking up the family.

Then we went to the shaft and waited for the blasts to go off, intending to go below to arrest the two leaders as soon as the smoke had cleared away. We could hear the men gathering in the drift to eat their lunch. All at once there was a thundering crash down below, followed by a regular bedlam of howling, yelling, and crying, and in a trice every miner was trying to climb up the ladders at once. As we could not make out the cause of the commotion, we stood at the mouth of the shaft and arrested every man as he came up. All scrambled out chattering with fear, and every face was as white as a sheet, and that is saying a good bit for Mexicans.

Again and again I caught the words, "Dos hombres muertos, Madre Dios, Jesu, Maria, merci, merci!" When the last man had climbed out and had been arrested we managed to calm down a few of the crowd, so we could learn what happened. Bit by bit we pieced the story together.

Juan and Alexandro had taken their seats as usual on the ledge of rock under the overhanging cliff. The other miners sat below in the drift. When the two leaders got through eating they stood up, and Alexandro shouted, "Now, boys, we go to send the German to hell!"

With a sound as though the earth had been torn apart the overhanging cliff at that instant parted from the wall and crashed upon the two men below. None of their companions stayed by long enough to find out whether the buried men needed help; everyone felt certain they were stone dead—it was the punishment of God.

We went down the shaft to see if there was any hope for the two men, but the rock had done its work well, crushing their heads and breaking their necks. There was no sign of life. The Mexicans struck their breasts and groaned, crying out, "It is the way of God."

When we had moved the rock from the crushed bodies, we hoisted them to the surface. Adolph had heard the cries of the other miners and had come out to see what was up. He gave orders for the making of two coffins, to be ready by daylight. Before long the crowd scattered, but no one went back to the mine.

In a few hours a party of Mexicans came to my office, asking me to do what I could to have the bodies taken to Las Cruces for Christian burial.

"Why not bury them in the Catholic graveyard on the Mimbres?" I asked.

"Father Edwardo would not like it," declared the spokesman.

"He no like the crowd from Cook's Peak. He say we contaminate his good people."

"I am amigo for Father Edwardo," I told them. "We will go there. It is only about twenty miles from here, and if we get an early start we can make the round trip in a day. But I promised Father if I brought any one there for burial, no one would go along except the near relatives. Be sure to make that known to everyone. And warn them to behave and not get drunk. All guns must be left on the Peak."

"Si, si, Juez," and off they went.

About eight o'clock in the morning of the same day the funeral was ready to start. Adolph had furnished four wagons. In the first were the coffins; in the second were six women, all claiming to be the wives of the dead men; in the third was a drove of children said to be their offspring; in the fourth were crowded other near relatives.

Adolph and I headed the procession on horseback; behind us rode the eight pallbearers; then came the wagons in the order I mentioned above. When we were all under way I looked back and got the surprise of my life. I saw that every man, woman, and child of the community, not in the wagons, had fallen in behind them on foot.

Never have I seen such a rough-looking crowd. Many of the men were already half-seas-over and every one of them wore a pistol. They gave as an excuse that the Apaches were reported on the warpath. Mexicans, half-breeds, and whites who had not shaved for a year made up the mob. Most of the women and children were bare-headed and bare-footed, all laughing and seeming to enjoy the outing.

Near the end of the journey we reached the Mimbres River. Here the children scuttled into the water like ducks and were soon getting the first bath they had had in six months. All the water at the lead camp cost fifty cents a barrel and could not be spared for anything so useless as a bath.

Near the church we met Father Edwardo waving a white cloth. "Go back! Go back!" he ordered. "I will not bury renegades in my churchyard."

I rode ahead to speak with him.

"Why did you bring this mob, Jimmie?" he complained. "The devil owns them all. They'll ruin my congregation. Why not take your crowd back to the Peak and let me attend to the burial?

These criminals can't be buried in consecrated ground. I'll have to put them in the potters' field."

I explained to Father that it was part of my duty as justice of the peace to see that the dead were buried. I did not blame him for not wanting the Cook's Peak crowd around, for the Mexicans in his parish were a happy and moral lot of farmers and herders. In this rich section of the Mimbres Valley they lived in peace and comfort, producing all they needed to eat and wear.

Still out of sorts, Father Edwardo led us to the graveyard and pointed out the potters' field. In a twinkling the miners were busy with their picks and shovels, and the grave was soon dug. The people of the village, attracted by the crowd, also gathered in the graveyard. Before long the good and the bad had mixed like sugar and sand in a sack. The priest came forward and said a few prayers over the bodies before they were lowered into the ground. In a jiffy the clods of earth rattled on the rough wooden boxes. The priest went off to the rectory.

Later in the day I tried to round up the Cook's Peak crowd, but I might as well have tried to catch water in a sieve. Word had gone the rounds that a big dance was to be held in the village that night and they had been invited to attend it. With two empty wagons rattling behind us, Adolph and I headed back to the Peak.

The priest's fears were not without ground. The celebration got so wild that he and the *alcalde* had to send for a deputy to stop the carousal. For a week the crowd straggled back to the Peak in pairs. I was the hero of the hour for having got Father Edwardo to give in to the burial. Everyone called at my office to thank me, "muy amigo". And many a garlicky and whisky kiss I warded off, being at last forced to tack a notice on my door in Spanish: "No admission on pain of being shot."

Several months afterwards I met Father Edwardo. "If you ever bring a crowd like that into my parish again, I'll excommunicate you," he exclaimed, but I took note of the twinkle in his black eyes. "One of the many widows got herself married to a parishioner of mine within a week of the burial," he went on, "and I got a fat marriage fee out of it."

Adolph Sweitzer still drove his men as hard as ever until his lease ran out. When he left the Peak he was worth a half million dollars. Tim O'Keefe was still as poor as Job's turkey. Adolph went to Germany where his fortune melted in the stock market like snow on Cook's Peak.

"The mills of God grind slowly,
But they grind exceeding small."

In time we heard that Adolph and his two brothers had all made away with themselves. One went by the rope; one went by the gun; one went by sea. Tim O'Keefe died a natural death and was buried in a poor man's grave.

2. *Rita*

Everyone in camp knew Rita, and everyone in camp had been invited to her wedding. And what a wedding it was to be! Rita's Irish father and her half-breed mother were very glad to give their daughter to Manuel, for they had many children, and Manuel had many goats. He would take good care of her, and maybe he could teach her to obey. Who knows? What harm that Rita was but fifteen years of age? Had she not blossomed out like a rose under the warm son of Manuel's love? Nor did Rita's parents mind spending Manuel's money in making ready for such a fiesta as Cook's Peak had never before known.

It was told around camp that the bride would be dressed in white satin covered with lace and ribbons, and would wear a long white veil. All this finery, picked out in a big, thumb-worn catalog and ordered from San Francisco, would have to be packed by burro up the barren side of Cook's Peak. Rough tables and benches of pine wood were built and set up on the rocky hillside that sloped away from the door of the cabin. Orange blossoms and roses were ordered from Los Angeles. A first-class orchestra was engaged in El Paso to play for the dance.

At last everything was ready. A big crowd of guests drifted in, each in his shabby best, and stared at the stovepipe hats and the long-tailed coats of gamblers who were there. A little fat padre, brought to the Peak for the purpose, made the solemn couple man and wife, and blessed them and all the company. Then the orchestra crashed into the popular strains of, "Rita, Bonita"; there was a shower of rice and much kissing and hand-shaking. Mescal flowed freely. Before long the guests gathered around the long tables taking no notice of the yellow sun that smiled down on them; and everyone filled up on venison, turkey, hot tamales, *chili con carne*, *tortillas*, and *penoche;* and everyone drank grape wine and fiery mescal till he was ready to burst.

When the fiesta was over the dance was on. The cabin would

not hold all the dancers, so they headed for a bed of soft shale near-by, where they danced or shuffled around, depending on their size and the kind of shoes they had on. Manuel and Rita were still at the table with their friends around them. Rita got many compliments. She surely was a beauty, round cheeks all smiles and blushes, black curly hair, bright eyes, and small, white teeth, lips like cherries. Her mother was a half-breed, part Indian, part Spanish, and her father was an American soldier of Irish blood. Rita had inherited the good looks of the different races as well as some of their bad qualities. My first recollection of her was seeing her pass morning and evening on her way to and from school. I looked at her sitting there beside Manuel in her wedding finery. She was not yet out of short skirts, and she was married. I could not but wonder how it would go.

As Rita lifted her wine glass to her lips, her eyes met those of Miguel, the tenor singer from El Paso. This was the moment the dandy had been waiting for with his bold stare. A handsome fellow he was, in his blue and gold uniform, with black hair and turned-up, silky mustaches. Miguel was a regular soft-soaper, and under the very nose of Manuel the two began to flirt. Everyone took note of it except Manuel himself.

He saw only Rita. How had he, such a bashful, homely cuss, won the love of the liveliest and prettiest girl in the camp? But he had! And now she belonged to him "until death do us part."

Bursting with pride, he watched her swing off on the arm of the El Paso singer, to lead the round dance in which she could hold her own better than any girl in the section. Her partner was making eyes at her. Rita blushed, and all at once Manuel was troubled. I took note that a cloud had slipped between the sun and the gay wedding party. Manuel shivered and went up awkwardly to get his bride. He seemed to be aware of his sallow, pock-marked cheeks, his ill-fitting blue suit, and his high, choky collar. But Rita smiled on him, and his trouble passed away like the cloud that for the moment had hidden the sun. The day whirled by in a round of gaiety made up of music, laughter, and liquor.

Late in the night Manuel put his bride on a buckskin pony with silver trappings, his wedding gift to her, and led her amid many cheers to the cabin built for her at the edge of the camp. For a week a string of burros had been packing furniture up the steep trail, and Rita was busy for many days showing off to the women and the girls of the camp the nickel-plated cookstove, the rows of pots and pans, and the big walnut bed in the corner of the cabin. But the day after the wedding and many more days Manuel was away in the upper part of the mountain looking after his eight thousand angora goats. Rita soon got lonesome in the new cabin.

"After all," thought Manuel, "it is only a few months since she was in short skirts, bounding over the mountain like a young deer, with her black curls streaming behind her. Didn't I meet her for the first time way up on a crag, holding in her arms the injured kid I had climbed up to save?"

Soon he was trading goats for beautiful dresses, jewels, fancy fruits and flowers, to amuse her while he was away. Finally he gave in to let her have many parties, for which he sold a great many goats. He himself could not often be there. But the tenor singer from El Paso was always there; and often he was there when no party was going on. People talked. Manuel, taking note that Rita's cheeks were as rosy as the apples in his orchard, and her eyes as bright as the stars in the pool where he watered his goats, did not mind selling more and more animals.

One day when he had grown tired with the goat-clipping, he sat down to rest under the shade of a scrubby juniper tree. From his pockets he dug up handful after handful of pinon nuts and began to shell them, storing the kernels in a clean red handkerchief. Rita liked pinon nuts. After a time he heard two of his herders talking in low voices behind a clump of manzanita shrubs that hid him from them.

"I think somebody should tell Manuel, that girl she's only after his money. Before long Manuel he go broke," said Sam.

"No harm if Manuel spend his money on her if she love him, but she love *la chanti hombre* from El Paso," returned Tony.

"Why don't her padre and madre look after her. They know—"

Manuel's heart turned to stone inside him. Yes, it was true. They were talking about Rita. Their words were crushing his heart as surely as his powerful fists were crushing the nuts they held. He wanted to break through the brush and choke the herders with their own words, but he could not move.

"Yes, but the whole camp knows, Rita's padre and madre, they never can manage her, no. She always been like a wild goat. What she learn in school? Four teachers, all crazy over the *hombres*. All marry before school term is out. Rita's edication mean go after the *hombre*. Edication, bah!"

"I no want to be the man to tell Manuel, eh, Tony?"

"He kill that sweet-smellin' dude from El Paso. I no blame him, Sam, when he find out how those two hoodwink him. Come on, we look after Manuel's goats. We help him all we can." And they rode off.

What could poor Manuel do? It was not true. He would not believe it. Rita was a foolish child, and wicked tongues had made a mountain out of a mole hill. Soon he must build a cabin up here in the mountain and keep her with him. How she loves birds and flowers, and the little wild animals! He will order the wood for the cabin as soon as he goes to the settlement.

On his next trip to the cabin Rita was kind and good to him. She must pack the tobacco into the bowl of his pipe with her brown fingers; she must fasten on his buckskin coat a bunch of the kinnykinick he had brought her; she must go with him half-way back to his goat corrals on her little Indian pony. She seemed to love him more than ever. He would close those wicked mouths with his fists. Let them dare to say another word against Rita! But when he went back to his goats he carried for the first time since his marriage a bottle of frontier whisky.

Not long after that trip to camp one of his herders returned from there with an order from the bank for Manuel to count his goats. Soon everything would be gone, for the bank held a mortgage, and he could not pay. In a gloomy mood he rode into the settlement on a day that Rita was not looking for him. He heard the strain of the "Spanish Cavalier" being picked on a guitar as he got down from his horse. The fat was in the fire. In an instant he stood in the doorway, glaring at Miguel, who still kept his arm around Rita. Rushing across the floor, he seized the guitar and with might and brawn beat the pair from the cabin, running them down the trail, and throwing the broken instrument at the head of the dazed Miguel.

Going back to the cabin, he stripped it of everything he had bought for Rita. Hundreds of dollars worth of dresses, jewels, ribbons, and hats, he hurled through the windows and door, even the dishes that she liked so well. Stumbling out through the clutter of clothes and broken china, he turned loose the little buckskin pony with silver trappings that had been his wedding gift to her only a few short months before. Again he entered the cabin and threw himself on a chair beside the table. Down went his head on his arms, and the cabin fairly shook with his sobs. That night he emptied his bottle, and while he slept, Rita came back and picked up what she could from the ruin outside the cabin. She dared not go in.

For many days Manuel stayed in the cabin, leaving it only when his bottle needed filling. Tony came in from the ranch and tried to get him to go back with him, but Manuel drove him away with loud, bitter curses. At last he fell into a long sleep, and woke up sober. What was it he had been dreaming? Oh, yes. Rita and he stood before the Spanish padre; they were saying words after him: "In riches or in poverty, in health or in sickness, till death do us part." He turned to take Rita's hand, but she was not there; instead he looked into the face of his little mother, framed in the old, black mantilla; "My son," said she, "go back to your goats. Learn to forgive, and some day Rita will come back to you."

That day Manuel settled up with the bank. Then he rode to the upper part of Cook's Peak. Gathering into his mountain corrals what was left of his flock of goats he began again to build up the herd. Many long months went by before he could bring himself to ask anyone about Rita. At last he mustered up courage to say to Tony, who had just come back from a trip to Cook's Peak camp, "Have you heard of her?

"Rita," began Tony, not looking at him, "she live no longer with that El Paso dude. He no have money enough for her; he no have love enough for her; he a regular ladies' man; his love is as free as the air to any *dona* or *senorita* that smile at him with his guitar. But she no learn good sense, and that judge, he edicated with the college, bah! He worse than Rita. He crooked as a snake. He sell Rita a bill of separation so she can marry that singin' Miguel for five dollars; now that same judge want a hundred dollars to divorce her from Miguel and marry her to Franz. You know Franz, Manuel, him that sells the fruit and vegetables to Cook's Peak Camp? Ah, Manuel, that Dutchman, he soon tame that little wildcat, I bet. Some day, Manuel, you see, she come back to you on her knees."

Manuel did not say a word, but turned away and went on shearing the goat he held.

Some months later he had to ride to Cook's Peak Camp on business. He did not want to go, for he was afraid he would meet Rita. Sure enough! He saw her in the street. Hiding himself in the nearest doorway, he watched her pass. Her black curls were drawn tight around her head; she wore a bedraggled dress, that had once made every girl have green eyes at a party she gave; and over her muddy arm she carried a market basket filled with fresh vegetables. All at once the truth came to him. She was peddling for the German! For an instant Manuel only remembered his love for her. She was still beautiful in spite of the way the German treated her. He wanted to rush from his hiding place, throw the basket into the street, and crush her to his heart. But no, she ought to suffer; he hoped the German would punish her more; and he turned away with a bitter curse.

Later in the day he came face to face with Franz. He wanted to knock him down. Instead, he straightened out his clenched fist and took the hand the stolid German held out to him.

"Ach, Manuel," said Franz in his guttural lingo, "I voot not take your Rita from you. I take her from that vicked Miguel, only ven she force me to. Vun night I come home, and mon, vot do I hear? A Spanish love ditty, yah, and there is Rita in my house, vich she has made all shining clean, as the German likes it, yah, and in one corner set up is her double bed; and in the other corner set on the shelf is her statue mit the Virgin Mary and the Child; and set up on the table is vun goot meal mit sauerkraut and vieners. Vot can I do? Next day I go and pay the Judge one hundred dollars, and he give the bill of separation to Rita, and I marry her. But Manuel, ach, I vish many times she be married yet mit you."

"Keep her," said Manuel as he turned away.

A year passed by. Manuel did not go to town again, and he heard no more about Rita. But it was springtime, and though he did not want to think about her, he kept wishing that she could see the funny, gangling kids that staggered about in the brown earth, or rolled in the new grass. He knew what she would do if she could see them. She would clap her brown hands and laugh like a bell till the goats would lift their heads and bleat in answer. And Franz had put that child to work in his fields. The brute! How could he do it?

One day as Manuel fed from a bottle a kid whose mother had died in giving it birth, Tony, the herder, came and stood beside him.

"From Rita," said he, pushing a soiled paper packet into Manuel's hand. Turning his back, Tony began to count the goats.

Manuel took his time to open the packet, and then the big tears filled his eyes, and rolled, one by one, over his pock-marked cheeks. Wrapping the paper around the sprig of kinnykinick, he slipped it into his pocket and brushed away the tears with the back of his hand. At last he called Tony.

"What do you know?" asked Manuel.

"Rita she in a lot of trouble again," began Tony. "She sneak away to many parties. Franz get mad, and he whip her like a beast. Then Rita get worse stubborn, and sneak away to a dance, and she dance with a nigger top sergeant, because he good-looking in his soldier's uniform with his skin shining like a blackberry and his lips the color of cherries, and Rita think she spite Franz. Franz was away, but his wagon break down, and he come home unexpected and find out where Rita is and what she do, but he does not let on. Then the nigger top sergeant come to Franz to buy vegetables for the troops, and Rita promise to meet him in the orchard where apple blossoms are all out, and again Franz know all, but he does not let on.

"Franz and his men hide in the brush and when the nigger top sergeant tries to throw his arms around Rita they jump on him and throw and hogtie him, and fasten him to his horse with a letter around his neck telling all, and send him back to the fort and he's top no longer. Next they tie Rita to a tree and Franz beat her with a quirt, and then he turn her loose and tell her never to come back. Her padre and madre not let her come back home; they say she very bad girl and spoil all their children like a bad apple spoil all the good ones in the barrel. Now Rita she go sure to the dogs. She got no home. She stay with a neighbor and say she walk soon to Silver City. Her pony she sold him long ago, and her clothes they nearly all gone."

"Can you get along without me this afternoon," asked Manuel, still fussing over the kid.

For answer Tony took the bottle from Manuel's hand, and opened the mouth of the bleating kid. "I think Rita give the little kid his bottle to-morrow," he said to himself as Manuel swung into his saddle.

Late in the afternoon of that same day Manuel and Rita looked me up in my office. "Rita want a bill of separation from Franz," explained Manuel. "She want to be my wife again."

And then I heard the whole story that I had known in part for several years; for I had been elected justice of the peace in place of the scoundrel who had given Rita the so-called divorces.

Most of the judges in these isolated districts did not know what the word honor meant. The position was elective, and the judge was something like the alderman or squire in a small town in the East. The judges appointed deputies, and did the marrying and divorcing. I believe many of them appointed deputies who would pack a gun to kill some enemy and get him out of the way. The judges held inquests, buried the dead, and settled mine disputes. In fact, the judge was virtually a king in these isolated districts. Most of the cases that were brought to them never reached the courts. All the gamblers, tin horns, and cutthroats in the section paid them tribute. Of course there were many fine men who filled the office and did a world of good, but they were the exception and not the rule.

Manuel and Rita were surely surprised when I explained that Rita had never been properly divorced, and that she could go home with Manuel without any charges and be his wife according to the law.

"I know she still my wife. All the time she live with other men she still my wife. The Spanish padre say, 'till death do us part.' But I afraid the American law make us pay for all Rita's sins."

At that, Rita threw herself into Manuel's arms. She was a bad child, but she had suffered a lot. "Oh, Manuel, I promise you, always I will be good. Every night I pray the Virgin Mary to help me, and I never, never leave you again."

And she kept her word. Years later when Manuel's flock of angora goats was one of the finest in the State of New Mexico, I stopped one day at his ranch to eat dinner. Manuel was very proud of Rita, for she had learned to behave and made him a good wife. She was better-looking than ever. Five big, strapping sons gathered with us around the table.

3. *The Bones of Sing Lee*

In Western mining camps I met many strange people and had many strange experiences, but nowhere was this truer than on Cook's Peak. There as justice of the peace I was called upon to meet all sorts of people in all sorts of conditions. The justice of the peace in an isolated district like Cook's Peak was not only asked to settle all fights and look after the poor, but he was also expected to visit the sick and to bury the dead. When it came to burying the dead I had my hands full, for the Peak is one of the most barren spots upon the face of the earth. Its formation is mostly a dolomite limestone cut with porphyry dikes. For miles there is not earth enough to bury a cat.

A well-known character in the camp was Sing Lee, a feeble and half-starved Chinaman, a regular bag of bones; he barely made a living even in the camp's best days, at odd jobs of cooking and washing. Two camp characters, as different from Sing Lee as day from night, were the gamblers known as Chatham Street Jim and Tom Terrible. Whenever a big game was going on or visitors were in the camp the two rogues lived in clover, for they had a knack all their own of getting money from their luckier neighbors. No camp ever had a more good-for-nothing team of scalawags.

When the bodies of ore played out the mines closed down, and everyone who had the means struck out for better fields. The two gamblers, down to bed-rock as usual, had to stay on in the camp, with not even a chance to fleece newcomers in future. Both were taking, in mine parlance, "a side leap at a rind of bacon." Among those who had to stay in the camp because they were too hard-up to move was poor Sing Lee. I also had to remain there, as I was postmaster, and the Government would not allow me to leave until the office was closed.

One day Sing Lee was reported ill, and I set forth on the trail to pay him a visit. When I got near his cabin, whom should I meet but Chatham Street Jim and Tom Terrible. Jim had a habit, always worse in excitement, of talking through his nose and twisting his mouth to the side of his face. Seeing his mouth working harder than usual I knew something out of the way had happened.

"Judge!" he exclaimed, "Old Sing Lee is deader than a door nail. All shriveled up like an apple. Me and Tom have jest come from his shack. Ain't it so, Tom?"

"Well," said I, "I'll have to view the body to be certain."

The two scamps turned around and went with me back to the cabin. It was true. Sing Lee had passed in his chips.

"What does the county pay for buryin' a corpse?" asked Jim, twisting his mouth so fast I thought he must be trying to get the money from the air.

"Four bucks, but remember, the body must be put out of the sight of man."

"Leave that to us, Judge. When do we get paid?"

"When you have put the body out of man's view."

"That's whatever!" said Tom. "We sure will do that!"

As I left the cabin I stopped for a moment to gaze at a small plot of grass not far above it. It was the only bit of green to be seen for miles. Several years before a deep shaft had been sunk up there, which did not pan out very well. In order to keep men or animals from falling into the hole, Poe, the owner, had fenced it in. The softening of lime on the near-by dump explained the patch of green. On a later day I was to see more of that spot.

Shortly after sunup the next morning the two vagabonds appeared at my cabin, and made affidavit that they had put the body of Sing Lee out of sight of man. I asked them where they had buried it, but they only hedged and stumbled, saying over and over that "everything was all right." I handed them the four dollars, and later collected from the county.

As soon as the postoffice was closed on Cook's Peak, my partner and I leased a mine near Benton, Arizona. For two years after that we shipped no ore and made no money. We were surely down on our luck but a day came at last when we were paid up for our hard work, for we struck a rich body of ore. As it was a kind of ore we did not know much about, and as our assays were high, my partner wanted me to go along with the first shipment to see it sampled. The day after the two carloads left the side track I boarded a passenger train for Lordsburg, expecting to change trains there for Deming. As I had three hours between trains in Lordsburg I went over to the mercantile house where I had dealt years before, to buy some supplies.

After I had given the manager the glad hand, he asked, "Weren't you judge at Cook's Peak a while back?"

On learning that I had held that office, he went on, "There have been some high-toned Chinamen about here looking for you. I have an idea they are agents of the Six Companies that make it their business to bury Chinamen in their own fatherland. They're probably looking for the bones of some Chink you buried on the Peak."

I felt sure the strangers were after the bones of Sing Lee, and I had a hunch there was trouble ahead. As it was near noon we went together to the Chinese restaurant for dinner. There was a lot of excited jabbering among the Chinamen when we went in. Some of them came to meet me.

"You bury Sing Lee on Cook's Peak?" asked the proprietor. "Two China boy wanta catcha him bones, send back to China. You know place catcha him bones?"

"No," said I, "but I'll try to see the men who buried him."

"Me telegraph Deming you come on seven o'clock train."

At the depot in Deming I was made known to two well-dressed Chinamen, by the owner of a Chinese restaurant who knew me. Sure enough! They were looking for Sing's bones. Taking care not to let them know what a fix I was in, I told them I would look up the men who buried him and tell them the next day if anything turned up.

That night I went from saloon to saloon asking for the two scamps. No one knew the whereabouts of Tom Terrible, but I heard that Chatham Street Jim was living on a goat ranch about thirty miles north of Deming on the road that led to Cook's Peak.

Next morning, bright and early, the two Chinamen looked me up in the hotel where I was stopping.

"I have got track of one of the men who took care of Sing Lee's body," said I. "Sing Lee may be buried very deep, so you will need to hire a team and wagon. Load up plenty of rope, a bucket, some picks and shovels, and enough lumber to build a windlass. Of course you know that you will have to pay all costs including the hire of men?"

But the Chinamen did *not* understand how it could cost so much to dig up the bones of one small man. After a lot of singsong gab they finally agreed to bear all expenses.

A few days later, after I had seen the ore sampled, I made arrangements to go with the Chinamen to Cook's Peak. The load on the wagon would make anyone think we were striking out for a new mining excitement.

About noon we reached the ranch and found Chatham Street Jim at dinner. Not without reason had I brought along the half gallon of whisky which I soon passed to the ranch hands. As I had hoped, Jim took several long pulls. While we sat at dinner his tongue loosened up, and I asked him where he had put Sing Lee's body.

Twisting his mouth around and giving an eye to the Chinamen he burst out, "Judge, we threw old Sing's corpse down Charley Poe's shaft. But honest, Judge, we let him down with a rope. You mind that bunch of grass that was growing on the dump, don't you? We threw down enough sod to give him a green blanket, same as if he was buried in a graveyard. With the paling all around the shaft, what better grave could a man want? Sing Lee'll have no trouble getting out on the day of judgment, for he was a good sowl, and he'll be pervided with wings when Gabriel blows his horn."

The fat was in the fire, sure enough.

"That shaft is ninety feet deep," I told the Chinamen. "I might have known better than to trust Sing Lee's body to those scamps. I was afraid they had played fast and loose when they came for their pay, but they would not own up to it, saying they had fullfilled their part of the bargain by putting the body out of the sight of man. That is why I wanted you to bring a wagon-load of equipment. Perhaps you would rather not try to get Sing Lee's bones if they are in the bottom of the shaft?"

"Wella good, you bring wagon. We must catch 'em Sing Lee's bones."

About dusk we reached the abandoned mining camp. The fence that once surrounded the shaft had blown down in a storm; the snow and rain had caved in the upper edges of the hole and a lot of the dump had washed into it. However, we set up a windlass the next morning. When the rope and roller were made fast one of the ranchers offered to go down in a bucket. A pick and a shovel were next lowered for him to use. The driver and one of the ranchers hoisted the dirt and the rock, which Chatham and I dumped. We went over it, looking for bones. The two Chinamen stood by as solemn as judges.

After a couple of hours some coarse, black hairs began to come up in every bucketful of debris. These we pulled out and laid to one side. The Chinamen stepped a little closer. Bones now showed up in each bucketful. These we laid beside the hair.

The Chinamen came still closer. Each time the bucket came up there were more bones, but I soon smelled a rat, for they kept getting bigger and bigger. Before long I tumbled to the truth, but I came to the conclusion not to let on to the Chinamen. Pulling as long a face as I could I said to them, "Soon we will have all of Sing Lee's bones!"

"But Sing Lee is vella leetle man. How he have such vella big bones?" asked the older man with his eyes popping out of his head.

"Maybe the lime has acted on the bones in the shaft," said I.

Chatham Street Jim just then got a bad fit of coughing and sniffling that drove him behind the dump.

"Better look out, Jim," I warned him. "You'll get your death from this bad dust."

Up came the shin bone of an ox. I put it on the pile of bones. The mystified Chinamen stood by making motions and shaking their heads. Up came the hoofs. The younger Chinaman cried out in terror, "Him no Sing's bones; him debble bones!" Up came a skull and horns.

"Oh, no, Judge," exclaimed the older man showing his teeth in a regular Chinese grin. "He no Chinaman bones, he cow bones."

All the time I kept on saying that the bones belonged to Sing Lee. By this time there were enough bones to fill two coffins. The Chinamen jabbered and grinned, and Chatham Street Jim got over his fit of coughing.

"Judge," said Jim, "those are the bones of the ox that old man Grover lost last year. I know it by the horns."

In the meantime the men kept hoisting, and they finally reached other and much smaller bones, which we piled to one side. The Chinamen, watching them closely, came to the conclusion they belonged to Sing Lee.

At last the man below called up that he had reached bottom. In the last bucket came up the skull of Sing Lee. One of the Chinamen then went down in the bucket to look around for himself. I was very glad it did not dawn on either of them there ought to be two hundred and six bones! When the Chinaman came up he brought out a paper which Chatham Street Jim and I signed, to prove that Sing Lee's bones had been taken by them. When they had loaded the bones into a box they had brought along, and paid all expenses, the two Chinamen seemed perfectly happy.

I have known these Chinamen, who gather the bones of their countrymen to ship back to China, to search camps deserted for years. At that time no Chinaman signed up with any company to come to America unless there was a clause in the contract providing that his bones could be returned for burial to the Celestial Kingdom.

For some years after this, every time I went into a chop suey joint in the Southwest, the owner would give me the glad hand and set before me free of charge an immense bowl of chop suey, chattering and grinning all the time he waited on me.

"Judge him vella good man. Catch him Sing Lee's bones, Charley Poe's shaft. Catch him big cow bones. Tell him China boy him Sing Lee's bones. Vella good! Catch him one big cow head. Big horns! Allee samee debble. No fool China boy. China boy go bottom of shaft. Then he catch Sing Lee's bones. Send him back to China. Vella good! Judge, Cook's Peak, no foolee Chinaman!"

Radium Wells

1. *Little Mountain*

IN the forepart of the year of 1882 I left Lake Valley where I had been prospecting and headed for Eureka, a recent discovery in the Hachita Mountains, which lie in the southwestern part of Grant County in the border country of New Mexico. The Santa Fe and Southern Pacific Railroads were at that time working towards the spot where the town of Deming now stands, expecting to meet there before long. If water could be found at the junction of the two railroads it was planned to build a town there.

Barney Martin, a foreman on the Southern Pacific Railroad, believing that water was near-by, put several Chinese track layers to work sinking a well. A good flow of water resulted at a depth of forty feet, and the spot was called Deming in honor of a vice-president of the Southern Pacific Railroad. I happened along a few days after the discovery of water.

Having a good saddle horse and a Mexican pack mule, I came to the conclusion to stay at the well-site for a few days in the hope that a good partner might turn up. Quite a rush had followed the opening of the well. No partner came along, so I struck out alone for Eureka. There I met an old friend, Bob Anderson, who had made a strike and had many locations. I was in the dumps when Bob told me that everything for miles around had been located. But he did me a good turn.

"Jimmie," said he, "I'll give you some rich float that I found about twenty miles east of Hachita in the locality known as the Jog in the Mountains, and also as Monument 41. You'll have hardship aplenty, but if you can find the body of ore that this float came from, you'll be sitting pretty in no time. The range is very low, and there is no water nearer than Cedar Grove. It's a favorite pass for Indians and smugglers, and you'll have to keep on the lookout for your stock and your food supplies."

When I had examined the float I came to the conclusion that tracing it would be worth the danger. The ore was so soft it could be cut with a knife, and I felt sure it would run up into hundreds of ounces of silver to the ton. The next day I bought two five-gallon kegs and stocked up with food. Turning back to Cedar Grove I got two barrels from a Mexican family I knew. I hired the sons to fill the barrels and kegs with water and to haul them for me to Little Mountain, where we pulled in about five in the afternoon.

On our way we had passed Jack Doyle, better known as Wind River Jack, who was digging a well. He had struck water at shallow depth and told me of his intention to put sheep to pasture in the vicinity. His well lay only three miles north of the Sierras where I expected to camp. I had a streak of good luck, for he offered me the use of the water hole.

The Mexicans went back to Cedar Grove, and I pitched camp on Little Mountain, setting up a small tent that I usually carried with me when prospecting. After getting myself a bite to eat I picketed the horse and turned the mule loose for the night. Fagged out by the long trip, I turned in early, taking no stock of my surroundings. I woke up at the first peep of dawn, feeling like a new man, and I soon had breakfast. By the time the sun was up I was on the hill prospecting. The hills being low and the rich float in my pocket a goad, I covered a lot of ground in a short time. Near Monument 41 on the border I found float plentiful, but it was a poorer grade than that Anderson had given me.

About four o'clock that afternoon I pulled back to camp to change the horse to better grass and to water both animals. After getting a bite to eat I again struck out with my pick, for the days were mighty long and lonely unless I kept busy.

Not more than a hundred yards from my camp I struck a rich piece of float. I saw it was on a par with the specimen I carried, as it was pure bromide of silver. Its roughness showed that it had not come far, for then it would have been smooth and round. Little Mountain being thickly covered with grass and shrubs, I found it hard to trace the float. I was so taken up with my search that the sun dropped behind the mountains before I knew it.

I hurried back to camp in the thick dusk of a mountain evening, in high feather over my first day of prospecting on Little Mountain. After changing the feeding place of the horse I turned in early as on the first night, using my saddle for a pillow. I slept like a log. When I got awake the next morning I soon found out that the good saddle under my head had been changed for an old Mexican saddle, that my animals were missing, and that all my supplies were gone except part of a loaf of bread and a small piece of cheese. I was foot-loose in a dangerous country.

After a light breakfast I struck out for Cedar Grove, where I got the Mexicans to go back to Little Mountain for what stuff the thieves had left there. Then they took me and my load to the well-site now known as Deming. Although the parties who stole my outfit wore moccasins, I felt sure they were white men. The Apaches would not have spared my life. I stopped several days at the Deming well, hoping that the thieves would turn up with my horse and mule, but they must have gone south.

While I hung around there, some prospectors drifted in who needed money, and they were glad to sell me their outfit. Once more I headed for Kingston, the new mining camp in the Black Range. Having made a small stake there I invested it in a team and wagon and again struck out for Little Mountain.

In the meantime Wind River Jack had built a cabin and fenced in his well, which was now guarded by three vicious bloodhounds, making it very dangerous to get water unless Jack was there. As the whole section was overrun with cutthroats and outlaws I did not stay there long, knowing I would again be afoot or lose my life if I did so. I had not found the rich float but no locations barred me from looking for it again when I got the chance.

2. *On the Water Wagon*

I pulled back to Kingston, but I did not forget Little Mountain. In the late eighties our Government came to the conclusion to set up a new boundary line with cement monuments every league. As Indians and outlaws still infested the border country, troops were ordered to go with the surveyors. Drivers were needed for the water wagons. Realizing that I might have a chance to do some prospecting near the border, I asked for a job as driver and set out with the troops from El Paso.

The officers were mighty interested when they found out my reason for joining them and promised to let me off where the country looked mineralized; they even offered to supply water and a guard if necessary.

When we reached Potrillos I prospected for a few days, finding much copper float and many caves filled with bat guano. But the railroad was too far away to make it worth while to ship either product.

The next place where we camped for any length of time was at Palomas, or Dove Lake. There we filled up on roast ducks and plover. From this point I prospected in the mountains known as the Three Sisters, isolated peaks rising side by side from the desert floor near the town of Columbus, which put me in mind of the pyramids of Egypt. I found a number of miners at work in these mountains, shipping a considerable tonnage of lead-silver ores.

Living in the vicinity of the Three Sisters at that time was a negro ex-trooper who owned about five hundred head of hogs, which fed on wild parsley and rattlesnakes. These mountains were alive with rattlesnakes, the thickest and most venomous that I have ever seen, often measuring four inches in diameter. Sometimes we found a whole jackrabbit in a rattlesnake when we cut him open.

The borderland country of New Mexico lies almost entirely in the Lower Sonoran Zone which has some queer plants and animals. Thousands of desert rabbits feed on greasewood and sagebrush. The rattlesnake has an enemy here in the roadrunner, or chaparral cock, which is a regular clown at times. His brown and tan feathers, so much the color of the ground, are a big help in hiding him from his enemies. He uses his long tail as a windbreak, throwing it up when he stops suddenly. Even the crest of sharp bristles on his head he uses to show his feelings. His habit of turning his head all the way around to gaze at you with one eye adds to his comical look, especially if his tail is raised at the same time.

He is known by several names: the "roadrunner," because of his habit of running ahead of horses on the trail, sometimes keeping in the way for a quarter of a mile like a mischievous boy; the "chaparral cock," because he is found mostly in desert thickets; the "lizard-eater," because lizards form a principal part of his food; and the "ground cuckoo," because he cannot fly high or far. The roadrunners are lone birds, not often seen in pairs except during the mating season.

I hold that the rattlesnake has an enemy in the roadrunner, though it is a fact often denied or doubted by those who are up on bird lore. At one time in Lake Valley my partner and I watched a pair of roadrunners in the springtime. Morning after morning we met them outside the tunnel where we worked. Not far from the mouth of the tunnel a rattlesnake used to climb on a rock to take a sleep in the early morning sun. It soon became plain to us that the roadrunners had spotted the rattlesnake. One morning we saw them making a corral of cholla joints and thorns around the snake. How quietly they worked until the circle was nearly three inches high! Then both birds ran with a strange cry towards the cholla corral, waking up the rattlesnake, which struck instantly. Hundreds of fine sharp thorns were buried in the tender underside of the snake's throat. The more he twisted and turned the deeper the spines of the cholla worked into his neck. After a half hour of writhing he lay still.

The roadrunners hung around long enough to make sure he was dead; then they hacked him to pieces, which they carried off to feed to their young.

Prospectors always kept on the lookout for rattlesnakes if they took note of a pair of roadrunners in the vicinity of the camp.

3. *Cazzarillo Springs*

At Cazzarillo Springs, now known as Hermanas Station, on the El Paso and Southwestern Railroad, we pitched our next camp. The Cazzarillo Springs were then owned by a man named Reed, of Las Cruces, the father of a large family, whose wife was a Spanish dona, also from Las Cruces. A large herd of Reed's cattle watered at the Springs, where the big flow of water almost formed a creek. Geologists claim that these springs are a part of the sunken Mimbres River, which rises again in the lakes of northern Mexico.

The Springs, located on the road that led to the mines in Sabinal, Old Mexico, were a favorite stopping place for packers and travelers. At that time there was no water nearer than Apache Tejo, on the old Butterfield stage route, near the spot where the town of Hurley now stands. At Apache Tejo the Government had stationed a platoon of cavalry for the protection of mail and travelers.

As Reed had been attacked many times by the Apaches, he built a system of rock corrals, which he used as fortifications. I took note of a small cannon mounted near the house. It was very hard for the Indians to surprise him without great loss of life. The cattle seemed to know a band of warriors from ordinary travelers, for even when no herder was with them, they would run to the corrals at scent or sight of an Indian.

Reed lived most of the time at Las Cruces, leaving the care of the cattle to his sons and the hired help. Some of the herders did considerable hunting and prospecting. As deer and antelope were plentiful, the walls of the living room were decorated with many antlered heads. On the shelves of a large cabinet hundreds of specimens of ore that had been picked up on the range were on display. My attention was taken up with two slabs of silver which had been found below the border after a fight. It was believed the metal was from the Plancha la Plata, or Plates of Silver Mine near Sabinal.

Taking note of my interest, one of the herders showed me a bar of silver he had found in a cave known as Boca Grande about three miles below the border. While hunting for cattle that drifted across the line he came upon fresh burro tracks, also moccasin tracks, made either by squaws or young bucks. The signs led to the main caves. As it was close to sundown he returned to the Springs.

The next morning he picked up the tracks and followed them up the canyon for a distance of five miles. A grove of alder trees at that point convinced him that water must be near-by, but though he looked about in the gulch he could not find the source. Hanging on the alder trees were a number of Indian skeletons still covered with dry flesh and wrapped in a papyrus made from cottonwood fiber. This made him think he was in a sacred canyon. With the bodies were many bows, arrows, and other Indian relics. On one side of the canyon the trail apparently led up to a number of caves.

Hoping to find a water tank under a sandstone cliff, the herder headed for the caves. As he went up he came upon the tracks of a cougar which led from the cave up the main canyon. The cave that he went into was so large and dark he could not see the end of it. Around the walls were ledges of rock which had been used to shelve sacks of grain and bolts of calico, but it was so long since the goods were stored there that the cloth crumbled to dust under his touch. He believed the cloth and grain had been stolen by Apaches from a train of packers on their way to Sabinal, Mexico, to trade them off for silver bullion.

The herder struck a match so he could look about. A bit of the burning match dropped on a bale of cloth, starting a fire he had a hard time to put out. Thousands of bats let go of the roof and rushed from the cave with a loud, whirring noise. Two young cougars ran towards him out of the dark, sniffing at him, not knowing whether he was friend or foe. Feeling along the shelves in the darker section of the cave after he had put out the fire, he laid his hand on something cold. It was the slab of bullion he had shown me. It weighed about forty pounds.

As he carried his treasure from the cave he took notice that his horse was excited, with ears lying flat and eyes directed up the canyon where the cougar tracks led. In a twinkling the herder had leaped into his saddle and was racing down the canyon like the wind, with the cougars crying after him. But he reached the ranch in good shape.

The next day he and two other ranchers went back to the cave, but they found no more bullion. They killed the two old cougars and brought the kittens to the ranch, selling them shortly afterwards to a circus in El Paso.

After hearing the herder's tale and examining the float specimens that had been picked up on Little Mountain, I got leave of the commanding officer of the surveying outfit to prospect ahead of the surveyors. He not only let me go, but gave me the use of a team and wagon to haul my bedding and several barrels of water. He advised me to go first to Little Mountain, so he could keep in touch with me.

4. *The Hidden Well*

As Little Mountain near Monument 41 was about the same distance from the cave as Cazzarillo Springs, I came to the conclusion to visit the cave first and prospect afterwards. I made an early start for the sacred canyon, taking a canteen of water, a few iron rations, my rifle, and plenty of ammunition, as I expected to stay overnight in the vicinity of the cave.

I walked fast having made up my mind to be across the alkali flat before the sun got high, as both the glare and the dust were hard on the eyes. Reaching the mouth of the canyon about ten o'clock, I sat down to rest a bit.

People who live in an Indian country become very sensitive to sight, sound, and smell. I had been resting but a few minutes when my ears warned me that some one besides myself was in the canyon. Crossing to the opposite side, I took note of fresh moccasin tracks, the prints having been made, I thought, by squaws or young bucks. The burros' dung I judged to be not over a day old. The tracks led up the main canyon. As I stood there listening, I heard a crackling sound. The hills were covered with sotol, and I came to the conclusion the Indians were gathering it to make the drink of the same name, a liquor something like mescal.

I became wary, keeping on the lookout for burros and squaws. I had gone about two miles up the canyon when I got a whiff of smoke. As I did not want to be discovered by a sentinel, or look-out, I kept in the shade of the canyon. Besides, I was afraid the burros would get my scent and warn their owners. A short distance ahead I saw a grove of sotol, putting me in mind of a squad of soldiers at attention. Beyond the grove was the fire.

Standing before the fire were two Indian maids, the elder about sixteen years of age and the younger about thirteen. As they looked very much alike, I took them to be sisters. Both wore bright blankets and buckskin leggings; their black hair was bound in by beaded bands. They were eating the roasted heart of a sotol, which tastes a good bit like cabbage when roasted or steamed.

When the younger girl was through eating, she looked up and down the canyon as if to make sure that no one was about. Then she picked up a lariat and a large olla and started across the canyon. All at once two burros came in sight and trotted up to her. She now seemed to be tapping the canyon wall with a rock. The next minute my mouth fell open, for she seemed to walk right through the canyon wall. Then I saw an opening in the wall I had not taken note of before. She soon came back with the large olla full of water and gave it to a burro. She went back several times to refill the olla.

In my excitement I kept on until I was near enough to see that the opening led into a cave. An egg-shaped slab of rock about seven feet high formed the door and fitted, top and bottom, into the hollowed edges of the wall like a ball into a socket. When it had turned in its socket, this egg-shaped door made a narrow opening on both sides of it about a foot above the ground, one edge of the door putting into the cave and the other extending outward about two feet. I had once seen a rock farther north in the Rockies, which stood in a stone basin like a ball in a socket, turning just so far and then turning back again. The Indians must have made use of some such freak of nature to close the cave.

When she had done her chore the Indian girl gave the egg-shaped door a slight push and it swung tightly back into place, sealing up the canyon wall. Stooping, she lifted a cluster of trailing hop and grape vines and arranged them over the door. No one would have taken note of the door, although he might have suspected water on account of the green spot that hid the mouth of the cave.

Fearing the burros would get my scent, I began to make my getaway. The prospector knew that an Indian's horse or burro would snort and jump if he got the scent of a white man, and that the white man's animal would act the same way if he scented an Indian. I had not gone far when one of the girls caught five burros on the hillside and tied them up. The other girl was covering the burro tracks in the canyon. I knew by these signs that they soon would be leaving the canyon.

I believed the spring lay in a sacred cave which might contain a cache of valuables as well as a supply of sotol. I came to the conclusion to come back and look around the first chance I got. I could not make out why Indian maids had been sent to distill sotol unless it was that the cave was known only to a certain family and not to a whole tribe.

On the way back I came upon some mule bones; I also found a part of a Mexican *aparejo,* or packsaddle. Had the mule been killed by Indians, or had he wandered away from his packers with the piece of rope tied to his halter and got caught in the brush to die of starvation? I took note of a pile of waste that looked like ore sacks, but being in a hurry, I did not stop to examine anything.

As I was still a good way from the American side of the boundary I did not let the grass grow under my feet, for I did not know whether or not my American officer had got me a permit from Mexican authorities. Just on the line I met a company of Mexican rurales and learned from their *capitan* that I had the right to cross the boundary.

"Have you ever been in that canyon?" I asked the *capitan,* pointing in the direction of the sacred canyon.

"A short distance only," said he. "Indians claim it is a sacred canyon and go not often into it. I no think there is mineral in that canyon. Too much volcanic rock and sandstone. See high peak yonder? Indians say he been in action in the memory of their oldest people. Me, I sometimes see smoke come from peak. On hazy day he give off sulphuric smell."

I said nothing of the Indian maids and the burros that I had seen. Having pulled back to my camp in Little Mountain, I decided to wait till the surveyors reached Monument 41 before I went again into the sacred canyon.

That night, as usual when camping out, I slept like a log. When I got cold towards morning, I tried to pull my bedding closer around me. Something was holding it down. In a twinkling I was wide awake. What a fright I got! Lying close beside me was a large black and white skunk. As he was sound asleep I slipped from between my blankets and let him have my bunk, realizing that to disturb him meant the ruin of my bedding. Soon I had stirred up the fire into an immense blaze. Missing his side partner when he woke up, the skunk trotted off.

The nights are cold even in summer in the higher altitudes, and Mr. Skunk, if he comes across a camper bedded down, will surely snuggle down alongside and make himself at home. If one has no dog it is hard to keep him away. This section is the favorite haunt of the little spotted or hydrophobia skunk, so much dreaded by cowmen.

The trade rat also visits the camper, helping himself to his forks and spoons, and leaving in their place, usually chips of wood or dung, bits of bark, or pine cones. Where the pinons grow the trade rat builds his nest of pine cones. The nest is often the size of a barrel. When the cones become dry, the small nuts, about the size of cherry stones, drop to the ground. Knowing this, the Indians rob the nests, often getting a peck or more of nuts from a single nest.

Prospectors seldom kill these desert varmint at camp or cabin; being often alone and seldom with anything to read, the old sourdoughs become interested in their habits. Like a child, the trade rat will drop whatever he is carrying, when something brighter catches his eye. This is the reason he is called the trade rat. An old timer who missed anything, from a tin cup to a razor, generally knew where to find it.

On the desert the pack rat, or the trade rat, builds a big pile of sticks over the mouth of his tunnel, arranging them so that no rain can go through the wood stack. The wise prospector, taking note of this, knew where to find dry wood in rainy weather. Still other trade rats build their nests among the rocks with runways leading to the opening between hedges of cholla joints. A pair of rats will sometimes drag hundreds of these spiny links to the vicinity of their hole, spreading them about in a radius of several feet from the opening. It would take a lot of daring for the enemy to cross a cholla thicket after the trade rat.

The trade rat has large round ears and bright black eyes, set in a gentle face. He keeps his diggings clean, and he is clean about his food, which is mostly grass seeds stored in a separate underground room. Often the only water he gets is through nibbling bits of leaves and grass, and this for months at a time. The Indians used to like the flesh of the trade rat, but they got ashamed to eat it when they saw the whites would not touch it.

In the border country is found in moist clays, a dangerous bug, *nina del terre,* or child of the earth, the bite of whose sharp fangs is claimed by the Mexicans to be poisonous. It looks somewhat like a large potato bug.

Tarantulas, scorpions, centipedes, water bugs galore, and snakes of many kinds are found in this section. Among the rattlers is the sidewinder, a small horned snake that is no bigger than a fancy biscuit when he coils up. He does not play fair like most rattlers, but strikes without a warning. In this section the wise traveler never drops in the shade of the brush without first making sure that a snake is not wrapped about the lower branches close to the roots.

The bite of the tarantula, an overgrown spider, whose velvety, black body would often cover the palm of one's hand, is not supposed to be deadly, but like most Southwesterners I would rather not have his two rows of teeth buried in my flesh. These big spiders with hairy legs were first named in Europe hundreds of years ago, because it was supposed the bite brought on tarantism, a disease that caused the victim to dance without stopping till he dropped dead. In the United States two kinds of tarantulas are found in the South and in the West.

Some tarantulas live under stones or rubbish, and others burrow in the ground, at times covering the opening of their hole with a lid, a perfect trapdoor. This trapdoor is woven in two half circles, which meet on the middle line of the opening like a pair of folding doors. The tarantula has a cunning enemy in the tarantula-wasp, which knows how to open the spider's trapdoor with its sharp, scissors-like antennae.

Hundreds of birds fill the air with song and gladden the eye of the camper with their bright colors. The mockingbirds nest even in the high mountains of the Southwest. If I had a cabin near a clump of brush, they were sure to build their nests there, bringing up two broods in a season. When the moon is full they sing all night. But I must get back to my story.

The next morning I climbed to a high point from which I could see into the sacred canyon, but though I watched for two days, I saw no sign of the squaws. On the fourth day I went over to the mouth of the canyon, cutting sign, but I found no fresh tracks. Watching me from the hillside were hundreds of antelopes, with a look of wonder on their gentle faces, proving that they had seldom been hunted by man.

When I went back to camp that day I got leave from the company officer to drive a team and wagon into the sacred canyon. I told him about the squaws but said nothing about the hidden well. He gave me a driver, a Cornish miner, saying he might be of aid in locating mineral. The officer also saw to it that we had plenty of food and several barrels of water and promised to post the troops to watch for Indian signs.

5. *A Night in the Hidden Cave*

About sunup the next morning we left the surveyors' camp, going first to the spot where I had seen the mule bones. There we unhitched our mules, giving them a taste of water before hobbling them, so they would come back to the wagon when they got thirsty. As the grass was good we did not suppose they would stray very far.

The Cousin Jack, as everyone called the Cornishman, offered to fix up the camp a bit, while I started up the canyon saying, "I expect to be back in four or five hours. If you hear shooting, and I am not back by then, I want you to hitch up and pull back to the surveyors' camp. Notify the company officer, and ask him to hunt me up and send word to the Mexicans rurales to be on the lookout."

About a mile up the canyon I reached a small grove of sotol, or giant yuccas. Going through it I came face to face with a large cougar. He almost turned head over heels trying to make a getaway up the canyon, so I felt there was no one in that direction. At last I got to the squaws' camp and soon learned from the old signs that they had gone south in the direction of the high Sierra Madres.

The Indians must have used this camp for years, although there were no signs of tents. In rainy weather they probably used the hidden cave for shelter. There were no shells, beads, or arrows lying about, but immense roots of sotol were scattered everywhere, from which the Indians had drawn out the juice to make liquor; many pits lay open in the soft rock where the juice of the sotol trunks had been drained through beds of charcoal.

Though I went over the canyon wall where I had seen the mysterious door, I could find no sign of it. Had I been dreaming? No, for cougars had passed by apparently looking for water, the burros' signs were not above four days old, and that patch of green was still there against the canyon wall. The wall behind thevines when tapped with my prospector's pick gave forth a hollow sound. Putting my ear to the wall I heard a drip, drip, drip, as of water, and then a long-drawn, mournful sigh.

Bracing my shoulder against the wall, I tugged at the grape vines trying to loosen them. All of a sudden, with a handful of vines, I fell backward through the very opening I was looking for. The pressure of my shoulder had turned the egg-shaped door in its socket. Getting my balance, I found myself in an immense, dark cave. I could not yet see any water, but its trickle echoed in the cave louder than the tick of a grandfather's clock in an empty house; a warm dampness seemed to wrap itself about me.

While I stood near the opening trying to get used to the darkness, a low, mournful sigh came to me from the deeper section of the cave, getting louder and louder until it ended all of a sudden in a wild shriek. In a twinkling I was outside the cave. I gave the big stone a slight push and it swung easily about, closing the cave. The socket in which this egg-shaped tufa, or pumice stone turned, had been hollowed out of obsidian, or volcanic glass, the work of either wind or water erosion or of the Indians. It was so easy to turn pumice stone in this socket, that a child could have opened the cave.

Scattered about over the volcanic floor of the canyon were many large pumice stones, so light in weight that I could lift without any trouble a rock as big as a barrel. The mountain was of sandstone formation, but it appeared to have been thrown up from a very active volcanic base.

While going back to the wagon I picked out a trail through the canyon, so we could drive the team almost to the cave. As I got near our camp I took note of Cousin Jack dragging towards me behind the mules.

"Oh, Jimmie," said he, dropping heavily to rest on the nearest boulder, "why didn't you tell me those bloomin' mules would make a getaway? I didn't miss them till they'd been gone quite a while. When I cut sign I knew I'd have a bally good chase before I caught up with them. They went south through the canyon lookin' for a water hole they seemed to know about. At last I located them about two miles away at the mouth of a small canyon. They were grazin' on a grassy knoll and didn't even take alarm when a gray wolf ran down the hill a short distance away. The bloomin' mules kept right on feedin', but they let me put their halters on.

"On the way downhill," he went on, "I ran into an old camp. Man alive! First we stumbled over the dry, rotten saddles, then over the bones of the mules, piled up around a circle of rocks. Inside the circle were several human skeletons and a pile of empty rim-fire shells; stocks and gun barrels were of a make of the early sixties. The boots had been badly chewed up by wolves or coyotes. When I lifted a boot the bones dropped out with the flesh dried over them.

"The fight must have lasted for hours, and I doubt if a livin' soul was left to tell the tale. Every little ways on the hill I found the skeletons of the attackers. Pans, kettles, bones, and rotten saddles were left to tell the story. At the foot of the hill I tripped over this pig. Is it silver or lead, Jimmie?"

He held out the bar of metal I had been wondering about while he was talking. It was a slab of silver, hacked and cut, and badly eroded. Perhaps the outfit that had been attacked had been loaded with silver bullion from the mines near Sabinal, on their way to the coast to ship the silver to Swansea, Wales.

After we had examined the bar of silver, wondering if other bars were scattered over the hillside, I told Cousin Jack about the hidden well where the Indians may have cached some of their stolen treasure.

"We'd better stay here to-night," said I. "If we tie one of the mules to the wagon, the other one will not go far for mates seldom drift far apart. These army mules become very fond of their drivers, Cousin Jack, and you needn't be surprised if you feel the cold nose of a mule rubbing your face in the night when we're out on a trip like this. If they smell Indians or dangerous animals they'll surely wake up their driver, and by their looks and actions will almost show him where the enemy is."

"They're like their bloomin' father, the jackass, eh, Jimmie?"

"You're right. They never forget and they never get lost. If once they travel through a section, no matter how much it is changed, even years afterward they will make for your old camp, and almost force you to stop there again.

"The smell of blood doesn't seem to excite them as it does a horse. A mule will go without food and water longer than a horse;

he will live on brush and grow fat, while a horse, and even a cow, would starve to death. Your mule will get along at times on a flapjack or a crust of bread. Mules are very fond of children and dogs. Sometimes their actions would almost convince you they had been planned."

"By King George's tooth, Jimmie, I'd have no trouble in believing those bally mules you're so fond of, planned to walk the legs off me this day. They're full of bally tricks if you ask me. I'm starved, old son. Can't we eat?"

After a light meal we went at once to bed, for we were both fagged out. About midnight I was awakened by Cousin Jack, who had grown very restless. "What's wrong?" I asked.

"That's what I want to know," he growled. "Some bloody beast is stingin' me. I feel as if some one was sticking needles into me. What bloody bird or animal would attack me like that, Jimmie? Is it those bally mules, do you think?"

"There's electricity in this pass," said I.

"I say, old son, I believe the place is afire. Even the grass feels like a bunch of nettles. Run your hand along it, and explain that to me."

I ran my hands over the grass and got a shock. "Have you ever been in the tropics near the ocean?" I asked him. "If so, you certainly have seen the lights on the water, of a dark night. You'd have taken note of the same thing in marshy places in the southern United States."

"Sure, old son, I was a whole year at Durban, Africa, before I went to the Kimberley Mines. Believe me or not, old son, myself and some other lads were bathing in the surf one night, when along comes a big wave, tucks us under his arm, and throws us right in the middle of one of those patches of bloomin' light. Don't talk to me about bein' in the lime light. I never felt so ashamed in my life, old son, for bathing suits were not in style, and that light showed more than the top of our heads to a crowd of girls on the beach. But there's no light here, Jimmie."

"No, although this place is about as spooky as a swamp with the lights moving over the water like spirits, in this mountain pass electricity is the cause. Do you see how it is shocking the mules? Run your hand real fast over the grass and you'll see the sparks fly. This place is a regular dynamo, and the air currents act as a receiver. See those dark moving clouds. I expect as soon as they pass over we'll be rid of the electricity, and then we can go back to sleep."

Hearing our voices, the loose mule came trotting up to us to be petted, but fearing to make a contact and give her a shock, I did not touch her. She walked over to the wagon, hanging her head, and touched the wheel with her nose. How she snorted and jumped from the shock!

Shortly after this a still breeze came up, and we got rid of the prickly sensations. A time may come when these passes that attract electricity are put to use by scientists, either for the treatment of disease or as power plants. Mexicans believe they are vents from hidden volcanoes. They take care not to camp in one of these passes.

"Jimmie, old son, I could have believed I was trying to sleep in a bed of cactus," said Cousin Jack, getting sleepy again. "I hope it wasn't a blasted warnin' to us to get out of this canyon."

Following the dry electric storm, the air became cold, as though we had had a hail storm. These electric storms are known among old timers as weather-breeders. I told the Cornishman we must make an early start; otherwise, we were apt to get caught in a bad sandstorm. I wanted to reach the hidden well as soon as possible, for northers as well as sandstorms were common in this section.

Even in summer one suffers with cold in a norther, as it generally brings hail and sleet with it. When caught in such a storm the wise traveler stops in a gully till it is over, taking care to cover up with his bedding to avoid being chilled to the bone.

The sandstorm is more common. At times the trails are buried under sand which whirls around the traveler, biting and stinging, like snow in a blizzard. The landscape is blotted out, and the sun is hidden behind thick curtains of brown sand. In such a storm it is easy to be lost. During these high winds droves of Russian thistles, or tumbleweeds, race by, each one trying to pass the other, ahead of the sand spouts.

The storm usually ends up with a light rain. Cattle will drift with the storm, sometimes crowding up against a barbed wire fence, where numbers of the herd are killed. Most cattle learn however, to hunt a gulch or a canyon, but even there the sandstorm is bad for the herd, if it lasts two or three days, for the cattle cannot reach food or water.

The cold nose of the mule woke me up the next time. Both

animals kept looking up the canyon where Cousin Jack had found them grazing. I saw by the Dipper that it was almost morning. I got up to look in the same direction as the mules. A signal flashed from the high Sierra Madres, which was instantly answered by one from the Big Hatchets. Had a stray band of Apaches discovered we were in the canyon, or were they signalling to each other on the hunt? In a little while the mules lay down again, and I went back to sleep. Cousin Jack had not stirred.

Cousin Jack had breakfast ready shortly after daybreak. While eating, I told him about the flashes. We had been thinking of driving first to the old battlefield he had discovered, but we now decided to go at once to the hidden well, as I knew the Indians would not enter a sacred canyon even when on the warpath.

About a mile from the well we unloaded the wagon, packing as much as possible on the mules, including plenty of rope and five lanterns which the surveyors had loaned us. Cousin Jack led the mules, while I went ahead, scouting as far as the alder trees where the Indian skeletons swayed in the wind in their cottonwood wrappings. I told Cousin Jack to wait for me at the sotol thicket where I had seen the Indian girls making sotol.

When I got back I found him there, boiling coffee and frying bacon. He was glad to hear I had found no signs except cougar tracks. After eating, we built a barricade around the door of the hidden cave, stacking up the sotol roots which lay about in hundreds. Inside the barricade we unloaded the mules and made up our beds. Before closing up the barricade we hauled in some brush for fire, and a good supply of fresh sotol, so the mules would have browse in case we were attacked by Indians or outlaws. By building our barricade against the canyon wall, we knew we could take the mules with us into the hidden cave if we were attacked.

When all was ready for the night I showed Cousin Jack the secret door to the hidden well. He agreed with me that it would probably be safer to go through the cave by night. After it got dark I opened the door. Cousin Jack's eyes almost popped out of his head when he saw the big stone turn in its sockets. We carried in the tools and the bucket, and lighted two lanterns.

Then we went down the drift into the cave and soon reached a turn, where we were almost blinded by a sudden flash of light. There followed the sound of water dashing against rocks. The light was gone with the speed of lightning, which it was like, though it was brighter than any lightning I had ever seen. How pale was the light of our lanterns after that brilliant flash! As we went on down the draft the flash was repeated every so often, each time followed by the roar of waters.

As we went deeper into the cave a rushing wind swept about us when the flash came. At each flash we could see the roof, on which were hundreds of hand prints. We could also see plainly the bones and veins in our hands.

A sudden turn to the right brought us to the hidden well. It lay below the floor at least six feet, steps having been cut to reach the water. The pool was about twenty feet across. The flashes showed a few fish and a frog in the pool, the light being so strong we could see every bone in their bodies.

We put on our dust glasses to protect our eyes. At each flash the water in the pool rose, dashing from side to side, throwing a heavy spray over us, but never overflowing. Then would rise from the drift a pitiful moan which put me in mind of a person in agony. It gave us both the creeps. "Oh! Oh! Ohee! Ohee! Mercee! Mercee!" began the low, sad cry, getting louder and louder and ending all of a sudden in a shriek as a rush of cool air swept about our legs.

"There must be a volcanic vent near-by," said I. "It all puts me in mind of geysers I've seen in action in Yellowstone Park."

"Damme, old son, I'm afraid it's the bloomin' Tommy Knockers! The bloody bounders! I've heard them in the tin mines of Cornwall, England, on the ghost shift, knockin' warnings to the miners to let them alone. When they make the rat-tat-tat, it's time for the Cousins to pick up their tools and pull for the top. Come along, come along, old son! Let's get out of this bloody cave."

"It's neither ghosts nor spirits," said I. "You're not going to give up, are you, till we've looked for that cache of bullion?"

At mention of the bullion he forgot his terror, and we pushed on down the drift. As we went down the noises grew louder and louder, and the air became heavy with sulphuric and other gaseous odors. When we had gone down about a thousand feet we came to a side drift, with its mouth almost closed from a fall of rock.

A short distance down this drift we stumbled over a pile of skeletons, at least a dozen lying close together. Had the victims died of bad air or of starvation? Searching about we found nothing but broken Indian crockery. Pictographs on the wall may have been the story of their death. In this drift we neither saw the flashes nor heard the moans, but the poisonous air soon made us drowsy.

Going back to the pool, we examined the ollas standing around it. All had lately been filled with sotol. The fresh marks on the wall near-by may have been made for visiting Indians. We tasted the sotol, which is a good deal like mescal, though it is much stronger. It was something like Scotch whisky with a strong, smoky flavor added to it.

Outside we found everything as we had left it. Cousin Jack helped me carry some boulders into the cave, which we piled up, so I could examine the hand prints on the roof. The marks seemed to have been burned in with a branding iron, or impressed there at a time when the sandstone in the roof of the cave was still moist. I have spoken with many Indians since, but none ever seemed to know the meaning of the sign.

The flashes kept on. One of my legs had been badly broken some years before, and it still gave me much trouble. I got the idea that since we were able to see through the fish in the pool we might be able to see through our bodies. Stripping off my clothing, I pointed out the weak spot and asked Cousin Jack to watch it during a flash.

"Jimmie, old son," he exclaimed, "at that point your bone looks as if it's hanging together by a cobweb."

Cousin Jack now wanted me to look for a bullet in his body that had never been found by the doctors. He said he sometimes got a pain in his shoulder, and he suspected the bullet was there, though it had entered his body near his heart. Sure enough! When he had pulled off his clothing the flash showed the flattened lead against his shoulder bone as plainly as if it lay in my hand. I marked the spot with an indelible pencil he dug out of his pocket, and later on the bullet was cut out by an army surgeon.

Our bodies seemed to be affected by the light. "Old Son," said Cousin Jack, "I feel as if I could run like a deer." But before long we were both in a big sweat. The Cornishman being a great smoker, his body gave off the smell of tobacco.

Fagged out with excitement, we dressed and headed for the opening of the cave. How fresh was the early morning air! Yet we nearly fainted from the change when we first left the cave. Tired as we were, we built a fire and boiled some coffee.

After we had a bite to eat, I said to Cousin Jack, "You turn in now, and I'll keep an eye on the camp. I'll cook a mess of beans, so we can have a good feed before striking out for your battlefield."

He needed no coaxing, and in a few minutes he was dead to the world. After watering the mules and putting the beans on to cook, I decided to time the flashes in the cave; but my watch had stopped, and I soon found out that it would not run in the cave. In order not to drop off to sleep I had to keep walking.

The sun was over six hours high when Cousin Jack woke up, feeling, he said, "like a fighting cock."

I then lay down, telling him to be sure to call me if there were any signs of danger. Many hours went by before Cousin Jack woke me up, to say that the mules were excited. With ears laid back both animals were staring up the canyon. Climbing on a boulder, I looked over the barricade but saw nothing. The mules had probably scented cougars.

In this section it was hard to raise a colt on their account. The cougar is very strong. I have seen him slaughter a three-hundred-pound colt, throw it over his shoulder, and trot down the valley as lightly as if he toted a feather.

As it was near sundown we made ready to leave, but we first ate a big mess of beans and finished our Army bread. While Cousin Jack tore down the barricade and packed our supplies I did some more scouting. When I got back we covered all our signs and fixed the vines over the secret door. Then we were off.

This canyon was not often used, for the trail was very dim. The mules needed no whip after we hitched them to the wagon, and we rattled along the trail as if the devil were after us. That night we spent in our old camp in the electrified pass.

The next morning we went to Cousin Jack's old battlefield, looking about for bullion, but we found only a few scraps. The history of that battle was written more vividly upon the landscape than I could ever tell it. Whoever had attacked the barricaded party paid dearly for victory, judging from the number of skeletons scattered over the hillside. The knoll was a natural fort from which we could see a long distance. As we started downhill we caught a glimpse of a company of United States troops on horseback, galloping through the canyon. I signaled them by firing my rifle, and they soon rode up to us.

The sergeant in command handed me an order from the company officer, bidding us to go back at once to the surveyors' camp. We learned from the soldiers that a renegade Apache, known as The Kid, had left the reservation with a crowd of bucks, killing two men near Lordsburg and stealing some horses not far from Hachita. He was thought to be somewhere along the border.

The Kid had been educated at Carlisle, Pennsylvania, and could speak both English and Spanish. Several times he had left the reservation, and each time he had kidnapped a squaw before he went back. One of these squaws, snatched from a chief, had been killed by him on the Gila River; a young Mexican girl had been stolen by him on the same river and murdered later on in the Sierra Madres in Old Mexico.

The Kid knew southern New Mexico well. Dashing into a settlement, he would kill several persons, rob a store or two, and make his getaway with a beautiful girl thrown over his horse. In the end he was killed by the officers of the law.

We went back with the escort to the surveyors' camp. I gave the company officer an account of our trip, showing him the bullion, and describing the scene on the old battlefield. I said nothing of the hidden well. He was very much interested in this strange country and felt sorry that Congress was not going ahead with the survey. The agent at San Carlos had sent word that a number of bucks had left the reservation to join The Kid, and that there was a lot of unrest among the Indians who remained. It was decided to stop the surveying for the time being.

I made the most of every minute that was left, prospecting on Little Mountain, but without any luck, for the brush at that season was so heavy I could not find any float. When the men were paid off we went to Lordsburg. From there I set out on a course of wandering that lasted many years, carrying me into Nevada, Idaho, California, and back again to New Mexico.

6. *The Old Lady From Little Mountain*

At Cook's Peak I was leaded and after that spent all I had saved from different stakes, trying to get back my health. At Lake Valley I sold a half interest in a mining claim to Jack Glasson, whom I knew to be as honest as the sun and a fine mining man. He was to pay for his share of the ores we took out. As the time of my lease would soon run out I asked the company for a three-months extension, which was refused.

When our time was up the company operated the mine, taking

out, it was said, a million dollars worth of ore. The new superintendent, who had refused to lease us any more claims, even ordered Glasson to move his family off the company's ground.

We stayed in Lake Valley waiting for the returns of our last shipment, intending to try our luck in some other camp. The returns seemed delayed, and as I was footloose, I was generally at the station when the mail train came in. One day a little old woman got off the train, looking about her in a dazed way. She spoke to the station agent in a real English accent. The agent pointed to me, and the old lady came up to me, asking me to direct her to my partner's house.

Thinking she was a relative of his, I offered to go with her. On the way it turned out that she was a stranger who had been directed to the Glassons by the railroad agent in Lordsburg. Her mind appeared weak, for she kept saying over and over, "It was no Indians; it was cowboys; and they murdered my husband for his ranch."

In a red bandanna, which seemed her only luggage, she carried something heavy. I offered to pack it for her, but she hugged it to her as though I were trying to rob her. The day was warm and she staggered with weakness, but she would not have the help of my arm. She was surely an independent old lady. When I told her that Mrs. Glasson was a good wife and mother she brightened up a lot. We found Mrs. Glasson bathing her two children. After reading the note from the Lordsburg agent, Mrs. Glasson brought the old lady into the cool front room and took off her hat for her. I went back to town where I met Glasson, but he could not imagine who the old lady was.

A few days later when I called at the Glassons I found Mrs. Griggs, the old lady, full of talk, and fairly cheerful, though the story she told was a sad one. Her husband, an Englishman, and his German partner had lived many years in Texas, owning a large flock of sheep. A drought came to that section of Texas, and it was soon plain that all their sheep would starve unless they moved them.

The German made a trip to New Mexico and found a good range near Little Mountain where I had once picked up the rich float. Neither of the partners was a citizen, but both had taken out their first papers. They moved their sheep to the New Mexico range, intending as soon as they were settled to take out their last papers, and prove up on the land.

Arrangements were made with Doyle to get water until such time as they were able to find it and drill for it on their own land. A surveyor was brought from Las Cruces to measure off two homesteads, but he told them that Little Mountain was mineral land and could not be filed on as a homestead, so they got the numbers of the quarter sections and filed on the mineral land.

They had taken an option on Doyle's place, only to learn that the cattlemen would allow no sheep on this range and that Wind River Jack himself would soon be pulling out. This cattle outfit had herds on both sides of the border and intended before long to drill for water on Little Mountain. The Englishman and the German paid no heed to Doyle's warning.

Soon they had built a cabin and an outhouse, and when all was ready they fetched the old lady from Texas. The sheep fattened quickly on the rich grass. She was happy in her three-room cabin, listening all day to the song of the hammers, for her husband was busy building corrals. Out on the range the German herded the sheep.

But one day the German came home early, wildly excited, saying that the cowmen had stampeded the sheep and ordered him to vamoose. They accused the sheepherders of ruining the range and threatened to fill them full of lead if they did not leave at once. When the sheep were again rounded up it was discovered that most of the ewes had been either crushed in the stampede or had died from exposure.

The German wanted to move out right away, but the Englishman was stubborn and would not give in. Instead, he moved the sheep to another part of the range. Nothing more was heard from the cowmen for many weeks, and the partners concluded that the trouble had been made by drunken cowboys on their way south.

In the meantime the Englishman had found some rich silver ore not far from the cabin. He had sunk a hole on the spot, saying he would record his discovery the next time he went to Deming, the county seat. A few feet from the cabin he set up his rock monument. Soon afterwards a cowboy rode up, saying he had filed on the quarter section where the corral stood. Hot words flew between the two men. The Englishman gave the cowboy the number of his claim and dared him to try to put him off. The cowboy swore a blue streak and rode off, saying that this was a cow country and that any damned foreigners who put sheep on it would be sorry.

Doyle faded out of the landscape shortly after this, and it was believed he had been bribed to do so by the cowmen. The troubles of the sheepherders began to multiply. One day a party of travelers, going from Texas to Arizona, stopped off at the Griggs' cabin to spend the night. From them it was learned that the Apaches were on the warpath. They wanted the Englishman to cut port holes in his cabin, but he took no heed of their warning.

Another day an outlaw stopped at the cabin, asking for something to eat. He told the old lady that the cowmen had no use for her husband and his partner because they were sheepherders. From him she found out for certain that Doyle had been driven out by the cattlemen. Before leaving, the outlaw told the old lady to do all she could to get the two men to leave the country. Then he looked up her husband on the range and warned him also. He ended with bitter words against the cattlemen, "I wouldn't be an outlaw to-day if it weren't for those damned cattle outfits."

About two weeks later, during a heavy rainstorm, a band of horsemen dressed like Indians dashed up to the cabin. No one heard them coming as it was a noisy storm. Breaking the windows and bursting in the door, they went into the cabin, and killed both men. They cursed and acted like fiends, finally driving the terrified old lady out into the storm. The sheep in the corrals were then stampeded by the raiders, and last of all they set fire to the cabin and rode off, shrieking like madmen above the roar of the storm.

The poor old lady hid in the brush for hours, drenched with rain. Towards sundown she crept up to the ruined cabin, where she covered the bodies of the murdered men, too dazed to shed a tear over the body of her husband.

She then set out for Lordsburg but made little headway during the night, for when the sun came up in the morning the ruined cabin was still within sight. Apparently the poor creature had traveled all night in a circle. She went back to the cabin to get a bite to eat. In the wreckage there she picked up the red handkerchief in which her husband had wrapped specimens of the rich silver float. Once more she set out for Lordsburg, spending two days and a night on the trip.

Miners from Lordsburg went out to Little Mountain to bury the two men. When they got back they told the old lady the cabin had been looted and the horses and sheep driven off. One of the Mexicans who helped to bury her husband said to her, "No

Indian kill your man. White man's work. No want sheep on range. No cow will eat after sheep."

The people of Lordsburg had treated the old lady very kindly; but fear, sorrow, and the long walk over the desert without food or water had affected her mind. The agent at Lordsburg, thinking she would get better among her own countrymen, had raised a small sum of money to send her to the Glassons, whom he knew well.

The old lady showed the ore specimens to Glasson and begged him to go down to Little Mountain to work the claim for her, saying that all she wanted out of it was a sum big enough to carry her back to England. When Glasson showed me the specimen I knew it at once for the same grade of ore I had picked up myself on Little Mountain.

Glasson got me to go down to Little Mountain with him. "If we find the ore it's good-by to the cattlemen," said I, "for it will mean a rush of miners into that section."

After scouring the countryside we finally made arrangements with a man who owned a team and wagon, to go with us. The old lady told Glasson she thought her husband had recorded his discovery in Silver City, but there was no account of it there nor in Deming.

With a ten-days supply of food we headed for Little Mountain. There we found the partly-burned cabin, with the door and window frames missing. A cot still in good shape stood in a corner of the bedroom. Some distance up the valley a well was being drilled, and a herd of cattle wandered over the flat. Then we knew the old lady's tale was true.

Doyle's well was filled up with debris, and the fence had been carried off. The drillers told us we could find water three miles across the border. We filled our barrels there the next day. Though we prospected every foot of Little Mountain we had no luck. The only spot left untouched by our picks was under the outhouse. At the end of a week I sat on the doorstep of the ruined cabin feeling down in the mouth. Hearing a creepy noise, I looked into the room behind me, just as a large rattlesnake slid out from under the cot. He crawled back in time to miss my bullet. Getting a long pole I tried to roll him out but disclosed instead a heavy cigar box filled with rich ore.

Again we began the search, staying on Little Mountain till our food was gone. Before leaving we located and monumented a large section of Little Mountain, believing the sheepherders' time was up, even if they had a right to the property.

Hoping to get the old lady to return with us, we pulled back to Lake Valley. There we learned that she had borrowed five dollars from Mrs. Glasson and set out for El Paso. The poor soul had decided to employ a lawyer there and sue the suspected cattle company for damages. A few days later I was notified by El Paso officials that Mrs. Griggs had dropped dead on the street. They had buried her in El Paso. In her purse they found my address.

In the meantime the superintendent of the mine had a change of heart, giving a new lease to Glasson and me. In a short time we made a neat sum of money. Once more I moved from camp to camp, crossed the Pacific in the Spanish-American War, and eventually wound up again in New Mexico.

7. *Toppy*

I took up with Charles Gearhart, who had been with me in Idaho, and we leased an old mine near Stein's Pass. We got our water and supplies from the station on the Southern Pacific Railroad. The ore on the dumps was good jigging ore; and we were in high feather when the rains came early, filling up several old shafts with a good supply of water.

We made use of an old cabin at the mine, set up off the rocks on posts about two feet high; so we had good circulation of air during the long nights of an extra hot summer. Probably in order to keep cool, snakes, centipedes, tarantulas, and a variety of poisonous insects made their headquarters under our cabin. As meat was cheap we bought it by the quarter, hanging it uncovered on a tree at night and wrapping a wagon sheet around it by day to keep off flies and insects; but every time we got a fresh supply we were sure to kill two or three rattlers and a dozen centipedes that had been drawn from under the cabin by the smell of blood.

Apart from these unwelcome visitors we often saw no living creature but ourselves for weeks at a time, though our cabin door was always open in keeping with the custom of the times. How pleased we were to find a visitor waiting for us in our cabin who knew the latest news.

One day when we came in at noon we met on the porch Toppy Johnson, a well-known outlaw of the Southwest, the man who had helped me years before in Kingston when I was down and out.

He had served a term or two in prison since then, and each time he was released he gave the cattle outfits a world of trouble. This time a big reward had been offered for him and he was, as he put it, "on the hike."

After we had given each other the glad hand, Toppy said, "I am going to make myself useful after we've had a bite to eat. I'm going to smoke out the varmint from under your cabin and nail it up around the bottom. It's a wonder the rattlesnakes didn't get you before this. I saw an immense rattler crawl up through a knot hole in the floor while I was sitting here waiting for you. But that fellow won't bother you again."

"If you think we have many rattlers here," I said, "you should have been with us in the northern end of the Black Range a while back, eh, Gearhart?

"Nowhere have I seen so many rattlesnakes as in that section," I went on. "It was the fall of the year and they were lying by the dozens on the rocks about us, following us with their unwinking stare, but too lazy at that season of the year to coil up and strike; though I will say we did not try to pet them.

"We had made our camp close to a cave with a narrow opening about ten feet long and three feet wide. How deep it was we could not tell. At dusk millions of bats, so it seemed to us, rushed from the cave, a fact which explained the number of rattlers, as bats are their principal food."

"I'll bet there's tons of bat guano in that cave, Jimmie, don't you?" Gearhart asked me.

"Help fasten this rope around me, and as soon as the bats are all out for the night you can let me down, and we'll soon find out. Bat guano will bring us thirty-five dollars a ton right now."

But I had reckoned without the rattlesnakes. Seeing so many above ground, it had not dawned on either one of us that there might be some in the cave. Gearhart had not let me down more than fifty feet when I realized they were there on every ledge and every jutting rock. My headlight focussed on one pair of beady eyes after another and showed up hundreds of snake skeletons lying on heaps of guano. There must have been tons of bat guano but I had lost all interest.

"Gearhart," I yelled, "haul me up." But he did not hear me and kept on letting me down faster than ever.

The cave was narrow all the way down, with drifts or openings, running off into the sides. Every minute I expected to land on the bottom in a nest of squirming snakes. Finally I made a leap for a ledge of rock where I could see only two snakes lying rather far back. I tugged at the rope with all my might——.

"And I hauled him up," said Gearhart, "and he'll never be whiter when he's dead. It was a narrow escape he had that time. We kept watch by our fire all night; it was too risky to go to sleep. Well, how about some grub?" he ended entering the cabin.

Toppy was a well-educated Texan, tall, straight, and lean. His bald head had less hair than a billiard ball and was a fine mark for the officers of the law who were out to get him. He was the last man in the world I would have picked for an outlaw.

"Boys," said he, while we fell to and cleared the table, "I've been accused of many a crime of which I did not know a thing. There was a time, as you will remember, Jimmie, when I owned a fine ranch with plenty of grass and water for my two hundred head of cattle. I expected to marry and settle down, and I'd be making a good living for a family to-day if it weren't for the big cattle outfits.

"The big cattlemen wanted me out of the way. First they accused me of branding their calves, and then they ran off my cows and calves to pay me back, so they said. Finally they burned my cabin while I was away and framed me in a shooting scrape. As long as I was under a cloud I made up my mind I might as well have the game as the name. The big cattlemen made me an outlaw."

I believed Toppy and so did many others who knew him in better days.

"But what about you, Jimmie, old son? Did the Indians finally let you alone?"

"They haven't bothered me much since they got Johnny," I told him, "but Charlie, there, will never forgive the California Indians for the boiled-dog dinner they gave him. It was the time we came down from Idaho driving a team of mail horses. Will you ever forget those horses, Charlie? They were two large bays, Oregon-bred, one named Sankey and the other Moody. They had been hauling the mail from Winnemucca, Nevada, to Silver City, Idaho, and it seems after they crossed the Ohyhee River, from there to the railroad they had been in the habit of stopping every time they met or passed a person on the road. They would stand stockstill till the person came up to the coach and got his mail. As there was a fair going on there were hundreds of wagons, men on horseback, and people afoot, in the road. We sure had a time with those two animals. At last some man gave us a bunch of papers that looked like letters, and told us to pass them out to everyone we met till we got to the railroad. He told us old Sankey knew every sheepherder from Ohyhee to White Pine, Nevada. We took his tip, and after that we had no more trouble to get the horses to move on.

"Well, Toppy, I was going to tell you about that boiled-dog dinner. We followed the Central Pacific Railroad west to Lovelock. Close to this valley was the sink of the Carson River. At this time there was not a drop of water in it. Some Indians from Walker Lake Reservation told us we could save forty miles or more by crossing the sink. They said we could follow their wagon tracks, for they had crossed the night before. The moon was full and they said it was as light as day in the sink. One of them offered to drive us over to Wabuska for five dollars, but as we were not very flush we tried to jew him down to two dollars. He refused, so we asked some ranchers what they thought about it. They told us the long road was sandy and advised us to cross the lake. The sun was too hot in the daytime and we had to drive over at night. That evening we headed into the sink, one walking ahead, following the wagon tracks. Gearhart did most of the walking. Shortly before daybreak we could see a light on the western edge of the sink. At times we could see people moving around it, so we knew it was a camp fire. Then a wind would carry to our noses the smell of soup. We were both tired and hungry and it was a smell to make the mouth water. Every little while Charlie would say, 'Oh, what I'd do to a pot of that stuff.'

"Finally the dogs got our scent, and then what barking and howling. At last we had a glimpse of the campers—a small band of Digger Indians. There must have been at least twenty-five dogs and puppies around the camp. I suspected what the soup was made of. A large caldron was sitting over the fire. It must have had two gallons of the slumgullion in it. At times one of the squaws would throw in some red chili peppers and a handful of barley, stirring it up and tasting it, pouring at times more hot water into it. Gearhart could hardly wait till we unhitched the horses, could you, old son? One of the bucks handed him a large gourd filled with the soup. It was so hot at first he could not drink it, but he soon gulped it down and held out the gourd to the buck for more.

"By this time I had got out some rye bread from the grub box and was soaking it in the soup. The Indians all sat around filling themselves up. Finally an old buck seemed full enough to burst, and Gearhart was nearly as bad. The buck kept rubbing his belly, saying 'Heap good! Heap good! Fat puppy!'

"Gearhart looked daggers at me. 'You knew that was dog,' said he.

" 'Why,' said I, 'Do you see any goat or sheep around here? What do you think they raise those pups for—to bark? It's good filling, and it won't kill you.'

"We stayed at the agency three days. The agent told Charlie he would about as soon eat young dog as chicken or ducks. A man travelling amongst Mexicans or Indians don't want to be too fastidious about his eats, so among old pioneers a boiled-dog dinner is some feast."

"Well," said Toppy, "and when a man is on the jump ahead of the law like I am most of the time, he can't be too fastidious, that's sure. I've seen the day I'd eat rattlesnake with relish."

"By jiminy," said Charlie, "you two can have all the dog and rattlesnake you want, but I'll take mine in beef or mutton. I sure never will forget how I felt when I knew I was full of dog."

"What kind of luck did you old sons have up in Idaho?" asked Toppy.

"Well," said Gearhart, "I had a brother up in Silver City, Idaho, I had not seen in twenty-five years. I heard from him every once in a while. He told me that himself and two other fellows had leased an old mine and had struck quite a good body of high-grade ore. He wanted me to come on as he believed there was more show up there than in New Mexico. It was the month of March when that letter came, so Jimmie and I disposed of our lease. We bought tickets to Nampa, Idaho, and staged it from there to Silver City. When we pulled in we found that section covered with snow two feet deep. My brother, Taylor, met us at a hotel. He told us he wanted to run a tunnel on a piece of ground adjoining the Black Jack, a very rich producing mine on Florida Mountain near where he was working. He said this land was vacant, for the law of Idaho made a locater have mineral in place before he could record the claim. No one had ever found any mineral in place, although the ground was covered with rich float. My brother could not show us the float on account of the snow, but he offered to put up along with us, and get us bed and board in a hotel near-by. If we struck ore we were all to have equal shares in the location. All the mining men told us if we ever found the lead we would be heeled as far as money went. We moved to the cabin on Blue Gulch, which was almost air-tight. We soon found out it needed to be, in that section. The snow sure got Jimmie up there about as bad as the dog meat got me in California."

"I'll say it did," said I. "Never will I forget those days. As Taylor Gearhart had all kinds of tools we soon were driving a tunnel into Florida Mountain. We could cook and sleep in the cabin but we carried a lunch up the mountain to our mine. The weather kept good till some time in May. We made great headway. The old snow was almost gone, and we could at times see the float which panned very good. We were now over one hundred feet under cover. As wood and water were close, they both being covered with almost air-tight sheds, why, we were thinking we would not be much troubled in stormy weather. But one morning we woke up and saw the whole mountain covered with a deep snow. We saw we would not be able to reach the mine unless we snow-shoed, so we pulled to Bonnersville about one and a half miles away on Jordan Creek, staying there about a week.

"The weather then warmed up again and we went back to the cabin and to driving the tunnel. The mountain soon was covered with growing wild oats and rye. Even the sunflowers came out. Then came a blizzard, and it snowed eight days. We had burnt up almost all our wood before the storm let up. At least four feet of snow must have fallen and we were snow-bound. But the sun came out, and as it was now June we soon warmed up again. The minute we opened the doors, in rushed hundreds of field mice. Oh, what a time! On to our cots, into our pockets and blankets, and if you would reach into your pocket or lie down on your blankets you would run your hand into a mess of young mice, slimy and without hair. I believe we killed a thousand before we got shed of them.

"A chinook wind coming from the west, the snow ran off the mountain like a flood. We continued running the tunnel till the middle of July. No snow being on the mountain we concluded to look the ground over. We believed the float had been forced up the hill instead of washing down from the top. We ran some open cuts below our tunnel and found the vein. It was small and not so rich. We started taking out ore, but before we got a good mill-run it set in to snow again. We were not prepared for the long winter of Idaho, so we had what ore we had taken out hauled to Silver City and milled. It now was snowing hard and as we had lived a good many years in the Southwest we decided to pull out for a warmer clime."

"And that's how you got in with Digger Indians and dog meat," laughed Toppy.

"Well, boys," said Gearhart, "I hate to say the word, but it's about time we pull back to the mine."

Toppy went with us to watch us at work in the mine. "Boys," said he, "why don't you go down to Monument 41 about fifteen miles east of Hachita? I saw an Englishman there digging pure silver out of a hole just back of his cabin. He was killed shortly afterwards by a cow outfit. It was given out that he was killed by Indians, but I know better, for I've seen his wagon and mules on a cattle range that I can name. If I weren't in trouble I'd go down there and locate the ore, but I guess from now on I'll be on the jump till I die with my boots on."

I told Toppy how many times in the past I had looked for that very ore without any luck. He drew a little sketch for me, showing me the direction of the ore hole from the ruined cabin.

Toppy stayed with us for several days. Noticing that his feet were almost on the ground, I made a trip over to the store in the Pass to get him some boots and some tobacco. He thanked me with tears in his eyes. That night he lit out, and we heard afterwards that he had joined Black Jack's gang, all of whom were killed or captured about two years later.

Shortly after Toppy left us we had an accident with our water supply and came to the conclusion to make use of Toppy's tip about the ore on Little Mountain. As I mentioned before we were getting our water from an old shaft that had filled up during the summer rains. It seems that the water had kept fit to use because a pair of green snakes lived on the insects and tadpoles that would otherwise have turned it green. Now, it happened that at the time, I was accountable for the comings and goings of a nineteen-year-old lad, who had been sent to me through my cousin, the mayor of Pittsburg, in the hope that a wholesome out-of-door life would make a man of him. He was the only legitimate son of a father who had about twenty children, but that is another story, and is neither here nor there. It is enough to say that Bill was costing me about a hundred dollars a month in Lake Valley, what with running after the girls and playing the dandy, so I sent for him to join me at Stein's Pass, thinking he'd have plenty of room to blow off steam in that section for awhile. He brought along a friend of his, and the first thing they did was to kill the two little snakes that had safeguarded our water supply for so many weeks. Within a week the water began to stink. I concluded to send Bill back to his people, for it seemed to me that he was a chip of the old block, and would sooner or later get into trouble.

Gearhart went with me to Little Mountain. A railroad had been built through that section since I was there last, and a station stood close to Doyle's old well. The country had been fenced and was dotted with windmills, but not a spear of grass could be seen for miles. The ranches were deserted, and we had to haul feed for our animals. Nearly all the quail and rabbits had disappeared. From an isolated rancher we learned that there had been no rain for three years. The railroad hauled water for their employees, and a water train ran through the section.

On Little Mountain we found a sparse growth of brush and grass roots. The cabin was still there. The international boundary line was fenced with barbed wire six strands high. A cowboy we met told us that all the cattle that had not died had been driven into Mexico.

About three o'clock my partner set out with high hopes to do some prospecting. I stayed behind to keep an eye on the stock. It was nearly dark when Gearhart returned. He was down in the mouth, for he had been to a dozen holes on the hill and had not found even one ounce of float.

The next morning we came upon a man from Deming at work on Little Mountain, but none of his diggings showed any rich ore. Still hoping to make a discovery, we prospected a week longer. Then my partner said that he had had enough of that section and backed out on his promise to visit the hidden well. There was nothing for it but to pull back to the Black Range. Near Hermosa we located and leased until the outbreak of the Mexican revolution under Madero.

8. "*Black Buffaloes*"

Fearing trouble, our Government had stationed troops along the border, one of the main camps being at Hachita, New Mexico. Most of these troops were negro cavalry of the Ninth and Tenth Regiments. They were good fighters and the Apaches did not like to run against them, calling them "buffalo soldiers." The commissioned officers were whites, graduates from West Point, and most of them were very strict with the soldiers under them. Negro veterans certainly knew their duty and were always on the job. No better troops could be found along the border. Details were posted from Columbus to Hachita, one group being located in Little Mountain pass. The sergeant in charge was as black as midnight.

Believing that in the unsettled condition of Mexico some good chances might turn up in the border mines, we came to the conclusion to go once more to Little Mountain. With so many troops in the vicinity it would be easy to get food and water, and maybe an escort. But the ruined cabin where we expected to camp was no longer there. Four small shacks had been put up near the old cabin site. About a hundred feet back of the cabin site stood a large gallows frame and a hoist house. A dump near-by showed that considerable work had been done.

We passed on to the windmill where we found the negro troops in camp. A trooper opened the corral and offered to take care of our outfit for us, telling us where we could wash up for supper. The sergeant gave us the glad hand, saying, "Mr. Jimmie, I knows of you for a long time, for I've been in these parts myself for twenty years. Come in, sahs, and have a good piece of Armour's beef, for you prospectors don't get it often. I'll set you white men by yourselves, for I knows you don't like to eat with the black folks. I'll see that you have a good place to sleep, and a man will be detailed to feed and water your horses."

Most of his men were rookies, although I took note that a corporal and two first-class privates were veterans. What tricks the vets used to play on the rookies! After supper the men gathered to play cards and shoot craps. At ten o'clock the lights were put out, and all went to their bunks except those on guard, and a man whose duty it was to keep up the fire. Holes had been cut in the cabin, and four men at a time were on guard.

One night which I will never forget, a number of wild animals came through the pass—coyotes, wolves, and bobcats. This put one of the troopers in mind that he had seen that day an animal which he thought was a black cougar. It is known as the Mexican jaguar and is seldom seen that far north. The trooper and the sergeant talked about it most of the evening, evidently considering it an omen. Taking note that Jackson, a rookie, was listening with his eyes rolling in his head, the troopers told several cock-and-bull stories about cougars.

It was claimed that a cougar had been known to snatch a trooper from the fireside and carry him off into the brush to eat him alive. The old vets gave one another the wink; when it was time to turn in the sergeant said, "Corporal Jones, you are to put Wilson Monroe and Jackson on the ghost relief, and Jackson is to take the outpost."

Oh, what growling! "But, Sarge, sah, I ain't feelin' well to-night," groaned Jackson. Complaining was a waste of air.

"I'm sorry, son, but it's duty. No nodding or smoking on guard either—that's a case for the old man at Hachita."

The outpost was at the farthest end of the cabin, facing the pass that led into Mexico. Jackson's eyes rolled in his head when he thought of the black jaguar. Lights were put out, but there was a good deal of smothered laughing among the troopers.

"Silence!" ordered the sergeant, "or Mr. Jackson will be relieved."

From the whispers that went on around me I gathered that Jackson was a big blowhorn by day, and the old sergeant had come to the conclusion it was time "that yallow boy turned white for once." The sergeant could fall asleep at will, but the noise of a falling pin would wake him up in times of danger. The yellow boy, having gone to bed, could be heard rolling and tossing nervously.

About five minutes before the hour set for ghost relief, the sergeant got up and went out to examine the tie ropes of the horses. Coming back just on the dot, he ordered Jackson to be called. But Jackson was very hard to rouse; he allowed he was too sick to go on guard duty. It was no use. Jackson got up and the sergeant himself went with him to the outpost. I heard him give Jackson a last warning. "Don't raise any alarm unless you're sure it's necessary. You don't want those white men to think we're a bunch of cowards. Remember, no smoking!"

The sergeant went back to his bunk. In the deep silence that followed, the breathing of the horses could be heard. In a few minutes the sergeant whispered loudly to an old vet for Jackson's ear, "I'se afraid of nights like this—puts me in mind of the massacre at Apache Tejo."

Oh, how dark it was! All of a sudden from the brush where Jackson was posted came the scream of a wild animal, bringing all the horses to their feet. Then the camp was again as silent as the grave. Not even the chirp of a cricket could be heard. In about a half an hour the old sergeant went slipping around the posts. By this time Jackson was asleep, snoring like a pipe organ, dead to the world and to his guard duty.

The sergeant took away Jackson's carbine and pistol, putting them out of reach. An old vet took his stand between Jackson and the horses to prevent a possible stampede. Then the stillness of the night was broken by a blood-curdling Apache war whoop. Jackson leaped through the slit that had been cut in the tent for the guard in case of danger, losing his hat and shouting, "Lord Almighty, save this yellow boy!"

The sergeant grabbed him just as the shrill screams of a jaguar were added to those of the Apache. Jackson tore loose from the sergeant, raced around to the cabin door, dashed in, and dropped to the floor in a swoon. The sergeant followed and threw an armload of greasewood on the fire, which flared up, showing the white face of the yellow boy, who was chattering and weeping. How those negroes did laugh and roll their eyes at the sight of the daytime hero in such a fix.

The next day Jackson had to be taken to the hospital in Hachita. It was three weeks before he got over his scare. The old sergeant finally got him to go back to his post on Little Mountain and eventually made a man of him.

This old sergeant had been in the service twenty-five years in the Southwest. Well-versed in military laws, he won his point many a time in an argument with new commanders, who tried to impose on "his men." He was known and respected by all the Army officers of the Southwest.

9. *I Hear of Cousin Jack*

The next morning the sergeant made us known to the owner of the mine on Little Mountain. "I believe I know you," said Buck Davis, giving me the glad hand. "Weren't you with Cousin Jack in this section some years ago?"

That broke the ice and he was soon telling me about Cousin Jack. "I was his partner in Alaska, and he talked of you often and of the hidden well where you spent an exciting night. I was prospecting near Harrison City, being down to bed-rock as far as finances went, when I met him. Crossing a ridge I fell in with him and a tall Missourian, who had a contract to furnish the river boats with cord wood, but they were not to get any pay until a certain number of cords were delivered.

"They showed me some coarse nuggets which they had found in the roots of a blown-over tree. Nearly every tree on the hillside where that tree lay showed gold in exposed roots. The two men had kept it dark and located on the hillside. As they were anxious to finish delivering their order of wood they hired me to help out, promising to pay me with a share in their locations. I was sure it was a bonanza and took up the offer.

"In two weeks the wood was delivered and we pulled out for Harrison City to stock up with supplies. As it was August we expected to get in a good month's work before the snow flew. We sunk several holes to bed-rock, all panning out big. We cleaned up in coarse gold about twenty-five thousand dollars before the snow stopped us.

"The next spring and summer we made a good clean-up, selling out our holdings for a half million dollars to a Canadian syndicate. The Cousin and I had batched together during the winter months with the Missourian and a hired man. During the long winter nights we talked on many subjects. Cousin Jack was never done telling about Little Mountain and the hidden well. He talked of going back the next year to cure his bloomin' rheumatism by the flashes in the cave.

"After we sold out we all went to Dawson City. A dame in a dance hall soon got all of the Missourian's money. The Cousin made up his mind to sail for England to visit his old mother, intending to go from there to New Zealand to take up the sheep business. I went to California, got married there, and lost all my money in stocks. I left my wife at work there and headed for Little Mountain.

"It seems a few months before I came here, there had been a bad cyclone. It blew down windmills and stations and uprooted trees and brush. After the wind the floodgates opened and Little Mountain was among the hills that were washed clean of all brush in the downpour.

"The Englishman who built the cabin and found the rich float, being afraid he would lose his location on account of not having his citizenship papers, had decided to keep the source of the ore hidden, so he moved the outhouse he had built for the use of his wife, setting it over the ore hole. He knew the last place anyone would expect to trace the float to would be to such a spot.

"Now during the storm I've been telling you about this outhouse was upset, the water loosened the cribbing, and some of the rich ore washed down the hill. I came along after the storm and traced the float without any trouble. It was easy to get a lease, and I paid for the whole mine on my first shipment of ore.

"The mine soon petered out, but I had made a neat sum of money. I am now planning to visit the hidden cave that Cousin Jack told me about. I have no doubt the flashes mean there is radium in the mountain. The value of radium was sure a great discovery the Curies made in '98. I have enough money to get a concession from the Mexican Government. I'd like to take you in as a pardner, McKenna. How about it?"

Of course I was more than willing to join him, for I had never lost interest in the hidden well. The old sergeant got us a detail of troops under several Army officers to act as escort. The day before we left Little Mountain we took note of a skirmish in the valley near Ascension, between the Insurgents and the Federals of Old Mexico. There was a lot of shooting and yelling but more running away from each other than real fighting.

In a day or so, on our way to the hidden well, we passed over the scene of the battle, finding one dead Insurgent and twenty-five live chickens. We headed for Cousin Jack's old battlefield, but I soon realized that the section was changed. The gullies and canyons seemed to have shifted, and in many places they were filled almost to the top with rock and debris.

The battlefield had disappeared. The skeletons had rolled downhill in a rockslide and were buried deep in a gully. The canyon that once led to the hidden well had been closed up. We rode along a boulder-strewn area, but the mountain where the hidden well had been seemed solid all the way through.

Deep crevices reached so far down into the mountain that a stone sounded for many seconds after it was dropped. Canary-colored boulders that weighed tons balanced on the mountain slopes and tilted on narrow ledges. The entire surface of the mountain was covered with red ash and volcanic glass. Coming up from the fissures was the strong odor of pitch. At last we reached a high point from which we could see through the field glasses the volcanic glass that covered the earth for many miles.

There was nothing for it but to pull back to Little Mountain.

In time to come the volcano may break forth again, bringing ruin to wide stretches of country. Near the border we met a party of Mexican refugees. When they saw the specimens of volcanic glass and pitch that I was carrying they made the sign of the cross. Pointing toward the mountain where the hidden well had been one of them said in Spanish, "Mountain of fire. No good. House of the devil. Boom! Boom! Boom!"

That was my last trip to Little Mountain but I have never lost interest in that strange country. I have asked mineralogists and scientists if it could be possible to find a body of pure radium. Some claim it could happen, but that the rays would be so powerful they would destroy the one who tried to reach it. It is well known that radio-active substances exist in certain New Mexico ores, in particular, in pitchblende. Pure radium has not often been found in Nature and then only in small amounts. A pound of pure radium is worth millions of dollars.

Will radium wells at some future day be opened in the hidden cave? Was the hidden well, perhaps, Ponce de Leon's Fountain of Youth?

SPIT AND WHITTLE CLUB

Old Kentuck's Dream

1. *The Spit and Whittle Club*

OLD KENTUCK threw an armload of juniper wood on the fire and hung the smoky bean pot on the tripod; then he stirred up the mess in the pot with a big iron spoon, tasted, and added a good dash of red chili and a handful of salt. Next he broke off some straight twigs from the limbs of an old juniper that gripped the steep hillside with feet spread like a stocky giant. These twigs he built into neat piles at each end of some long rough benches standing under a clump of live oaks. When he had done all this he was ready for the Sunday afternoon meeting of the Spit and Whittle Club. Then he shambled over to the shade of a big pine tree and stretched himself with a sigh of content on a bed of brown needles. He locked his long, powerful hands under his gray head and watched a pair of nuthatches back down the trunk of the pine, picking their meal of bugs and twittering to one another. And all the while Danny and I watched him.

Pickett's Spring is famed for its sylvan beauties. Kentuck could not have picked a better camp site. Clear water gushed from the hillside, and its gurgle reached him where he lay. Mighty oaks, junipers, and yellow pines filled the canyon and climbed to the brink of the surrounding hills, forming a windbreak and making cool shade for the summer meetings of the Spit and Whittle Club. Several hundred yards below the spring was a grassy park, a regular paradise for leg-weary burros. Many wild flowers grew in the canyon and even in the park in spite of the burros' browsing. Kentuck raised himself on his elbows to gaze at a clump of Indian paintbrush that had pushed up among lichen-covered rocks; he smiled to himself at sight of the scarlet flower, saying to Danny and me how glad he was he had come to the conclusion to settle for a spell at Pickett's Spring. He seemed fagged out, and in a few minutes he dropped off to sleep.

The Spit and Whittle Club met wherever Old Kentuck pitched camp, for he was a regular leader. Everyone always stopped to listen when his deep, burring voice was heard. Old Kentuck always had something worth while to say, for he had been up and down the world looking for gold and silver, and he had picked up in his wanderings a good bit of learning.

The Spit and Whittle Club met every Sunday to give the old sourdoughs and desert rats a chance to swap tales of their Indian, outlaw and mining experiences. Each prospector had his own place on one of the benches, depending on the number of years he had been a rover in the hunt for metal and the extent of his journeyings. When a member arrived he took a tin plate from a shelf that had been wedged into an oak tree and ladled himself a helping from the steaming pot of red frijoles, or Mexican pinto beans; then he picked out several juniper sticks from the pile and took his regular seat on a bench. When he was filled up with beans he pulled out his sack of tobacco and packed his left jaw till it looked as if he had a billiard ball under it. Next he opened his jackknife and stropped its longest blade on the sole of his shoe. Now he was ready to listen or to take part in the talk as the case might be. The only one who did anything different was the one from Tennessee—he would strop his knife blade on the palm of his hand; then he would pull forth his snuffbox, take off the lid, dip up a bit of snuff on the tip of his knife, and put it on his tongue. Of course every prospector's pockets would be bulging with specimens of ore which his comrades would pass from hand to hand during the meeting with a lot of head-shaking and many wise cracks.

On this particular Sunday afternoon Danny and I had been the first to get there. Kentuck slept on. After a while we turned our burros into the park and helped ourselves to the beans, taking our places at the end of a bench, for to these old timers we were only pilgrims, though we had been in the country a number of years.

"I say, old son," whispered Danny to me, "doesn't Old Kentuck look more like Abe Lincoln than any other homely cuss you ever seen in your life? Sure he's got the same scrubby beard on his chin and the same kind of a mouth."

"Yes," said I, "and he's just as gangling with his six feet, four. His cheeks are sunken in like Abe's, too, and he's got deep-set eyes that seem to hold fun and sadness at the same time. Old Virginia always makes me think of Abe Lincoln, too."

"Here comes Pete Kitchen and Sheba Hirst, old son," said Danny, peering through the trees. "Pete's wearin' his stove-pipe hat as usual, and I can see the curl in his mustache from here. That long face of his hardly fits a sawed-off human like Pete. I say, Jimmie, Pete must be about seventy-five now, don't you think?"

"Yes," said I, "he's a good deal older than Sheba. I don't think Sheba will ever be anything but a tenderfoot in looks, though he's knocked around a darn sight more than a lot of other hard-boiled hombres I've met."

"Sheba's wearing his gray suit as usual, and his mustache is trimmed like a duke's. That little derby of his beside Pete's stove-pipe is like a toadstool alongside a pine tree."

As the two men pulled into camp Danny held his finger to his lips and pointed to Old Kentuck who was still dead to the world. Danny and I had another plate of beans with the two men. We were too busy for a time to wake up Kentuck with our jabbering. Before we were through eating, however, a booming voice broke the silence in the canyon.

"Hello! Hello! old sons. Glad to see you all, you old sourdoughs, you old desert rats, you old devils! No Cousin Jacks around? Those birds sure do stick in my craw, and they spoil the day for me when they're around."

It was Gassy Thompson who came tearing through the brush like a bull on a rampage. "Did I wake you up, Kentuck? Sorry, old sourdough."

"I'd as lief try to sleep with Gabriel blowin' his horn. Son, where did you get that bugle of yours?"

"Big chest! Big voice!" roared Gassy, pounding himself till the echoes came back. Gassy had a breast like a horse. He always wore bib overalls and a blue shirt with a big jagged tear in the right sleeve as though it had been ripped in the brush. He had muscles like a Greek god, and he loved to show them off.

"Me for a tin of pinto beans," he roared, tossing his hat under a bench and rumpling his thicket of light curly hair with a hand like a ham. As he made for the bean pot I saw him smoothing his sideburns of which he was as vain as a peacock.

"Well! Well! Look who's driftin' in now," said Old Kentuck. "Welcome to your old stampin' ground, Pickett." The newcomer came forward in a halting manner, nodding to the company as solemn as an undertaker. He took off his round peakless cap and dropped his very long swallow tails behind the bench when he sat down.

Quartzy Johnson and Deaf Jack were the last to get there. Quartzy always wore a long overcoat buttoned up tight summer and winter and even while at work. The pockets bulged with specimens of quartz, hence the name. When questioned on his peculiar habit of wearing an overcoat in summer, he would say with a shrug of his shoulders, "What keeps out the cold in winter keeps out the heat in summer."

Deaf Jack wore overalls with bibs to which immense pockets had been sewed by special order. His pockets, too, were crammed with specimens of ore. A bottle of red eye sticking out from his hip pocket gave away Deaf Jack's weakness.

"Well, now that the company's mostly all here," began Old Kentuck—"and I hope there's no liar among you—I'm aiming to tell you the queer dream I've been havin' this afternoon."

"How could you suspicion an honest bunch of humans like us?" asked Sheba Hirst, pulling a long face. Sheba could stretch the truth farther than anyone I ever met in my life.

"Well," went on Kentuck, taking no notice of Sheba's remark, "the last thing I remember before fallin' asleep I was thinkin' how that stalk of Indian paintbrush always put me in mind of a girl I knew in Denver. She was sure a peach, and she always wore red silk dresses. The next thing I knowed I was lookin' into the face of an old man with a long white beard reachin' down below his waist. I knowed it was Moses as soon as I see him, for his picter was in the family Bible in old Virginny. 'Kentuck,' says he to me, and then I see those horny rays of light risin' from his forehead, 'the Lord has sent me to tell you He has made up His mind to round up the prospectors of all time in a special place. These prospectors spend their lives goin' up and down lookin' for gold and silver. Now, when man gets these two metals he puts them to bad use: on account of them are wars, murders, rape, robbery, and a deal of other crimes. Nations gather these metals to add to their power and to bring ruin on the rest of the world. Now, I'm aimin' to show you, Old Kentuck, how in every age a certain kind of humans known as prospectors have helped to add to the evil in the world by findin' this treasure; it's true some good is done with the money, but the evil uses outnumber the good ten to one.

" 'These humans, the prospectors, are men with good brains and great imagination, but they are a race of liars, too, not wicked liars who do harm or scandal with their tongues, but enthusiastic liars who tell of the great finds they have made, of lost diggings, lost leads, and lost cabins; of caves filled with gold and jewels; of silver reefs and cliffs in sections without water, beset by savage

Indians—and some of what they tell is true, and some of it ain't true. The prospectors like to tell of the times they struck it rich, and how they blew it in on dizzy dames and faro games—and sometimes it happened and sometimes it didn't.

" 'Now, Kentuck, the Lord is not aimin' to let them critters into heaven; neither is He aimin' to send them to hell; for in truth, although these men have been bitten by the imagination bug, they have suffered a lot and borne a lot of hardship and done a lot of hard work. And seein' they're not such a bad bunch in more ways than one, the Lord is settin' apart a certain section of the other world where they can play pitch, high five, smudge, and penochle. I allow He'll likewise let them play some keno and faro games. There will always be a pot of red frijoles hangin' on the tripod and plenty of sourdough and black coffee will be pervided for all hands and sundry. There the old timers can swap lies to their hearts' content.'

"Now, sons, when Moses had shown me the prospectors' heaven where I see there were plenty of shade trees and many mountains and canyons and rivers, he led me up into a mountain; then he drew apart the curtains of the future, and I saw immense birds with men ridin' in their bellies, and the birds made a queer whirrin' noise, the like I never heard comin' from a critter with wings. And them birds passed from planet to planet, and daggon-it, if one of them didn't swoop down, and Moses pushed me into it, and I see it was a man-made contraption. We spun away into space, and before long we was wanderin' on the streets of Mars, and sons, the streets were made of silver, and we stumbled over gold nuggets as big as Gassy's fists. But nobody took notice to all this treasure.

"I learned from Moses that these metals had become worthless, war was unknown among men, and all hands lived in peace and plenty. Men had discovered chemicals that could be rolled into pellets, and one of them bein' swallowed would sustain a husky human for a week. Moses also showed me how the light of the moon shinin' at night was caused by the reflections of the sun shinin' on hills of gold and silver on the moon.

"Now, sons, come the most surprisin' part of my dream, for when that man-made bird dropped me and Moses on the mountain we started from, Moses pointed out an island in the Antarctic seas below Tierra del Fuego, and there was a volcano on that island spoutin' gold nuggets as big as Gassy's head, and an old man was busy pilin' up them nuggets, and the pile he'd built him was nigh as big as the mountain they spouted from. A native woman was helpin' him, and them two, I see were the only humans on the island; they had planted fields of grain and orchards of fruit trees and gardens of flowers—and they all grew in that latitude by reason of the heat of the volcano. And when I look closer I see that old man with the long beard is myself. I see him writin' a date on the mountain wall, and the date is 2001 A.D. I asked Moses if that meant I would be the last prospector on the earth. He told me I would be the last of the Black Range old timers except one, and sons, you'd never guess the other—it's no one but that little Jimmie Kinny, sittin' right there at the end of the bench!"

This was too much for Sheba Hirst. "A liar! a liar! a great big country liar!" sang he. "Kentuck, I can spin a yarn that'll beat yours all hollow—but mine'll be of real happenings of later times."

"Let us hear it, Sheba," said Old Kentuck, not giving ear to Sheba's jibes.

2. *The Days of Gold*

"It'll be the tale of Tom Moore who set the ball arollin' in the great gold rush of '49. Moore was one of Marshall's hands and helped to dig the ditches and finish the flumes to carry water across the hills and hollows to run the sawmill. Moore helped turn the water of the American River into the flume, and then he was set to cutting trees near-by, working hell-to-split, and when some of them California tree giants flopped over, the dirt from their hoofs flew into the flume. Now once a week it was part of Moore's job to clean out the flume. Before long him and Marshall notice there's a deal of black sand and sometimes pieces of quartz in the flume especially where the flume is roughest.

"So Moore puts a few riffles in the flume and gathers up all the snuff and quinine bottles in the camp, and the next Sunday when they clean the flume they fill all them bottles with black sand. It was the most exciting clean-up ever made in the history of the world. Of course, as you old sourdoughs know, this all happened on Captain Sutter's ranch—empire would be a better word for the big bunch of territory he laid claim to. The Captain, knowing what would happen when this news got out, begged the men to keep mum about their discovery. But such secrets soon break out of bounds like a bucking pony. Within three days San Francisco knew of the find.

"Commander Stockton had taken hold of California, his fleet being in the bay of Monterey, lying at anchor. In two days there was not a sailor left on his ship, all lighting out with top-notch speed to Sutter's Fort; and within two weeks people were on their way or getting ready to go there from all parts of the world. All the ships were mostly sailers and had to go around the Horn; no railroad nearer than the Missouri River, no telegraphs, no phones, no real cities nearer than St. Louis, no railroad across the Isthmus of Panama to shorten the trip. Most of this immense crowd of gold-seekers followed the overland trail, with snowy peaks to cross, dry alkali deserts with water unfit to drink, no wood for fire, having to use the buffalo chips for fire to cook by, not being able to scare up at times even one rangy jack-rabbit, no matter how hard they beat the brush. Many people passed in their chips in the terrible heat.

"The ships that carried the sea-going crowds were regular old sea-traps. How they ever went around the Horn with its devilish storms is a mystery. Many of these old ships went down in the bay of Frisco within a few days of anchoring there. Oh, what risks and privations and hardships! Many who came into Frisco had not a dad-blasted red left to their name; but the gold was plentiful, and many found the riches that had lured them from the ends of the earth. Over forty million was taken out the first year. San Francisco was a city of fifty thousand inside of two years. People hailed from China to England, and from Maine to Florida —the world was gold-mad.

"That discovery was the first where the burro, or donkey, became the prospector's friend. The native Mexicans had hundreds of them, and they were soon selling them to the newcomers at a shylock profit to pack their supplies to the diggin's. Luckily the climate was mild; this was the reason there were so few deaths from pneumonia. Within a year enough Chinese had drifted into that section to do the cooking and washing around most camps. The chinks raised garden truck and chickens, and eggs figured once more in the eats of the miners.

"As to Captain Sutter, the squatters did not recognize his rights, and the United States Government never gave him title to his claim. He lawed for settlement but never got a red, dying as poor as Job's turkey many years after the discovery. Marshall drifted from one settlement to the other, and he likewise died without a sou marquee. I imagine it was pretty cold comfort to him when the State of California set up a monument to him.

"Tom Moore, after blowing in the wad of dough he got for the gold he took from the flumes, kept drunk around Frisco as long as he could get bug juice, then drifted to Sacramento, hanging around there till the officers told him to vamoose. He struck off for the diggin's and had about reached where Hangtown now is; having a bottle of corn and being tired and half-seas-over he laid down in the grass at the foot of a tree near the trail; he never woke up till the next morning. Being as dry as the desert he made for a running stream near-by and drank his fill. After bathing his face he started back for his coat and hat, when his eyes fell on the roots of a big tree exposed in the bank of the stream; hanging to the roots he seen what looked like a round boulder of iron.

"Pulling the boulder from the roots with might and brawn, he took note of its immense weight, it being so heavy he could scarce lift it. Knowing he was near rich gold fields, he became terrible excited and broke off a piece of the boulder to test it; he soon made certain he had struck a nugget of real value. Covering it up careful with brush, he destroyed all signs of his sleeping quarters and lit out for Sacramento. He sneaked around among his old sawmill friends, taking care not to have a run-in with the officers of the law, and he managed to round up a few dollars. He made for a hardware store and bought him a wheelbarrow, the only one in stock. Getting a few blankets from his friends he struck off, wheeling the stuff, and taking no note of the snickers and jibes of the crowd of small boys afollowing him.

"Still pushing the barrow he reached by sundown the spot where he had left the nugget. He hid himself in the brush so no one would stop with him to spend the night. Lying down, he waited for darkness, intending to travel all night, for the moon was full. He was taking no chances on having some dad-blasted snooper look into the load he was trundling. The country was swarming with outlaws and cutthroats, and he knew his life would be snuffed out like a candle in a cyclone if anyone suspicioned what sort of a load he had.

"When night was on he loaded the nugget on the wheelbarrow, covered it with his blankets, and set out for Sacramento. About daybreak he pushed the barrow into a clump of brush, only stopping long enough to eat a raw-bacon sandwich, not daring to build a fire for fear he be found. All that day he pushed ahead with the barrow, always taking up into the brush if he heard travelers along the trail. Shortly before sundown he reached the outskirts of Sacramento, and there he went into hiding for the night.

"The next morning he appeared on the streets of the town, asking where he could find the best gold-dealer. As a matter of fact every restaurant, hotel, and saloon dealt in the metal, there being little real money in circulation. The United States had not yet set up mints. Finding one dealer who was said to hand out genuine I.O.U.'s and was A-1 in recognizing metal, Moore pushed his wheelbarrow into the place of business.

" 'I have a large nugget to sell,' said Moore. 'How much will you give me per ounce?'

" 'Nineteen dollars per ounce.'

" 'How much per pound?'

" 'If your nugget weighs more than a pound, I'll pay you at the rate of nineteen dollars and twenty-five cents per ounce,' laughed the other.

" 'Put this in writing and the nugget will be yours,' said Moore. 'Get your stilliards ready.'

"Seeing Tom was in earnest, the dealer signed. Then Tom pulled the blankets off and showed his find. The dealer tested the gold, finding it almost pure, and when he hung the nugget on his scales it tipped them at well-nigh a hundred pounds. Tom walked out of that dealer's shop worth thousands of dollars. A cast of the nugget was made and sent to a Frisco bank. So far as I know it was the largest nugget ever found in the United States.

"Another excitement was on, but not another grain of gold was found within thirty miles of Moore's treasure tree. Tom went back to Frisco, getting rid of his dough like a dad-blasted horse thief, never drawing a sober breath till it was gone. He drifted back to the placers, but his luck went back on him, and he was seen in every new excitement, almost always without shoes, wearing a hat without a crown, drinking corn when he could get it, and forever singing a stanza of the 'Days of Old and the Days of Gold and the Days of '49.' This song had been made about himself.

"It is said he fell into a shaft near Hillsboro, New Mexico, a couple of years ago and was killed by the fall."

"I knew Moore at Siskiyou," said Old Kentuck, "for as you know I come to California in fifty-two. Moore was never a blowhorn or quarrelsome and never asked a favor. He had more in his head than lice, but he was a bummer sure of the days of '49."

"Well, I be doggoned, who is this poppin' in in the middle of a meetin' if it ain't Old Virginia? Where did you come from, old sourdough? Well, I'll be jiggered! Jimmie'll turn your burro into the park with the other jacks. Get him a plate of beans, Danny, old son. You know all these old liars, don't you Virginia?"

"Do I? Sure, most of these old desert rats were in this section when them mountains were holes in the ground. I first heard of Sheba through Mark Twain, the writer; he told me Sheba was sure some liar, but a darn good prospector. I know Pete, too, and some of the stories they tell about him, such as that one about the adobe dollars."

3. *Fake Gold and Adobe Dollars*

"Suppose you tell us about your trip down to Altar, Mexico," went on Virginia. "When I last saw you in '78 you were hiring a four-mule team hitched to a Government wagon to go down there. I drifted up to Antelope Hills and I never heard how your claim turned out."

"Well, as you will remember, Virginia, I was flush at the time, having made considerable dust at Weaverville, and as I had been prospecting down near where the El Tigre Mine has since been found, I had picked up a nugget on what looked like a whole pile of the same thing. Sizing it up I says to myself that some one had made that stack, and more than likely had been killed or run off before he had a chance to tote it off. And I never rested until I had hit it up to Tucson and got ready to haul away my find.

"I reached the ore the fourth day out from Tucson. I had to move fast, for I had only two barrels of water left and the nearest hole I knew of was fifty miles away. It was about sundown, but I loaded up my ore and drove all night, hardly taking time enough to feed myself and the animals. The next day I noticed that our load seemed lighter, but I didn't stop to look it over. For three days and nights I drove those mules like the devil was after us, only stopping once to get in forty winks. When I had crossed the border I fell in with some campers; there I pulled off the wagon sheet and found out I had been driving them mules like mad with a wagonload of fake ore—horse manure it was, and the smell would knock you down! And that's how it's come about that when a fellow gets the worst of it they say he got what Pete Kitchen got in Sonora."

"I'll take your story with a grain of salt, Pete, for you take the cake when it comes to cock-and-bull tales, but I'd like to hear your version of the adobe dollar affair before you take a back seat," said Old Virginia.

"Yes, and these young tenderfeet are aimin' to hear that tale, too, Pete, as I see by the look in their eyes, so go to it," put in Kentuck.

"Well, as you all know, they had some big monte games in Paso del Norte—nothing on the table but gold and silver. They carried it fresh from the banks to the gaming tables in big sacks, both ends being open, they tying them in the middle with buckskin thongs, so the mosos could carry them across their shoulders. I had made quite a stake up at the Hassayanpa in Arizona, having in my belt over a hundred ounces in gold. I went to Paso del Norte and was soon in a monte game. I made big winnings—adobe silver dollars by the gallon.

"I broke one dealer flat, scooped my silver haul into a sack and paid a moso to carry it over to another gaming table. By five P.M. I had won at least twenty thousand pesos. The Mexican gamblers finally got together, and I was betting a thousand pesos at a time. By seven P.M. it was dark outside and things was looking dark inside, too. I could make out a little of the Mexican lingo, and the word rurale buzzed in the air; at last I made out they were going to raid the place. I knowed if I was caught they would seize all my winnings and then throw me into jail. I said to my partners, 'Let's put up what each has, the winner to get the pot.' 'Bueno,' said they. Of course I won. Scooping the pile into the sack I motioned for a moso to tie up both ends and hoist it to my shoulder. Away I ran for the Rio Grande River. It being at flood stage I shifted my bag of adobe dollars so that the sack where it was tied in the middle rested against the back of my neck with the ends of the sack balancing like wings, and I dove into the river. And that sack of adobe dollars acted just like a cork life-saver, and I swam like a fish with the bullets of the Mexican rurales whistling around me but not hitting me on account of my bag of dollars also acting like a shield.

"The Americans in El Paso hearing the shooting knowed it was some brother American in trouble and crowded down to the river bank. As soon as I drifted near enough they caught me and lifted me out of the water. A wagon and horse being handy they threw my sack into the box and took it to the Gem Saloon on El Paso Street. There they opened the bag, and when it was counted I knew I was forty thousand adobe dollars to the good. That was forty thousand silver ounces in weight. It was sure some load to tote across a swollen river."

"And do you expect us to believe that fairy tale?" scoffed Sheba.

"Why not?" argued Pete. "It's not half as crazy as that cock-and-bull yarn of yours about finding a whole forest of fallen trees petrified from gold, and wanting us to believe that when you tried to tote a log away it changed back to plain wood as soon as you got it out of the enchanted spot. Of course I lost my load of adobe dollars the next day and had to hoof it back to Silver City."

"How about having a little truth, now," said Old Virginia. "As I am the oldest of all the old timers at this meeting, I believe it's my turn to talk next."

"Virginia's the one I want to hear," said I.

4. *The Wanderings of Old Virginia*

"After '49 and '50 the placers getting run down around the American River and no longer paying over a half an ounce a day, and as living was terrible high, flour costing a dollar a pound, eggs a dollar a dozen, and ham a dollar a pound, I came to the conclusion to light out for better diggin's. The American River diggin's were being worked mostly by Chinamen. Some of the pioneers had gone as far north as the Frazier River in British Columbia. The Knight brothers discovered the rich quartz gold of Grass Valley, California, and Nevada City was attracting many prospectors. To this day the North Star and Empire Mines of Grass Valley produce rich ore at over a mile in depth.

"Some of the miners had gone back to England, going from there to Australia to raise sheep. Drifting thence into the Blue Mountains they discovered the rich placers of that section, causing another great rush. The English statesmen believed that gold would get so plentiful it might become worthless and passed a bill to demonetize it, but before it became a law the Civil War broke out, and then came the great discoveries of silver of which I was the leader. The finding of the Con Virginia Mine stopped the demonetization of gold. Up till then silver had been at a premium. Most of the mines in California were very low in silver, but the mines of Idaho and Montana from then on carried mainly silver, and it became the metal mostly found from '62 to the present day in western America.

"In the placers of the Blue Gulch, Idaho, a metal in the sluice box seemed as heavy as gold to the prospectors, and they sent samples to Frisco to be assayed. It proved to be the white metal, giving Silver City, Idaho, its name. But when Jordan went up on War Eagle Mountain, he found the bones of five men, who it is said killed each other. It seems they had discovered a ledge of almost pure gold, all arriving on the mountain about the same time. This ledge stood a few feet above the ground, and it is supposed each claimed the location and went to shooting at the other. Not one was left to tell the tale. These claims were named the Poor Man's Group, the War Eagle, and the Mahogany Mines, and millions were taken from them and many thousands from the near-by gulches. Ten or twelve years afterwards many thousands were taken from the Black Jack and Trade Dollar claims.

"At Wagon Town a few miles south from Silver City a man named DeLamar, a sea captain from Holland, drifted into this section and noticed on the dump of an owner named Johnson a black-looking metal; the Dutchman bought the dump and had it run for silver. Johnson had always happened to assay that which assayed very little, but the Dutchman's luck was good. He opened the mine and paid for it from the dump. He is said to have cleared millions from the mine.

"The hardships of these early pioneers cannot be put into words. Most of the time they were making 'a side leap at a rind of bacon'. Even when they packed as little as they could get along with it often meant struggling over steep mountains with a fifty-pound load strapped to their backs through rain and sleet, often facing blizzards even way below zero. Most of them knew ore to the queen's taste, but when they'd made a stake they were always pushin' on to some new excitement. Hundreds of miles from civilization, never in the world's history were such pioneers. This was the prospector's life for the past fifty years. These old sourdoughs and desert rats can sure walk circles around these up-to-date pin-headed mining engineers with their high-top boots and prospector's pick, looking wise.

"I was in the rush to Yankee Fork and Salmon River in Idaho.

When the Civil War broke out all the Indians seemed to know it, attacking the settlers in Idaho and Montana. Tribes that had been at peace for years suddenly broke out, and many a pioneer lost his life. In Nevada and California the settlers took sides and many crimes were committed in the name of the cause for the North and the South. Finally the Vigilantes were formed and many cutthroats and desperadoes were shot.

"As the winters on the Salmon River were very severe I pulled out and went back to the Feather River in California and from there to Sacramento. As agents for both the North and the South were hunting lead for ammunition, and as I had seen some a year or two before while prospecting in the Inyo Mountains of southeast California, I bought a horse and mule and outfit and struck out for these ledges. Crossing the Sierra Madre Mountains near Lake Tahoe, I went south, passing Walker Lake, the Indians there being on the warpath. I camped at the south end of the lake, finding other prospectors going south.

"I crossed over the borax marshes and thought it was a bed of alkali. Oh, the heat of these deserts and the cold nights! The alkali water nearly ruined our animals. We could not even make coffee from the water. In those days we could not get roasted coffee, and the green coffee that we packed, we ground by pounding it with stones, a stunt we learned from the Indians, having watched them crush their corn in the metate.

"Finally I reached Bishop Creek. Crossing over a small divide I came to the Owens River. There I found several settlements of squaw men and was able to buy some hay for my animals from them. They also had raised quite a few vegetables. When I got to Independence I found the mountains were filled with prospectors, and a stage was running from Los Angeles to the mines at Cerro Gordo, crossing the Mojave Desert. They made charcoal from the pine timber on the Sierra Nevada Mountains not a great distance away. I prospected around here for over a year making some locations at Panamint and Darwin, selling them to men looking for lead. I had crossed the Sierras above Walker Lake. I saw quite a bit of quartz afloat there, which, after seeing the Cerro Gordo ores, I thought might be silver, so I started back to make sure. If it was no good I intended to go on to the deep hole near Marysville, Montana.

"Before I left Independence they burned a man who ran a stage station near Owens Lake. It seems that many of the men who were reported killed or lost while crossing the desert had last been seen close to these stage stations. All these stations were at springs or wells, and most of them were run by just one man. It seems that the Governor's brother had left for the Inyo Mountains a year or so before, riding a coal-black horse. He was last seen at a place called Hayway Meadows on the desert, there being a stage station at this point. Near-by flowed a large spring which irrigated about a hundred acres. It was a beautiful spot with many trees and vines, and if the stage was late or delayed so passengers could not reach Independence for the regular mealtime, they were glad to eat at The Meadows. As fresh meat was scarce, most of the places would serve either ham or salt pork or perhaps corned beef. But it was remarked that the owner of The Meadows would serve pickled pork.

"Many prospectors stopped here and were never seen again though their horses and mules could be traced to the spot. At times the owner would go to Independence to fill up with booze, trading watches and ornaments for whiskey and other things that he wanted. After the Governor's brother disappeared, the Governor sent detectives to find a trace of him if possible. They found the horse and mule near Yuma, Arizona. Some one had tried to dye the horse, which they found at a stage station. They arrested the keeper, but he proved an alibi showing he bought the horse from a man going east. Some articles belonging to the Governor's brother were found in Cerro Gordo.

"Not long after this a doctor rode the stage to the new mining camp, stopping for lunch at Hayway Meadows. The pickled meat was put on the table, and the doctor thought the bones were not from an animal but from a human. Hiding some away, when he got to Independence, he made some tests and found they were human bones, sure enough. The sheriff and a posse going to The Meadows arrested the keeper. Searching the station they found many articles belonging to the Governor's brother and many belonging to lost prospectors. They got a confession, he showing them the graves of eight missing men, also testifying there was a gang from Arizona to California murdering nearly all single travelers who stopped at their stations. The Vigilantes burned the murderer alive. With the Civil War going on and all the regular troops gone east to the war front, these mining camps were almost all deserted and life was at a low value. With Indian outbreaks, with stage and highway robbery, prospecting was almost at a standstill till the Civil War was over.

"In a few days I pulled out, buying a new outfit. I came across Mackey and Jones, who said they were going back to Frisco. They said they would travel with me to Walker Lake. We all started next day. We met Comstock at a soldiers' camp on the lake. Jones and Mackay striking out for the pass, Comstock and I headed for the peaks near the sink of the Carson River. We kept west of the sink and soon came into a section of pinon trees. We panned these gulches and got a few colors, and we seen always in the pan a heavy metal we believed was silver. Soon we came upon muddy waters and we knowed some one was washing in the gulches above us.

"Coming to what is now known as Gold Hill, we stayed there overnight, going up the gulches next day, and there we found some Mexicans and a few Chilianos washing. Their sluice boxes were filled with a black metal that they were saving, saying it was "rico plata," rich silver. I says to Comstock that this was coming from a big lead which we must find and locate. The Mexicans were working at the head of a basin or cove, a large spring gushing its waters into it.

"Taking our pick, shovel, and pan, and going to the top of the ridge we soon discovered the richest gold and silver vein the world has ever known. Our first location was the Yellow Jacket, then the Savage, and then the Comstock, and I named one the Virginia, calling the district Virginia. We picked off about ten pounds of ore putting it into a small sack we had with us. The ore appeared to be a rotten granite filled with gold and silver. Taking it down to where the Mexicans were, putting it into their mortar and using their pestle to break it up, it seemed that one half of it was pure gold and silver. The Mexicans look on and say 'muy rico.' They had a little adobe smelter where they smelted the metal from the placer, forming it into bars, or bullion. They used the trees of pinon and juniper to make their charcoal for smelting the ore. They had quite a number of bars. This was a common practice in the mining districts at this time. Running the metal into moulds which contained about five ounces, they passed these in the stores and saloons for five dollars in value.

"These Mexicans also had several small mules and some yucca sacks. We dickered with them to mine some of the ore on the big ledge and also to smelt it, and to pack the bullion to Frisco, we promising them about fifty per cent of what it ran. Soon they were working hell-to-split, they packing it into sacks, mining in a jiffy about a thousand pounds. Then we loaded the mules, putting on them our blankets and supplies, and headed for San Francisco, going first to Sacramento, the railroad being finished to the last-named town. Arriving at this town we threw in with Jones and Stewart and many other prospectors, telling them of our great find, they taking our mules and burros after we had expressed our bullion to Frisco, and striking out for our big discovery.

"Myself and Comstock going to Frisco, dropped into Flood and O'Brien's Saloon, it being miners' and prospectors' headquarters. We showed them a few of the bars, they having the mint to test them. Results: over five dollars apiece, they having considerable gold in them. Oh, the rush and the excitement! We stayed in the city some time, came across Mackay and an Irish banker named Fair. They wanted to organize a stock company at once, money being plentiful, but labor was scarce. The Civil War was still going on, the C.P. R.R. was rushing the building of the road across the Sierra Nevadas, hoping to beat the U.P. R.R. to San Francisco, but the first-named company had a hard time getting men, having to employ mostly Chinese labor.

"As Mackay and O'Brien were practical miners, they went back with us to the Virginia District, but when we got there we found at least five thousand men around our locations, and over a hundred were working on them, having run open cuts along the veins for at least six hundred yards. They had laid out a townsite, calling it Virginia City. Everyone was taking out ore, and our Mexican friends were running eight or ten smelters day and night. Some of those greenhorns that struck it rich didn't know enough to carry guts to a bear. Fair and Flood, inside of four months had sold over a million dollars worth of stock, and had ordered some of the largest and best mining machinery the world has ever had, and all kinds of milling and separating machinery were being rushed to the camp. The ore was good milling, and as most of the ore that had been found in California was likewise milling ore, abandoned mines were scoured for machinery.

"Oh, my, the road building and the demand for mechanics! But the work went right on, and within three years some of the mines were over two thousand feet deep. Sutro had started his tunnel to drain the mines below two thousand feet. The tunnel was eight feet square and six miles long. It took millions of feet of timber for this tunnel and to support the mines. The miners demanded big wages and got them, too. All shifts were only six hours, and when you saw these men on the street after work hours you would think they were bigwigs, with their stove-pipe hats and cutaway coats, some of them driving to work in buggies or fine rigs. The mines were very hot and it made these miners' skin tender and white. Many of them were worth thousands one day and nothing at all the next day, all gambling in mining stock. Nevada was made a state, and the capitol located at Carson City; and a mint was set up there for all bullion west of the Missouri River. No paper money was used to the year 1880.

"By 1868 Virginia City had a population of over 50,000 and the state was ruled by that city, Jones, Stewart, Sharon, and other mining kings all being its senators. It is said that Flood and Fair controlled all the saloons and gambling dens. In fact the Big Four controlled the railroads and all the industries of the State. When the war ended in 1865 there was another rush in this section. By this time those immense bonanzas had been opened up, and everyone was betting on production. Mackay, Flood, O'Brien, and Fair, with Jones and Sharon were multi-millionaires. Myself and Comstock had millions at times, but the Big Four eventually got it all. We lost our interest, being froze out by some law that was passed by the stock legislature, and in stock gambling.

"By 1868 over $250,000,000 worth of ore had been taken out of this ledge. When the workings got below the Sutro drainage it became so hot that the miners and muckers had to work naked, and no one could work more than six hours at a stretch. Fair was in favor of short hours and high wages, saying they would get it all back from the miners by selling stock to them. San Francisco at this time was the greatest stock market in the world. It was there I seen you two old desert rats first, meaning you, Old Kentuck, and Pete Kitchen. Kentuck, you sure made many winnings. I knew Joaquin Miller and Sam Clemens there, too. I retired for a few years, but the stock market at Frisco got me, and I went back to the old mining game. The rich deposits had been worked out by now.

"Even before the C.P. and the U.P. had connected at Salt Lake the prospectors had found Eureka, Cherry Creek, White Pine, and Austin, and the deserts of Nevada were filled with prospectors and their Mexican burros. And now came disaster to the silver miners.

Financiers of the United States, backed by English money, had an act passed in our Congress demonetizing the white metal, and its great day was over. Oh, what a crime was slipped over the people of the United States! It took years to find it out, but the fat was in the fire, and these pioneers who opened the West were doomed. About this time I took the train for Winnemucca, staging it from there to Yankee Fork, Idaho, going from there to the deep hole country of Montana, a placer diggings near St. Mary's, from there to a silver find near Butte, Montana. But it being quartz mining, and an excitement being on near Fremont and Pike's Peak, Colorado, I went there, hence to Georgetown, meeting these two old sourdoughs again, we all going to work on the Pelican and Dives Mines where the veins came so close at the six hundred we could almost hear each other breathe."

5. *The Democrats Vote*

"This is where you come in, Gassy," went on Virginia. "Do you remember the fights between the Cousin Jacks and the American miners? You could sure lick the Cousin Jacks every time. They sure had a wholesome fear of you, old son, knowing you were the best man on a double jack that ever hit the drill. None of your single jacks for Gassy, and none of your bloody uppers. All back holes or lifters and a couple of side cuttings in holes, and then you gave the muckers some rock to move."

"And I can keep the muckers busy yet for another spell," bragged Gassy, "and I've never taken on any more love for the Cousin Jacks than I had in those days. All the foremen were Cousins, and they were always ready to take the bread from some American miner's mouth to put it in their own—the damnedest bunch of Clanishmen that ever walked the earth. Many a hefty American miner they did out of a job with their tricks. But they were good old days in spite of the Cousin Jacks. Oh, what high-grading, especially when we struck rich ore. Many a time the miners were forced to strip in a bath house to be gone over by searchers, who even combed the hair of their head looking for bits of ore, for a piece of quartz did not have to be very big to contain an ounce of gold. All the dinner and lunch buckets were searched, and at night if the watchman heard anyone pounding ore in a mortar he would get his walking papers at the mine the next day. Yet a deal of ore got away from the mine owners in spite of all their watching. Many times a foreman would let some well-known high-grader work a few shifts on a rich streak, they dividing the profits.

"As to politics in those camps those damn Cousin Jacks always voted the Republican ticket, and they all voted whether they were citizens or not. Georgetown, Colorado, had never gone Democratic until I came along. In fact, if a Democrat came to vote, those damn Cornishmen generally threw him off the porch. The voting was generally done on the second floor of a building reached from an outside stairway, and many a Democrat went away from the poll with a lump on his head as big as a turkey egg. Even if a Democrat did manage to cast a vote, it was thrown out when the votes were counted, for the Cornish knew just how many votes there should be. It was a common sight on Election Day to see an American thrown over the railing or kicked down the steps.

"Jack Reilly and I had made up our minds to vote the Democratic ticket in the election of 1872. Jack had shoulders on him like a wall. On the morning of the election we came along in time to see a friend of ours making a speedy landing from the porch of the second story. Asking him the reason we found out it was because them damned Cornishmen wouldn't let him vote Democrat. Then Jack and I made the rounds of the saloons and gathered up all the Democrats and armed them and lit out to vote. Up the stairs we went. In a few seconds there were Cousin Jacks flying out promiscus through the doors and windows, riding on Democrats' toes till they hit the stairs; after that they needed no man's help to reach the street. I never saw so many black eyes and broken noses in one town in my life. Of course, the Democrats of Georgetown carried the day the first time in its history.

"A contest was made, a judge being sent from Denver to hear the testimony. The first witness was Johnny Jones from Dolgouth, Cornwall.

" 'Damme, old son,' said he to the judge.

" 'Hold on,' said the judge. 'If you call me "old son" I'll throw you in the calaboose. Address me as "your honor".'

" 'Well, your honor, first comes Gassy Thompson, then Jack O'Reilly, they askin' for a ticket, sir. Evan Evans he asked if they be Democrats or Republicans, and then he tell them we don't take Democrats' tickets. "The 'ell you don't," says Gassy, and he grabbed Evans by the buttocks and threw him over the bannister, and he says to the rest of us, "Scooten, scatten, all abroad, you—"

" 'Hold on, hold on,' roared the judge, 'what do you mean scooten, scatten?'

"Johnny grinned. 'Why, damme, old son, don't you savvy plain English?'

"And so the judge fined him for contempt of court and put him in the jug, and the Democrats won.

"Did you know that Bill Nye, the writer, put me in his book for the tricks I played on the Cousin Jacks?" went on Gassy. "You know, General Grant read about me in Nye's book, and when he was coming home from his trip around the world he stopped off in Denver to see me. He sent for me to come to Boulder, and we had a great conflab whilst imbibing some first-class bug juice. Before we parted I told the General the next time I struck it rich I'd wire him to come to Denver and I'd show him a boiled-dog time. He said O. K. Sure enough, inside of six weeks I hit a good body of ore, and the first thing I did was go to a telephone to ask if I could send a telegram to General Grant. Answer, yes. Could I wire Queen Victoria? Answer, yes. Could I wire Emperor William? Answer, yes. So then I says, 'Wire them that Gassy Thompson has struck it rich and has the world by the tail on a downhill pull.' I never got an answer."

"Poor Gassy! Whatever'll you do if you meet Cousin Jacks in Old Kentuck's prospector heaven?" laughed Old Virginia. "The next excitement after the Colorado rush was in the Cimarron district," he went on, picking up his own tale again. "Some prospectors drifting south along the top of Old Baldy, some Indians showed them some copper ore, claiming they got it at the head of the Cimarron River, on what is known as the Maxwell Grant. There was quite a rush, and soon there were thousands in this field. Amongst them were two Irishmen named Foley and Lynch, who discovered the Aztec vein from which millions were produced. My, the cutthroats and thieves! They seemed to come here from all parts of the world. One of them named Kennedy is said to have murdered twenty-five men. At the new town called Elizabeth Town crime became so bad that Vigilantes were formed, and Kennedy was one of the first to be hung. The six-shooter was the only law. The stages were held up almost every day by such outlaws as Henderson, Coal-Oil Johnny, Joe McCurdy, and Stewart. The county officials offered three thousand dollars reward for anyone caught robbing the stage.

"Henderson and Coal-Oil Johnny planned to rob the stage on a certain day at a certain place, and McCurdy and Stewart, getting wind of it, followed them and hid in the brush. When Henderson and Coal-Oil Johnny leaped on the stage, the hidden men jumped out, killed their two old pals and brought the bodies into Cimarron, claiming the reward."

6. *Old Kentuck's Tale*

"I remember that right well," said Old Kentuck, "for I worked with McCurdy on the Aztec. I shall never forget him. One day while he was working on the lead he ran into a pocket of pure gold, it havin' about fifteen hundred dollars in it. As it was about noon he tied up his find in his neck rag. He told me he was quittin' for the day and climbin' the ladder alone, and he showed me the gold, sayin' it all belonged to him and all hell wouldn't get it from him. He went up and showed his treasure to Matt Lynch, darin' him to take it from him or to make trouble about it. Lynch knew better than to try, but he see to it that McCurdy was fired from the mine.

"I went from there to an excitement in Arizona, this vein havin' been discovered by a man named Nick Weaver, he callin' the place Weaverville. Weaver's vein was about a hundred miles east of the end of navigation on the Colorado River, a stern-wheel steamer carryin' freight and supplies from Yuma to that point on the river. Weaver had bought from the Government post at Yuma a four-mule team with harness and wagon to carry his quartz to a mill on the river, also gettin' his supplies and feed from there. As the Haulipas Indians roved through that section, Nick had considerable trouble with them on his trips back and forth, they attackin' him, killin' his mules, and destroyin' his supplies. As the profits were large, Nick kept takin' out the ore anyway, makin' enough money to overcome his losses.

"But he was aimin' to get even with the Indians in time, so he bought him ten six-gallon kegs fitted with spigots, fillin' them all with poison whisky. One day about sundown he pulled into a camp havin' a spring at it. After feedin' the mules he built up a big fire to attract the Indians, and then he set up the kegs near the wagon. As soon as it was dark he unharnessed the mules and led them into the near-by hills, tying them to the brush where they could not be seen.

"Sure enough? About sunup the next mornin' the Indians made

an attack. Nick watched from a distance until the whisky had done its work. Inside of an hour the Indians was stretched out, and Nick rode back, dispatchin' with his gun them as still lived. The Indians did not bother him again for a considerable spell.

"Late in the fall, however, they stole a pair of his mules. Again Nick had his revenge. He planted dynamite with cap and fuse in many of the favorite campin' sites of the Indians. Then he posted signs in English and Spanish, warnin' the whites to beware. As the Indians could not read, the whole tribe bid fair to be blown up. After that they let Nick alone, same as if he had smallpox.

"Weaverville was not a big field, and I soon drifted to other sections. There was another strike not far from there called Antelope Hills, which was, I am sure, found by a burro. A miner's jack disappeared, and the prospector trailed him to the top of the hill, findin' the burro lyin' on large nuggets of gold, some as big as pigeon eggs. In fact, there was no fine gold on this hill; all workin's were done without water or sluice boxes.

"Then Father De Smet, a Jesuit missionary, while he was in the East collectin' funds for the Sioux Indians, told that he had seen the Indians of the Black Hills with gold nuggets. The prospectors went in there, but as the gold-bearin' gulches were on the Indian reservation, they were driven off by the Government troops. It was not until General Custer met defeat and death by Sitting Bull and his warriors, who then fled into Canadian territory, that the prospectors had another chance. After this tragedy the Government moved the Indians from the reservation, and the prospectors began to make headway. It was one of the greatest rushes in history. Stage robbers and outlaws of all kinds were thicker than fleas on a cur's back. Such characters as Wild Bill Hickok and Calamity Jane made life more than excitin' for desperadoes like Deadwood Dick.

"The celebrated Homestake Mine was one of the discoveries, it bein' a mountain of gravel containin' but one dollar a ton in free gold, but it is still a payin' mine after fifty years, for the ore is run into a mill and separated. The Hearst estate gets a fair per cent of all dividends, and I suppose will still be gettin' them a hundred years from now. They run three thousand tons a day, savin' nearly all.

"Just before this excitement I was down near the Arizona line, it bein' said they had found diamonds down there. It sure was one big hoax, a regular mare's nest, if ever there was one. A large company was formed by Ralston of San Francisco, president of the California Bank. Just how guilty he was from the beginnin' is more than I can say. Some claims he had the wool pulled over his eyes by a friend of his who had brought back some diamonds from the African fields. Reports were buzzin' around about the great silver discoveries in the Southwest, and Ralston got this African miner and a man named Brown to go down there and look around. Brown claimed he had seen silver veins near the Burro Mountains, New Mexico, when he was surveyin' for a railroad. The two men went south, but they did not stay long on account of the Apaches; however, they brought back specimens of rich silver ore and managed to salt the earth with diamonds in the Burro Mountains. Ralston organized a stock company, sellin' most of the shares in England. In a short time he had rounded up five millions in cash. Here and there in the Burros, prospectors picked up real diamonds, and a rush was on from all parts of the country. When the Ralston men came back they found their claims had been jumped. Ralston got himself into money troubles and walked out into the bay of Frisco and drowned himself. All English investments were a total loss.

"I drifted from the Ralston excitement to Pinos Altos, washin' gold there and bein' on hand for the openin' of Silver City, this rush bein' the result of the Bullard brothers' find. They havin' some cattle around a spring noticed ore there and had some of it assayed. The Apaches made trouble for the Silver City settlers from the beginnin', but in spite of the danger some big piles were soon made. There was a general round-up of regular minin'-camp characters in the new town—some good and some bad; there were soon many stores with false fronts, and saloons and dance halls aplenty, where guns popped in short order as in other new minin' camps. They even had a newspaper run by Judge ——, and at times the Judge was so busy imbibin' corn juice at the Red Onion that he had no time to round up the news. On them occasions the newspaper would carry headlines informin' the public the news was the same as last week's.

"Then some old sourdoughs prospectin' on the headwaters of the Arkansas found a heavy metal stickin' to the pan. There followed the famous rush into Leadville. One of the men who became rich was H. A. W. Tabor. You've all seen him in these parts at one time or another. He's a New Englander. He came out to Kansas when he was in his twenties and took part in the border troubles there before the Civil War. In 1859 him and his wife and baby headed for Colorado and it took 'em three months to get there in their covered wagon. Off and on he tried his luck at minin' in the Colorado mountains but nothin' ever come of it for more than twenty years. His first wife stuck by him through thick and thin, cookin', washin', bakin' and takin' on boarders to help make ends meet. When the rich carbonates were discovered in Leadville Tabor was clerkin' in a grocery store, and he loaned a small sum of money to a couple of prospectors to help them sink a shaft, he to get a percentage of the profits. That was the beginnin' of his riches, and after that the dust rolled in, until he's got so much he can scarce count it now. He didn't aim to live like a poor man after that, and he soon helped himself to another man's wife, Baby Doe, as pretty a gal as ever set foot in the Rockies. Next he bought him a seat in the United States Senate, and all in all he's livin' like a prince in a story book for the past few years, even went so far as to fasten his shirt with diamond buttons, got received into society in Washington, too, and built in Denver the finest opery house this side of the Mississippi. But his luck can turn overnight for all that, and I would not be surprised to hear his millions had melted away like snow, what with extravagance and onlucky investments. He may die a pauper, yet, like many another that struck it rich.

"The next discovery of any great note was in the Black Range, as you old sons be aware. All the men who were workin' on the railroads kept an eye open for float, knowin' they were in a mineral country. In a valley called Hillsboro there was a sink always filled with brackish water and near-by a stream of fresh runnin' water. A man by the name of McEverts had settled there among the cottonwoods and walnut trees. Everyone goin' into the Black Range used to stop overnight at McEverts'. The Apaches tried to run him out but found him bad medicine and left him alone.

"A lone Chinaman who had been workin' at Fort Selden on the Rio Grande had quit his job, strikin' across country, aimin' to reach Silver City by takin' a short cut which ran near a high peak not far from the Mimbres River settlements. Somehow the Chink got lost and in tryin' to get his bearin's he come across a large outcroppin' of what he thought was iron. Breaking off a piece he took it along, soon findin' a trail which led him to the river and thence into the new minin' camp called Georgetown. The miners see at once he's totin' pure horn silver, and they try to wheedle out of him where he got it, but the Chink could never find the spot again.

"However, some of the bridge builders and carpenters who went searchin' for the spot found what has since been known as the Carpenter District. An engineer named Sawyer who was with them, discovered and named Sawyer's Peak, the highest point in the Black Range. Amongst those who had seen the Chinaman with the ore were two prospectors, Lufkins and Watson. These two believed the Chink had found the ore near McEverts' ranch, so they went through Gavilan Canyon and camped at Crystal Springs. Prospectin' south they came to a large quartzite dyke, there bein' a small valley to the east of the spot. Goin' through a little pass they came upon the outcroppin's of the Bridal Chamber, but of course they did not reconize it as such. In sinkin' they came upon good-sized boulders, takin' out the first day about one hundred pounds.

"Goin' back to their camp that evenin' they found that the Indians had raided it, burnin' up whatever they did not carry off. They went to the McEverts ranch for the night, he tellin' them how lucky they were not to have been there when Victorio and his Apaches passed by.

"They showed McEverts some of their rich strike, he agreein' with them it was almost pure silver. They arranged with him to have part of the load taken to Silver City to be assayed. Hitchin' his mules to his wagon the next morning McEverts went to the new minin' site and loaded up about a thousand pounds of ore and struck out, with the two miners. Arrivin' in Silver City they all went to the Red Onion Saloon to put a few bowls under their belts and then they were soon showin' samples of their find among the crowd that had gathered. A well-known minin' man named Miller who had been runnin' a sutler's store at Fort Bayard for quite a spell looked over the ore and offered to pay them a dollar and a half a pound, sayin' if they would turn it out of the wagon bed so he could judge the number of pounds in it, and see if it be the same quality all the way through, he would pay fifteen hundred dollars for the load. They agreed, and in a few minutes he handed them a big wad of dough. Miller had some of the ore assayed, and it ran as high as twelve dollars a pound. He sure made a good haul that time.

"In a day or two Miller went back with them, buyin' them out for twenty-five thousand dollars. He made a few other locations over there and then went east and organized a company, but before goin' he put a few men to workin' on the hole that Lufkins and Watson had started. My, what a find! They opened the celebrated Bridal Chamber within ten feet. It is said over three million ounces of silver were produced from it within thirty feet of the surface from a hole less than forty feet in diameter. One solid chunk is said to have been worth fifty thousand dollars. This strike attracted big minin' men from California and other western States. Marcus Daly of Butte, Montana, sent his brother to do some work. He believed it was an immense vein driftin' to the south. He started a shaft two hundred feet south of the big deposit, but before he made much headway he was killed by the Apaches in Gavilan Canyon. The western minin' men were disgusted with the Apache conditions and they sold out to eastern capitalists. Most of the ore lay within fifty feet of the surface. It is said over fifteen million ounces of silver have been taken from the mine to date. Many leasers, payin' as high as forty per cent royalty, made big wads of dough at Lake Valley. The two discoverers, Lufkins and Watson, both died without a red to their names.

"After the great finds of Lake Valley, those croppin's being mostly manganese of iron, all prospectors were lookin' for that kind of blossom. Whilst keepin' up the search, men crossed the divide in the Black Range, makin' big discoveries there which led to the foundin' of the town of Kingston. But ye are sittin' here listenin' to me in the very heart of the Black Range, and there ain't much I can tell you about this section that you don't already know. I came here from Hillsboro with Dugan, and he located the Iron King. I located above him believin' the best outcrops were on the top of the mountain, but the only thing I got out of that camp was the name they gave the mountain, callin' it Old Kentuck."

"Well," mused Old Virginia, "it would be hard to say which of us two has seen the most excitement, Kentuck. These tender-foot pilgrims, like Jimmie and Danny, have seen some hard times among the Apaches of this section, but they'll never have it as tough as the old timers of our day. Ain't it about time to break up this meeting of the Spit and Whittle Club? We're almost snowed under this pile of shavings we've been making, and the last stick in the pile has been trimmed to a feather edge."

"Yes," agreed Old Kentuck, "and judgin' from the number of times I've seen you packin' your jaws, one and all, except Jimmie there, I surmise you'd have to send some one into Kingston for a few packs of Dog Leg, Five Brothers, and Mail Pouch tobaccer if you hung around any longer. How be it we end up as usual with a verse of the Days of Old? That'll bring the burros into camp. It always does. Don't you old sourdoughs forget to make your location here next Sunday afternoon. I'll have the pot of frijoles on the tripod waitin' for you. Already now"—and for the next few minutes the valley echoed with the strains of the favorite old song.

"There is New York Jake, the butcher boy,
Who was fond of getting tight,
And every night that he got drunk
He was sure to have a fight.
One night he ran against a knife
In the hands of old Bob Kline,
And over Jake we held a wake
In the days of '49.
In the days of old
And the days of gold
And the days of '49."

And so on and on through many verses.

Hearing the song, the burros trotted into camp, and the old timers lit out for their cabins in different sections of the Black Range.

Nearly fifty years have slipped by since I listened to the tales of those old timers. Many of them have been a long time in their mountain graves. The last I heard of Old Kentuck was in 1901. He had taken on a partner from Patagonia, South America, and was bound for Punta Arenas where he expected to outfit a ship and head into the Antarctic seas for an island that was reported to have a volcano spouting nuggets of gold. So much, at least, of his dream came true. Whether or not he still lives there, I cannot say; if so, he and I are among a very few of the old timers of the Black Range days who still live. Am I going to be the last? And when I cross the last divide will I find my old friends gathered in the prospectors' heaven described by Old Kentuck? Who can tell?

Old Towns and Old Friends

NOVEMBER 8, 1934, I drove from Deming with two lady friends and their chauffeur to pay a visit to old friends in the Black Range country. Our route led from Deming to Lake Valley, Hillsboro and Kingston. Deming lies in the Mimbres Valley in southwestern New Mexico. The Mimbres River rises in the Black Range not far from the headwaters of the East Fork of the Gila River. The Mimbres has a good surface flow for about forty miles from its headwaters, then sinks through the sands, and after that does not come to the surface except here and there in rainy seasons. As an underground river the Mimbres makes its way to the great inland basin near the Sierra Madres in Old Mexico. This underground river has never been known to fail. It is easy to reach by drill and this has made it possible to irrigate a wide stretch of desert country. A fine highway runs through the Mimbres Valley, but we did not follow it that day. Instead, we took the one going north from Deming, always keeping the Rio Grande River to our right.

Lake Valley lies at the western edge of the Rio Grande Valley among the Black Range foothills, a distance of forty-two miles from Deming. The day was clear, the sky very blue even for New Mexico, and the air put new life into us. To our left as we traveled along, I pointed out to my companions, who were all pilgrims in this country, the Mimbres Range and Cook's Peak where I served for several years as judge. A distance of one hundred and ten miles to our right across the Rio Grande we could see plainly the big mountain mass, known from its likeness to the elephant as Elephant's Butte.

About midway between Deming and Lake Valley the Black Range came into view putting me in mind of piles of gray smoke on the horizon, its dark tones a real contrast to the golden tints of interlying ridges. As we got near Lake Valley the old volcanic Hat Mountain, or Sierra Sombrero, pushed into view; first its crown, then the rim of the hat, and finally the lizard that climbs the side of the "Hat"—head up, shoulders hunched, and tail dragging—a lava formation that is a wonder to man.

Lake Valley is a regular ghost town of the West. We stopped to explore the ruins of the Bridal Chamber, which I have mentioned several times in these chronicles. The roof of the mine chamber has fallen in, showing the tunnels made by miners in the eighties. Passing under the arches of the deserted section known as No. 25 Cut, we scared an immense owl from his hide-out. We took snapshots of the open caves, now empty of all treasure; and also of the adobe ruins of the old jail, with the lonely juniper tree on watch beside it.

From Lake Valley to Hillsboro the highway passes among the foothills. There is a big change in vegetation. The rich gramma grass of the plains, which fattens immense herds of cattle, sheep, and goats, gives way to thick brush—a tangle of mesquite, alderita, and manzanita bushes, yucca plants, ocotillo, and patches of sacatone. Along the creeks immense walnut trees flamed in autumn orange and yellow. Junipers, pinons, and oaks got more and more plentiful, and the heavily timbered slopes and summits of the Black Range got nearer and nearer.

Hillsboro, eighteen miles from Lake Valley, is a peaceful old town, with its mighty cottonwoods and walnuts bordering the bed of the Percha Creek, which still forms its main street as in early days. The town is safe on the low banks during most of the year, though sometimes in the rainy season mountain torrents have destroyed life and property there. When the Percha Creek was the main route from Hillsboro to Kingston the business men stretched a telegraph line between the two towns to warn heavily loaded freight trains when the cloudbursts filled the creek. Even at that, outfits were lost at times. Hillsboro is not a ghost town but a settlement of home-loving folks. City comforts are scarce, but the people do not seem to miss them. It is only a few years ago that the first bathtub was set up in the home of Mrs. Zollers, who told us that she was satisfied and happy in her adobe cottage, after years of travel around the world. Mrs. Zollers was one of three sisters brought by their father and mother to Kingston in the early eighties. All three girls taught school for a time, and eventually all three married bankers. Hillsboro is the Sierra county seat and has a fine courthouse and school and good hotels.

We found Fred Mister in his flower garden almost hidden by the zinnias which had not yet been touched by the frost. In all my wanderings I have never seen zinnias grow so large anywhere nor have such vivid colors as they do in our southwestern mountains.

Fred is known all through the Black Range for his old-time spirit of hospitality. Though crippled with rheumatism and fighting an attack of flu, nothing would do him, but we go through his winery just back of the house. For years Fred has given a lot of time to improving and aging different kinds of wine. He told me he had lately gathered bushels of alderita berries to make wine for a Texas friend who wanted that kind. I have never known him to sell any of his wines, but he always treats everyone who drifts in to visit him. We were glad to sample his grape wine while we chatted over bygone days. Fred was a mining man in the early eighties, but he spent many years from 1902 on, carrying passengers and mail from Lake Valley to Kingston. Promising to stop on our way back to pick up the gallon of choice wine he was giving us for sick friends near Deming, we struck out for Kingston cheered by our drink and the thought that the world still has unselfish humans. We headed up the main Percha Creek over what is now known as the Black Range Scenic Drive to Silver City, and were soon in a section rich in wild beauty and historic interest. The highway circles around the hills, and keeping above the creek bed, passes the celebrated Box Canyon over a bridge of steel, from which we caught a glimpse of the creek far below. In the early days of Kingston all passengers and freight had to pass through this canyon in danger of being ambushed by Apaches, or swept away by the cloudbursts of the Perchas.

My companions were filled with wonder, for we were going up fast, and pine-covered mountains, splashed with autumn tints that would shame a rainbow, whirled into view, one after the other. A well-kept ranch where they were picking mountain apples was a surprise to the ladies. Near-by I pointed out the site of the old tollgate and told them its history. In the early eighties a charter was granted to Judge Whitham and others, giving them the right to build a road from here to Kingston. A gate was set up at the beginning of the road and toll was charged for many years.

Not far from Kingston the highway leads across a little flat, which was at one time a great spot for horse racing and even for foot races. At the south end of this flat, or valley, was Toppy Johnson's slaughter house where animals were butchered to supply meat for Kingston and the surrounding section. It was a rendezvous for all the rustlers and thieves of the vicinity. It was said that nearly all the beef sold from this slaughter house was stolen, but men must eat, and at that time it was all we could get.

Toppy Johnson and his gang packed guns, so no one cared to nose into the matter too far. Toppy and most of the men who made this place their headquarters died with their boots on.

From the arroyo that leads into the town of Kingston I pointed out several mines now in ruins, among them the Three Square Mine, once owned by Forbes and Elliot.

The first building on our left as we entered Kingston was the Old Stone Hotel now known as the Victorio, whose yellow-leaved register contains the names of some of the best-known mining men of the world. It is now operated by people from El Paso and is doing fairly well. In front of the postoffice hangs a large bell between two posts, which is still rung when the mail comes in. The Kingston town-site, on the head of the Middle Percha, was first surveyed August 26, 1882, following Jack Sheddon's silver discovery at the spot named by him the Solitaire. By fall the town numbered eighteen hundred people.

We stopped to call on Jim Drummond and his wife, who have lived in this section since the early eighties. Jim is in his eighty-seventh year, and his wife told me he still likes to have his picture taken. She is younger than Jim, her dark eyes still as bright as when she taught her boys and girls in school "to tell the truth at any cost." Jim's ears are bad, but when he learned through his ear trumpet that we wanted his picture, he picked up his cane and made his way without help to pose for the snapshot, with the mountain known as Old Kentuck in the background.

Many of the stores and saloons lie in ruins, as there have been several bad fires in Kingston, but I pointed out to my companions the location of the Long Branch Saloon, the Forest Home, the Grand Casino, and Ed Doheny's old home.

Almost south of Ed Doheny's place, facing the main street east, lives my friend, Johnny Moffitt, a regular old timer, who can still tell wonderful Indian tales, and is quite a hand at swapping lies with his old pioneer comrades. For fifty years he has made his home in Kingston, having come out from Scranton, Pennsylvania, as a young Irish lad. His speech is still flavored with a dash of Irish, with what the old Irish granny called the "n-ya in his voice", when speaking of John McCormack. Johnny's rambling cottage lies at the foot of Old Kentuck. I would say that it is many a year since it saw a paint brush. Through a sagging gate we made our way up the rickety steps. Johnny heard us coming and was at the door to give us the glad hand.

"Well, by George, now! Come in! Come in! And don't you ladies be expecting too much, for I keep bachelor quarters here," said he, sweeping a packsaddle from one of the three rough chairs in the room. One of my companions who had been wanting to see a packsaddle surprised Johnny by asking him to show her how it fitted over the burro's back.

In a twinkling Johnny became the teacher. "Now just pretend the back of this chair is the back of the burro, and we'll put the saddle on this way. Here is how we fasten the cinch, ——" and so on.

"But you must all sit down," said Johnny when the lesson was over. "I'll close this window so you won't be in a draught, and then I'll round up another chair."

While he was gone we took stock of the room with its broken walls and bare pine floor. There was a round wood-stove, a table covered with an old-fashioned checkered cloth, and an assay cabinet. Magazine prints covered the unbroken sections of the wall. To judge from the styles, they must have hung there twenty-odd years or more. The only framed picture in the room was that of a battle which showed Irish dragoons in green uniforms driving the British from the field at the point of the bayonet. This room opened through a double doorway into another about the same size. In the doorway stood a homemade rack, decorated with paper flowers. The only furniture I call to mind in this second room was a cabinet with hundreds of specimens of precious ores. Atop this cabinet was an immense bunch of pampas grass and an old bullwhacker's whip. One of the ladies was holding the whip when Johnny came back.

"Ah, that's a relic you have there. 'Twas used to hustle oxen when covered wagons were all the style. But maybe you'd like to look over some of my pictures," said he, pulling open the drawer of the cabinet.

"Yes, we surely would, and the older they are, the better," put in one of the ladies.

We made for our chairs in the front room. "But before you get taken up with the pictures, I want Jimmie to see this button of silver," he said, lifting the dish with its silver deposit from the assayer's scale. "You'll agree with me, Jimmie, that I'll be running five hundred ounces to the ton when this deal goes through. It's a fabulously rich strike, and I'll soon be sitting pretty with at least two hundred dollars a day rolling in. By George, I'll be glad to have a piece of money to help my friends with. What do you say, Jimmie?"

"Johnny," said I, "I suspect you've been melting Uncle Sam's dimes in your assay furnace. It's a rich deposit all right, but I'd have to see the ore it came from and the spot the ore came from, too. But tell me," I went on, "whose picture is this I have in my hand?"

"Ah," said Johnny, "that's my mother's picture you have there." There were tears in his eyes, but he went on. "One hundred and four years old she is now, still living back there in Pennsylvania where I was born. My sisters look out for her, so I don't have to worry about her. Once when I had gone to New York to do a good turn for Ed Doheny he said to me. 'Tell me what I can do for you, Johnny'. I says to him, 'I want nothing myself. There's a little woman living in the mountains of Pennsylvania that I worry about at times. Now, I think if I could take her a little present, say, of five hundred dollars, I'd feel a lot easier about her.' When Ed found out I meant my mother he made a date with me at the bank, and, well,—you know Ed, he never does things by halves."

We spent considerable time in looking over the old photographs and calling to mind persons and incidents. Knowing that Johnny lost all track of time when he had a good listener and a tale to tell, I tried to head him off each time he began, "By George, now, let me tell you a story——,"

"How about that pot of coffee I asked you to have ready, Johnny?" I put in at one such moment.

"Aw shucks! Don't you worry about the coffee," returned Johnny. "I have a rib roast and some sweet potatoes in the oven, and we'll have dinner in plenty of time."

"Maybe so," said I, "but we want to get over the summit and out of these mountains before sundown."

"As I was saying," went on Johnny, "I may be superstitious, but I do believe, 'There's a destiny that shapes our ends, roughhew them as we will.' Take the case of George Lufkins. Now when he made his big strike in Lake Valley, if he had tunnelled just eight feet farther he would have run into the Bridal Chamber itself, over three million dollars' worth of dust right there. But he quit within eight feet of the richest deposit of silver ever found in the history of the world. Him and his pardner sold out for twenty-five thousand dollars, and much good it did them; for it wasn't no time till George was poorer than Job's turkey. Take the case of Ed Doheny, now. I can remember a day when I was sitting pretty after making a rich stake—a hundred thousand dollars, it was that time—and one morning I met Ed coming up the street. 'Well, Johnny,' said he, 'you're the very man I'm looking for, and I didn't know it till I set eyes on you. The doctor says I must get Carrie down to El Paso for treatment, and I don't know where the money's coming from. If you can help me out I'll pay you back when my stake is made.' It so happened that I had just broken a hundred-dollar bill to set up a few drinks in the Monarch Saloon, so I reaches into my pocket and pulled out a wad of dough. 'Here, take this, Ed, and welcome. It's all I have on me. Carrie is a good woman even if she is a bit excitable, and she deserves help. When I'm broke and you're flush you can remember this day.' Well, by George, now, I may be superstitious, but I'll always believe Ed and I were meant to meet that day. Many a time since I have turned to Ed for a ham-and-egg stake, and he's never failed me yet."

Just as this tale ended an old familiar sound broke the peace of the village. "By George, there's my pal. Excuse me please. I'll be back in a minute." And Johnny rushed from the room. "Come on up here, Nick," he shouted from the porch.

"That's the queerest auto honk I ever heard in my life," said one of my pilgrim friends looking puzzled, as the sounds again echoed through the valley.

"There's your auto horn and there's Johnny's pal," said I, as the owner of the raucous bray trotted up the hill.

"Come out and meet Nicodemus," called Johnny. "He's the best pal a man ever had," he went on, as we all appeared on the scene. "Good old Nick! I never lend my burro to anyone, I never whip him, and I feed him well. Here Nick, old man, have some apples," ended Johnny, tossing the burro about a half a peck of rosy-cheeked mountain apples. Nicodemus was surely a credit to his master. His full paunch, sleek gray sides, and bright eyes showed the good care he got.

Johnny stood for a snapshot with the burros — a stray animal had followed Nicodemus up the hill. Then I again asked about the coffee, and Johnny at last headed for the kitchen.

The two ladies set the table with such dishes as they could find. Cups and saucers did not match and plates were cracked, but everything was clean, and Johnny is a first rate host.

"Don't overlook that apple pie," he warned them, as he stood over the stove basting the roast. "I'm not telling who made it, till I see how it goes."

I made a stab at a sweet potato with a fork. "Man alive!" said I. "It would take two men on a drill to get through one of those potatoes. Did you dig them out of solid quartz?"

"By George, now, Jimmie, don't you worry. They'll be done."

The two ladies went out to explore the back yard while Johnny and I talked over the business that had brought us together. When Johnny finally made up his mind to serve dinner without the potatoes, I stepped with him to the door to call the ladies. We found one of them seated on a store box, and the other between the forks of a wooden horse. Johnny showed them his assay furnace and explained his water supply.

"I led a pipe from a spring on yonder mountain, and I get all my water by gravity. Down below, there in the gulch, I've set up a shower. It's a fine way to get a bath, and many Kingston visitors make use of it," he told us. "But come in now, before the roast gets cold."

"Where do you keep your apples, Johnny?" I asked him, sniffing the air, which was filled with their scent.

"In a room across the way. By George, you must see them after dinner. I've got about twenty bushels in a heap in there. I'd have more, but I don't take much care of my orchard."

We were soon gathered around the table close to the kitchen stove. Johnny stood to carve the roast. All of seventy, he is straight, strong, and active, with the same honest blue eyes that have won him so many friends through life. Still a fine figure of a man, he stands about six feet tall, broad-shouldered and clean-shaven, with skin fair, clear, and unwrinkled except for laugh-lines about his eyes. The drooping mustache, slightly tinged with gray, which he has a habit of brushing with his long powerful hand, was all the go in the early nineties.

My companions and I were soon working so hard with our garlicky meat that I had no more time to watch Johnny.

"By George, now, how do you like my beef?" he asked with a sly smile, as he pushed aside the platter.

"Beef!" said I. "I don't suppose it would be much older than Noah, but it surely must have been with him in the Ark."

Johnny laughed. He knew he could not fool me on goat meat, even if the ladies did not catch on. After opening a can of plums of his own raising and canning, he joined us at the table. Between operating on the roast and jumping up to put wood in the stove to hasten the baking of the sweet potatoes, he kept right on talking, till it became a feat to get a word in edgewise.

"I hear you buried Sophie," I told him when I could get my wedge in.

"By George, now, let me give you a tale about Sophie—may she be in Heaven this day. Now, as I've said before, I may be superstitious, but I don't believe we can get by unless we play fair, and Sophie's story is an example of what I mean. Well, you know, of course, Jimmie, that Sophie was a Danish woman who came to these parts when Kingston still boasted of its seven thousand population. And you know how she herded those cattle of hers afoot through these rough canyons and over the steep hills. Now, by George, about seven years ago Sophie got sick, and some of her neighbors believed she was going to die, and they cast eyes on her possessions. A visitor from the East wanted Sophie's place for a summer home. Some of the neighbors counted her chickens and cattle. But they sure got left, for Sophie did not die. It seems her title to the house wouldn't hold in a law court; it was just a squatter's right. Sophie didn't want to sell, but before long there were some quiet schemes afoot to take her property from her. She come to me with her troubles and told me if she had a hundred dollars she could save the house. I wrote her a check for that amount. It happened in the meantime that I was called to New York on a business deal. Soon after I got back Sophie stumbled into my house one morning, crying and shaking like a leaf—may she be in Heaven this day—and she told me she had been thrown out into the street. 'Whatever'll I do now?' she sobbed. 'There's nothin' left for old Sophie but a wagon sheet!' 'Oh, yes, there is,' I told her, as I pulled her to the door. 'Do you see that house yonder at the turn? Well, it's my property now for years, and it's yours as long as you live, if you want to stay there.' Well, by George, Sophie took up my offer and before night she was located.

"Now, as I say, I may be superstitious, but it wasn't any time until misfortunes began to fall on all those that had any hand in doing Sophie out of her diggings, law and all on their side. One fell from his burro and broke his shoulder blade, a second got in on a mine deal that went haywire, another rolled down a mountainside with a boulder after him and was nearly crushed to death. Soon after the last bit of bad luck came home to roost someone said to me that these people seemed to be down on their luck. 'By George,' said I, 'and don't you know the reason? Well, let me tell you what's up. Sophie's put the gypsy curse on that outfit, and they'll never have another day of luck until they make amends. You want to know how she could do such a thing? Well, by George, it's because she had the secret handed down to her in Europe. Oh, no, she'll never let her secret out to anyone, but I wouldn't want to be the person that wronged her.' Well, by George, didn't that story get about, though I only told it for a yarn, and the first thing you know, old Sophie that's been making a side leap at a rind of bacon, finds a juicy pie on her doorstep; the next day it's a sack of flour; the day after a hunk of venison, and so on. When I went to see her she told me the good news. I put her wise, and she promised not to give me away, if anyone asked about the gypsy curse. But no one did. By George, till the day she died she never was in want again—may she be in Heaven this day."

When this tale ended Johnny got up to pour the coffee and to cut the apple pie, which was a credit to him, and made up for the goat meat, and the potatoes that would not bake.

"Now I'll admit I may be superstitious, but I could tell many a tale to prove that there is such a thing as an act of God. And I believe in warnings, too. Now when I have certain dreams such as battling against rattlesnakes, I know they mean something. Now, a while back I told my two pardners one morning at breakfast, that I had dreamed about a rattlesnake every night for a week, but no matter how many times he struck at me he was not able to get me. 'By George,' I told my buddies, 'I have an enemy and he's trying to get me, but he might as well lay off, because he'll only be caught himself.' Now, about a year later didn't one of my pardners tell me that for a whole week before I gave out my dream the other pardner had been coaxing him to double-cross me in a deal, but when he heard my dream he played quits."

Before we left the table Johnny said to my friends, "Jimmie tells me you ladies are interested in the care of the t.b.'s. Now, by George, I can tell you how to bring about a sure cure every time. Just excuse me a minute, and I'll show you how it's done."

He came back with a whisky flask about half filled with broken garlic roots. "Now I can promise any lunger who'll take about a pint of this mixture every day in small portions a couple of hours apart, that he'll make the cure. I've seen more than one lunger,

KINGSTON IN THE OLD DAYS

given up by the doctors, get better on this treatment. And you'll never catch cold or flu while you take it either. Here, just taste it—it's easy to swallow." Both ladies swallowed a spoonful of the mixture and promised to remember the remedy.

We broke away from Johnny by force. "I can tell you one thing about your house, Johnny. It's a lot easier to get into than it is to get out of."

"And I can tell you one thing about yourself," said Johnny. "You're still as nimble as a squirrel, and you've not gone haywire yet."

"Don't you worry about me, Johnny. I can buy and sell the whole outfit yet, and I'll be eighty-one in a few weeks. Don't forget your promise to visit me in Deming," I ended, as I climbed into the car.

Everyone we met on our way told us not to miss the trip to the summit of the Black Range, so we headed up the South Percha Canyon. Circling higher and higher over the fine new highway that has cost Sierra and Grant Counties about $40,000 a mile in construction, we at last reached the heights from which, on clear days, one can see mountain ridges three hundred miles away. Here the pines and spruces often stretch upward a hundred feet from their mountain footing. Though we sighted no wild animals we knew there were bear, deer, mountain lions, coyotes, and wild turkeys hiding among the shadows. I believe the wild creatures have been, for the time being, frightened away, for the road is still under construction near Iron Creek. Almost the entire highway and all its culverts have been carved out of solid rock; and the noise of the blasting, added to the rumbling of heavy trucks and caterpillars, has done away with the peace of mountains and valleys.

I pointed out a park at the foot of Mount Sawyer, which in my prospecting days was the finest blackberry patch I have ever seen, and for that reason a favorite hide-out for bears, that filled themselves on juicy berries as big as pigeon eggs.

"What glorious colors! Some of those trees on the mountain side seem to be dripping with blood," said one of the ladies.

"You're thinking of Apaches now," I told her.

It was a trip I will never forget. How vividly it brought back the days when I climbed among these mountains, as a young man, often alone for weeks except for the company of my faithful burro. I sighted the Gray Eagle Mine about fifteen hundred feet below the highway, and a little farther on, at a depth of at least two thousand feet from the road, the old deserted Bennett's Saw Mill. The road turned slightly northwest, the curves being many and sharp, but it is plenty wide, so I knew we were in no danger.

I made out the head of the Percha Creek, which we had glimpsed time and again trickling along over its canyon bed. Reaching the divide between the headwaters of the Middle Percha to the east, and those of Iron Creek to the west, I realized we had climbed to an altitude of at least nine thousand feet. Far to the west beyond Silver City I could see the Burro Mountains. We lingered for a time on the summit near Iron Creek, and were sorry to turn away from the fine view of deep, wooded canyons and mountain ridges.

On our way home we stopped to take some pictures of the cemetery where many old friends lie in their rocky graves, surrounded by weather-beaten wooden palings, and watched over by pinons and junipers. At Johnny's we halted for the box of apples he had ready for us. Two more stops we made that afternoon—one at Fred's in Hillsboro to pick up the jug of wine, and the last in a grove of flaming walnuts near Lake Valley. Here we ate our lunch, while we watched the sun sink behind the mountains in a flood of orange and crimson.

Only known photo of the author, James A. McKenna, taken at Silver City Old Timers' Days, 1928. McKenna is in the second row, center, below and to the right of the number "22" later used to identify him..

The gravestone of James A. McKenna, Bay Pines National Cemetery, Bay Pines, Florida. *Courtesy Donald E. Florence whose research located it at findagrave.com.* Also clarified there, is his birth date of November 6, 1853 and his death date of November 4, 1940.